GENTLEMEN
EMIGRANTS

GENTLEMEN EMIGRANTS

From the British Public Schools to the Canadian Frontier

Patrick A. Dunae

Douglas & McIntyre
Vancouver/Toronto

Douglas & McIntyre Ltd.
1615 Venables Street
Vancouver, British Columbia

CANADIAN CATALOGUING IN PUBLICATION DATA

Dunae, Patrick A. (Patrick Alexander), 1950–
    Gentlemen emigrants

    Bibliography: p.
    ISBN 0–88894–324–5

    1. British in Canada. 2. Canada—Emigration and immigration. 3. Great Britain—Gentry.
I. Title.
FC106.B7D8   305.8'21'071   C81–091271–6
F1035.B7D8

Jacket design by Nancy Legue
Typesetting by The Typeworks, Mayne Island
Printed and bound in Canada by John Deyell

Frontispiece photo: F.C. Inderwick, owner of the North Fork Ranche near Pincher Creek, c. 1885 (*Glenbow-Alberta Institute*)

Which is the better for an English gentleman,
to use all the strength and valor that is
entrusted him—we are taught there will be a
reckoning when he must account for them—subduing
savage Nature, that the hungry may eat cheaper
bread, or lounging about a racecourse, shooting
driven pheasants...[and] wasting precious hours
in the reeking smoke-room of his club?

Harold Bindloss, *A Sower of Wheat* (1901)

ACKNOWLEDGEMENTS

During the course of researching and writing this book, I received assistance from many people on both sides of the Atlantic. Of those who helped me in Britain, I would like to thank Surgeon Captain H.E.B. Curjel, R.N. (retired), of Hollesley, Suffolk; Mr. H.F. Ferguson, Administrative Officer, H.M. Borstal, Hollesley Bay Colony, Woodbridge; Miss Margaret De Motte, Local History Librarian, Manchester; and Dr. Walter Mackey, City Archivist, Edinburgh. I also appreciate the cooperation I received from the headmasters, librarians, and archivists of the various public schools. Mr. J.A. Bentley of Haileybury College, Mr. Mark Baker of Wellington College, Mr. Patrick Strong of Eton College, and Miss Jennifer Macrory of Rugby School were especially helpful. To Gil and Val Speechley of London, and the gentlemen of Didsbury, Manchester — many thanks for your help, hospitality, ideas, and friendship.

In Canada, I am greatly indebted to Lewis G. Thomas, professor emeritus of The University of Alberta. Professor Thomas not only read portions of the manuscript and provided detailed information on gentlemen ranchers in the Alberta foothills; he also provided much of the inspiration behind this book. Similarly, I would like to thank Dr. David H. Breen, of the University of British Columbia, and Miss Sheilagh S. Jameson, formerly of the Glenbow-Alberta Insitute in Calgary, for their assistance.

The staff at the Public Archives of Canada have been unfailingly helpful in answering a host of questions concerning gentlemen emigrants in the Dominion. Staff members in the University of Saskatchewan Special Collections Library, along with staff members at the provincial archives of Ontario, Manitoba, and British Columbia, directed me to some valuable material. Mr. Garth Pugh, of the Saskatchewan Department of Youth and Culture (Historic Parks Division, Regina), and Mrs. Georgeen Klassen, of the Glenbow-Alberta Institute, also helped me considerably.

Since I began this project during my tenure as Killam Postdoctoral Research Fellow at the University of British Columbia, I would like to acknowledge the trustees of the Izaak Walton Killam Memorial Fund For Advanced Studies. In addition, I would like to acknowledge the Canadian Plains Research Centre, for providing me with a travel grant, and Judith Alldritt, for her editorial assistance.

Like many of the young men in this book, I relied on the support and enthusiasm of my family. My parents were particularly helpful and to them I extend a special thanks. Unlike most of the young men in this book, however, I was also fortunate in having a loving, patient, and ever-encouraging wife. To Leslie — critic, comma-hunter, and lady — I acknowledge a great debt and offer a very personal thanks.

CONTENTS

INTRODUCTION
I

I: Pioneer Gentlemen
13

II: Gentlemen Adventurers
32

III: Supernumerary Gentlemen
48

IV: Emigrant Schoolboys
67

V: High-Class Cowboys
87

VI: Nature's Gentlemen
106

VII: Remittance Men
123

VIII: Cloistered Colonists
147

IX: Mudpups & Premium Hunters
171

X: Old Boys & Old Colonials
192

XI: Pro Patria
215

NOTES
237

BIBLIOGRAPHY
253

INDEX
267

Alex. Staveley Hill's Oxley Manor, Staffordshire (top), and his New Oxley Ranche, N.W.T., 1885. A romanticized view of emigration

INTRODUCTION

Between the end of the Napoleonic Wars and the outbreak of the First World War, an army of British public school boys, retired military officers, university graduates, and aristocrats invaded Canada. Resplendent in Norfolk jackets, riding boots, and straw boaters, armed with sporting rifles, double-edged axes, and cricket bats, they trooped into the backwoods of Ontario, fanned out across the prairies, and poured into the valleys of British Columbia. Collectively, these well-born, well-educated British settlers were known as "gentlemen emigrants."

During the last century the gentleman emigrant was often described as a British institution. It was an apt description, for no other nation sent as many gently bred sons to the New World as did Great Britain. Few countries attracted as many of these emigrants as did Canada, and in few countries did the British gentleman have so great an impact. It was the gentleman emigrant who accounted for so much of the capital that was invested in Canada's fledgling industries; it was the gentleman emigrant who provided the colonies of British North America and the provinces of the Dominion with a large pool of capable administrators and educators; it was the gentleman emigrant who established many of the country's first artistic and athletic associations. It was the gentleman emigrant, more than anyone else, who made the Canadian West different from the American West, just as it was he who was responsible for the ambience and the attitudes that prevail in many parts of central Canada to this day. Yet despite the emigrants' contributions and their legacy, they have received very little attention from those interested in the history of immigration and settlement in the Dominion.

The emigrants have been neglected for two reasons. First, most of the gentlemen were English, and until very recently the English have not been regarded in Canada as a distinct ethnic group. Rather, they have been viewed as one of the country's founding "races," as a kind of core community around which other "ethnic" communities developed. As a result, in spite of the emphasis Canadians have placed upon multiculturalism, the English have never aroused the same interest or received the same attention as the Irish, the Scots, the Ukrainians, the Finns, and a host of other ethnic groups. The gentlemen emigrants have also been overlooked because of the vogues and vagaries of academe. Since most of them were drawn from the middle and upper classes of British society, they have been regarded as "toffs"; and toffs, however fashionable they may have been at one time, are not fashionable subjects among academics today. The academic community in Canada during the last few decades has been much more concerned with labour history, with women's studies, and with the social and political struggles of minority groups.

Admittedly, historians have always been affected by contemporary trends and developments, and the work recent historians have done on, say, trade unionism has helped to compensate for the emphasis that a previous generation of scholars placed on the country's political and commercial elites. Still, in swinging from right to left, from rich to poor, from men to women, from privileged to oppressed, scholarly searchlights have swept over some important ground. While shedding new light and generating new interest in some areas, they have—regrettably—detracted from and obfuscated others.

One of the intentions of this book is to rescue bourgeois and aristocratic emigrants from the shadows: in particular, to draw attention to the contributions they made and, in the process, to demonstrate that they were members of a distinct ethnic group. This book will also deal with the emigrants' experiences and their reputation in Canada, for as we shall see, British gentlemen formed a controversial as well as a colourful group. Finally, the book is intended to provide what might be called a trans-Atlantic view of the emigrant gentleman. Such a perspective is important, for only by understanding the emigrants' backgrounds can we begin to appreciate their expectations; and only by acknowledging their expectations can we assess their activities in Canada.

The emigrants we shall be considering were a diverse lot. Some were army officers who settled in Canada after long years of service in India; some were middle-aged bankers who had spent their lives in London. Some were clergymen's sons, others were the sons of professional men. Some came from mercantile families, some from arictocractic families who frowned on trade. Many of the emigrants were wealthy, others were comparatively poor. But whether they hailed from the middle classes or the aristocracy, whether they grew up in Elizabethan mansions or modest red-brick bungalows, our emigrants had one thing in common: they were all gentlemen.

As we use it today, the word "gentleman" is simply a courteous synonym for "man," but in the nineteenth century the word had a more limited meaning. It referred to a person of rank, to a man of substance, to an individual who held a superior position in society. Even so, the definition was not always clear, since gentility might be measured by a great many different criteria. Income, occupation, nativity, religion, accent, manner of dress, political inclination—any one or all of these factors might have a bearing on one's standing as a gentleman. The Victorians, however, rarely went to great lengths to define the term. Although they realized that the concept was flexible, they could recognize almost at a glance who was and who was not a gentleman. In making their assessment they used a simple yardstick: education. They assumed that a gentleman would have had the education of a gentleman—a proposition which, as one historian has observed, carried "the convenient converse that someone who had had the education of a gentleman was likely to be a gentleman."[1] In Victorian-Edwardian Britain, such an education was usually acquired at a public school.

The British public schools are anomalous institutions insofar as they are not "public" in the usual sense of the word. They are elite institutions which would be called "private" schools anywhere else in the world. A school's status—that is, its right to be called a public school—is based on a number of criteria, including curriculum, affiliation with the prestigious Headmasters' Conference (the association of British public school principals), and annual fees. For our purposes, though, a public school may be defined as an independent, privately endowed academy, established by bequest or by statute. Most British public schools are controlled by a board of governors, and most cater to students between the ages of twelve and eighteen.

At the turn of the century there were approximately one hundred first-class boys' public schools in Britain. Seven of them— Winchester (founded in 1382), Eton (1440), Westminster (1540), Shrewsbury (1551), Rugby (1567), Harrow (1590), and Charterhouse (1611)—formed the heart of the public school system. Known as "Ancient Foundations" or "Great Schools," the academies were established originally to teach grammar and good manners to humbly born scholars. Over the years, however, they developed into expensive boarding schools which catered to the sons of the aristocracy.

Although several prestigious colleges were founded during the seventeenth and eighteenth centuries, the most significant growth in the public school system took place in the early decades of the last century. The middle classes had by that time achieved a considerable amount of political and economic power and were in a position to provide their sons with the type of education that had previously been the preserve of young aristocrats. The vehicles for middle-class education were resuscitated grammar schools or, more frequently, newly established public schools. "Proprietary schools," founded by joint-stock companies to serve particular sections of the Victorian middle class, were among the latter. Cheltenham (1841), for example, catered to the sons of colonial civil servants and Rossall (1844) served the sons of Anglican ministers. Since virtually all the new schools were patterned after the Ancient Foundations, they did not alter or in any way detract from the elite nature of the public school system.[2]

The public schools—ancient or modern, endowed or proprietary—were easily one of the Victorians' most venerated institutions. As Leslie Stephen remarked in 1873, "Neither the British jury, nor the House of Lords, nor the Church of England, nay scarcely the monarchy itself seems to be so deeply enshrined in the bosoms of our countrymen as our public schools."[3] But as Stephen's friend, Thomas Hughes, made clear in his celebrated novel, *Tom Brown's Schooldays* (1857), the schools were admired more as "character-building" institutions than as places of scholarship. They were places where youths who were destined to hold leading positions in British society learned to be stoic, self-reliant, and morally upstanding. They were proving grounds where the young learned to revere the philosophy of *mens sana in corpore sano*—a sound mind in a sound body. They were spiritual centres, where boys were imbued with the "public schools' ethos"—an ethos that involved Christian manliness, loyalty, and respect for tradition.

It was possible, of course, to be a gentleman without being a public school alumnus, or Old Boy, and indeed many of the ex-army officers who came to British North America during the first half of the nineteenth century did not have the benefit of a public school education. Most of these officers were, nevertheless, well born and gently bred. They upheld tradition and respected authority, were well mannered and chivalrous, and had a keen sense of duty. They put high premiums on respectability, and they valued godliness and good learning above material wealth.[4] They were, consequently, recognized as gentlemen and were accorded the respect and privileges to which gentlemen were entitled in nineteenth-century Britain.

The obvious question—why did British gentlemen choose to emigrate, given the prestige they enjoyed in the Old Country—is one we will consider throughout this book, but the short answer is that emigrant gentlemen were motivated by both "pull" and "push" factors. For instance, many young Britons were attracted, or pulled, to Canada by the prospect of adventure and excitement, just as many were attracted by the prospect of wealth. On the other hand, many British gentlemen were dislodged, or pushed, from their homes because of socioeconomic pressures. Among the latter were the army officers who, having retired on half-pay at the end of the Napoleonic Wars, found that they were unable to maintain their position in society on their paltry pensions. Then there were the "broken-down" or "reduced" gentlemen who had large families but small incomes, and the liberally educated schoolboys who were unable to find suitable employment in an increasingly industrialized Britain. They, too, became gentlemen emigrants.

Unfortunately, because of inaccurate immigration records, there is no way of knowing precisely how many emigrant gentlemen entered Canada. The difficulty here stems mainly from the fact that most of our emigrants made the Atlantic crossing as first-class (cabin- or saloon-class) passengers. People who travelled in such classes were not required to provide authorities with the same information as less affluent steerage-class passengers. The latter were required to provide name, age, birthplace, occupation, destination, and reason for travelling, as well as the names of their travelling companions. The information was recorded on the ship's passenger manifest and was then presented by the ship's master to immigration authorities in Canada. But when interviewing first-class passengers, officials were deferential and discreet. If a saloon-class traveller appeared to be over fourteen years of age, he was recorded as "adult," and in the column headed "Passenger's Occupation," the recording officer simply wrote "gentleman." Aside from the passenger's name, no other information was taken. Thus we do not know, after studying these manifests, whether a particular passenger was a youthful or elderly gentleman, whether he was born in Britain or on the Continent, whether he was a dependent of some other passenger, whether he was a returning colonist, a tourist, or a transient. This is an instance where the historian regrets that rank has its privileges.

The problem of identifying and enumerating the gentlemen emigrants is compounded by the fact that ships' masters did not always provide immigration authorities with accurate information as regards the number of passengers they carried or the accommodation they provided. During the cholera epidemics of the 1830s and the typhus epidemics of the 1840s, for instance, it was not uncommon for a ship's captain to list all passengers as first (or cabin) class in order to avoid quarantine regulations aimed at disease-stricken steerage immigrants. Similarly, in the 1850s many shipping companies fudged their manifests, since vessels carrying only cabin passengers did not have to conform to parliamentary acts which laid down minimum standards for immigrant carriers. Figures that purport to show the number of first-class passengers landed in Canadian ports prior to Confederation are, therefore, often inflated. Even after Confederation the statistics can be misleading since government officials in Britain and in Canada used different methods of enumerating immigrants.

It is apparent, nevertheless, that a revolution of sorts took place among emigrants' ranks during the second half of the nineteenth century. Traditionally, general labourers had far outnumbered members of other occupational groups in the overall army of British emigrants. But during this period, the proportion of "higher-class migrants" (a group comprised of gentlemen and professional men) among the total number of adult male emigrants increased steadily, from 8 per cent in the 1850s to 15 per cent in the 1870s. Higher-class migrants then constituted the largest occupational category after general labourers. The proportion of elite migrants, as the gentlemen emigrants were sometimes termed, continued to increase during the last years of the century, and by the late 1890s these migrants constituted almost 27 per cent of the total number of adult male emigrants. They were, by that time, overrepresented in the emigrant army, since the educated, white-collar, and professional classes in England and Wales then constituted less than 22 per cent of the adult male population.[5]

The increase in the number of gentlemen emigrants was related to "push" factors such as declining incomes of the landed gentry and a tightening of gentlemanly professions in Britain. "Pull" factors, such as the opening of the Canadian West, were also important and help to account for the fact that at the turn of the century substantially more gentlemen emigrated to the Dominion than to the other white settlement colonies or to the United States. One authority, using figures compiled by the U.K. Board of Trade, has estimated that the Dominion claimed 18 per cent, or approximately 45,000, of Britain's "high-class migrants" during the last quarter of the nineteenth century. During the Edwardian years, Canada's share increased from 23 per cent (1906) to almost 40 per cent (1913). Over the same period, the United States' share fell from 40 per cent to 25 per cent, and South Africa's share fell from 13 per cent to 7 per cent, while Australia and New Zealand's share increased only marginally, from 13 per cent to 15 per cent.[6]

The Board of Trade figures include "merchants and commercial men," as well as "professional men and gentlemen," and the records are such that the two groups cannot be separated easily. Still, the total number of gentlemen among the migrants was obviously significant, considering the attention that both the British and the Canadian press devoted to this particular contingent during the late Victorian and Edwardian years. Furthermore, we have only to look at the many specialized guidebooks and settlers' manuals and the attention that Canadian railway, steamship, and colonization companies lavished on the well-educated Britons to realize that as far as contemporaries were concerned, gentlemen emigrants constituted a relatively large, and unquestionably important, group of settlers.

By 1914, when immigration to Canada was temporarily halted by the war, emigrant gentlemen were scattered across the whole of the Dominion. However, most were located in southern Ontario and the western provinces, regions that had traditionally attracted aristocratic Britons. Quebec and the Maritimes, in comparison, attracted relatively few of these emigrants. Halifax and Windsor, Nova Scotia, it is true did attract well-educated settlers during the Victorian period, as did Charlottetown and several hamlets in Prince County, Prince Edward Island. Gentlemen emigrants also settled in Loyalist villages in New Brunswick, in the Eastern Townships of Quebec and, as might be expected, in the English-speaking quarters of Montreal. But compared with the number of emigrants who settled west of the Ottawa River, the number of British gentlemen in eastern Canada was small.

The emigrants shied away from the East partly because of the climate, which was thought to be inhospitable, and partly because opportunities there were relatively limited. When the emigrants began arriving in British North America in the 1830s, much of the best land in the Maritime colonies was either developed (and therefore expensive) or in the possession of squatters and absentee landlords. In Lower Canada (Quebec), the most accessible land was held by long-established *seigneurs* and their *censitaires*. Besides, the principal economic activities of eastern Canada—lumbering, shipbuilding, fishing—held little attraction for the gentleman emigrant. He was more interested in practising the type of agriculture that developed in the West.

Emigrant gentlemen, particularly those who were members of the English gentry or the Anglo-Irish ascendency, also tended to avoid areas where there were high concentrations of Irish settlers. Even those who had been officers in regiments that contained a large proportion of Irish soldiers tended to be wary of such areas, for they recognized that there was a very real antipathy between emigrants who came from opposite ends of the social spectrum in the British Isles. Of course, as many well-born English settlers discovered, impoverished Irish immigrants could not be avoided entirely, for the latter were much too ambitious and energetic to allow themselves to be confined to any single region in the New World. Still, as late as the 1870s, some guidebooks aimed at the emigrant gentlefolk were advising readers to avoid certain parts of New Brunswick because of the rough Irish element, and clearly, many readers heeded the advice.

As for impoverished Scottish immigrants and French-Canadian *habitants,* they did not intimidate upper-class emigrants to the same extent. Nevertheless, English gentlemen preferred to be among their own kind, and whenever possible they preferred to settle in areas where they could pursue interests in keeping with their upbringing. Accordingly, they tended to direct their attentions to the English-speaking districts of Upper Canada and to the anglophile regions of the Far West.

Gentlemen emigrants arrived in North America in two dis-

tinct waves. The first group began arriving soon after the end of
the Napoleonic Wars. They settled principally around Lake Ontario where, from the mid-1820s to the mid-1830s, they secured
approximately 65,000 acres of free-grant lands. The ranks of the
gentlemen pioneers were reinforced in the late 1850s when veterans of the Crimean War began their exodus from Britain. With
the discovery of gold in the new colony of British Columbia in
1858, a sizeable portion of the vanguard was diverted to the
Pacific coast.

By 1871, when British Columbia entered Confederation,
many of the gentlemen who had come with the first wave of settlers were comfortably settled and enjoying successful careers in
southern Ontario or on the southern tip of Vancouver Island.
Many of those who had emigrated a generation earlier held high
government offices or owned profitable farms or businesses. As
successful and experienced colonists, they were in a position to
assist the second wave of gentlemen emigrants—a wave that
began swelling in the late 1870s and reached flood proportions
during the early 1900s. Generally speaking, the emigrants who
made up this second and larger wave were younger and less
worldly than those who had pioneered in Ontario and B.C. In
fact, many of the "Tom Browns" who came with the second contingent were scarcely out of school. Nevertheless they were an
ambitious, adventurous, and energetic group—as they showed
when they made their spirited assault on the wheat fields and
rangelands of the newly opened North West Territory.

The gentlemen who settled in the prairie West, like the gentlemen who settled elsewhere in the Dominion, imported, im-
planted, and nurtured a great many of the institutions, traditions, and rituals associated with their class in the Old Country.
They laid out cricket pitches and race tracks. They founded hunt
clubs and literary guilds. They clung resolutely to *The Times*
and the Old School Tie. As a result, they were a conspicuous
group within Canadian society, and because of this, they aroused
considerable interest. Government agencies followed their economic progress, colonial churchmen reported their religious
activities, local newspapers kept tabs on their social calendars.
Fellow settlers also observed their habits closely and passed on

to their children a fund of anecdotes concerning the fortunes and follies of the gentlemen. But while pioneers' reminiscences, contemporary newspaper reports and the like are indispensable in charting the emigrants' careers in Canada, these sources provide us with only one side of the picture, and one that is sometimes misleading since the observers did not always understand or appreciate the expectations and the dispositions of those they observed. To complete our picture of the emigrants we need records from the emigrants themselves. Happily, such records are abundant.

Gentlemen emigrants were Canada's most literate settlers and not at all reticent when it came to expressing their ideas or chronicling their experiences on the frontier. They wrote voluminous letters to their families and friends; they kept detailed account books and diaries; they published essays, settlers' manuals, sportsmen's guidebooks, personal memoirs, poems, and autobiographical novels. This vast and varied body of literature constitutes a singular record which is all the more valuable because it reveals so much about the emigrants' personalities. Cockiness, confusion, loneliness, euphoria—the literature reflects a whole spectrum of emotions. And it does more than that, for the authors of this literature had a good eye for detail and a keen appreciation of history. They were well aware that they were taking part in a crucial phase in the country's development and cognizant of the fact that they were laying foundations for future generations. They had, perhaps more than any other group of settlers, an acute sense of time and place. Their writings, consequently, are important not only for what they say about emigrant gentlemen but also for what they say about the Dominion during its formative years.

Since this book is intended to illuminate various aspects of Canadian society during the country's formative years as well as provide a portrait of a particular group of settlers, a final word regarding the title and focus of the book may be helpful. The chapters that follow deal with a patriarchal age and a male-oriented society. Many of the individuals we shall consider in the book were graduates of masculine institutions; most came to Canada without their wives and sweethearts; all pursued what were regarded as manly vocations. Our study, then, concerns gentle *men*.[7] As for the use of the term *emigrant* instead of *immigrant*, the former is more appropriate since the subjects of our study always referred to themselves as *emigrants*. And so they were, for even those who spent most of their lives in Canada and who embraced fully all aspects of Canadian life retained certain attitudes and mannerisms that marked them as being British. Few of the gentlemen settlers turned their backs completely on their heritage or severed their emotional and spiritual ties with the Old Country. In this respect, they were forever emigrants.

CHAPTER I

PIONEER GENTLEMEN

The *Anne,* which set sail from Leith for Quebec City on 1 July 1832, was typical of the small vessels that plied the North Atlantic routes. A square-rigged, two-masted brig of just under 200 tons, she normally made the crossing in about six weeks. On this trip, because of unfavourable winds, it took her nine weeks to reach Lower Canada from the Edinburgh outport.

The seventy-six passengers aboard the *Anne* were also typical. Most of them were impoverished emigrants from Scotland and Ireland who were fleeing pestilence, enclosures, famine, and unemployment. Crowded together on rough wooden bunks in the orlop deck, the men, women, and children who were travelling steerage class endured sour water, rancid food, and cholera in hopes of building a new life in the colonies. Above them, comfortably ensconced in private cabins, were a few gentlefolk who were emigrating to Canada in order to avoid the ignominy of having to live in reduced circumstances in England. Among the first-class passengers were Lt. J.W.D. Moodie, late of the 21st Regiment, Royal (North British) Fusiliers, and Moodie's twenty-nine-year-old wife, Susanna. Despite the incessant rolling of the ship, Lieutenant Moodie remained in good spirits during the voyage, and he devoted much of his time to writing verse and playing his flute. His wife, who was accompanied by their infant daughter and a maidservant, was less enthusiastic. She spent most of the crossing glowering at the *Anne*'s captain, a bluff North Country sailor, and thumbing through a copy of Voltaire's *History of Charles XII*. She derived little satisfaction from either activity.

John Wedderburn Dunbar Moodie was thirty-five years old when he emigrated to Canada. The youngest son of a landed Orkney family, he had fought with distinction during the Napoleonic Wars. He retired on half-pay in 1816 and for two years received an army disability pension for a wound he suffered while storming a French redoubt in the Low Countries. When the pension was terminated, he moved to South Africa to join a brother in the Cape Colony. During his ten years there he enjoyed the salubrious climate and no end of "wild sport." He failed, however, to establish himself in a trade or a profession, and in 1820 — after being mauled by an elephant during a hunting expedition — he returned to England. Two years later he married Susanna Strickland of Reydon Hall, near Norwich.

Susanna was the youngest of six daughters born to Thomas Strickland, a wealthy merchant and warehouseman. Like her sisters she was privately tutored in the genteel arts and in the religious principles of the Church of England. Like her sisters she was literary minded and at an early age wrote short stories and verse. Unlike her sisters and her three younger brothers she was reserved, moody, and pessimistic. She was inclined to be prissy, haughty, and dogmatic in her opinions. Her disposition made it difficult for her to adjust to the economic depression that followed the Napoleonic Wars and that all but ruined her father's business. Her disposition also made it difficult for her to adjust to the rough characters and primitive conditions she encountered in British North America.

Lieutenant Moodie — whom his wife described as "a lover of ease, a man of books, of refined tastes, and gentlemanly habits" — had not intended to emigrate when he married. But once Susanna became pregnant, it became clear to him that he would have to take steps to provide for his family's welfare. The money he received as a half-pay subaltern and the royalties he earned from a few essays gave him an income of about £100 per year.[1] This would have been sufficient to provide him and his wife with food and rented accommodation, but it would not have provided them with any luxuries or protected them from what Susanna called "the vulgar sarcasms [of] purse-proud, commonplace" neighbours.[2] Nor would Moodie's income allow him to provide a respectable education for his children, who eventually numbered six. Emigration seemed to be his only recourse, but he faced the prospect with equanimity. He had, after all, survived French grenadiers in the Netherlands and outraged elephants in the Cape, and he had no doubts that he could survive the backwoods of Canada. Whether his wife would be able to leave her family and friends in England was another matter, though Moodie was optimistic. As Susanna later reported, he told her: "the sacrifice must be made, and the sooner the better. My dear wife, I feel confident that you will respond to the call of duty; and hand-in-hand and heart-in-heart we will go forth to meet difficulties and, by the help of God, to overcome them."[3]

When Moodie made this statement, sometime in 1831, there was a veritable mania for the Canadas. In that year alone 58,000 Britons emigrated, mostly to settle on the free-grant lands of Upper Canada. The following year, social and economic pressures accounted for an even larger exodus which was encouraged by colonial emigration agents who toured the depressed agricultural districts and market towns of England, Scotland, Ireland, and Wales. The agents tailored their appeals to their audiences. Destitute labourers and mechanics were told that in Canada they would be landed proprietors and would be free from the social and political constraints they endured in the Old Country. Better educated audiences were told that, whatever their incomes, they would be the vanguard of a new aristocracy and would be accorded a pre-eminent place in colonial society.

Lieutenant Moodie and a friend, Tom Wilson, attended one of these meetings in Norwich in the spring of 1832. Wilson, the younger son of a local squire, was an eccentric spendthrift who, by his own admission, had previously spent seven years of "valueless existence" in New South Wales. Considering Wilson's poor track record, Moodie was surprised that Wilson was intent on going to Upper Canada, and as they left the Norwich meeting he ventured to suggest that his friend was perhaps unsuited for colonial life. Wilson disagreed. He retorted that if either of them were unsuited to the backwoods it was Moodie.

"You expect, by going to Canada, to make a fortune, or at least secure a comfortable independence," Wilson said. "I anticipate no such results; yet I mean to go, partly out of a whim, [and] partly to satisfy my curiosity whether it is a better country than New South Wales." Wilson predicted that Moodie's "refined habits and unfortunate literary propensities" would make him and his wife objects of mistrust and envy in the colony. "Thank God! I have no literary propensities," he exclaimed. More ominously, Wilson predicted that his laziness and Moodie's eagerness and energy would, in the end, amount to the same thing. Both men would probably fail in the backwoods, and both would return to England, disgusted and disappointed, within a short period of time. "But as I have neither wife nor child to involve in my failure, I think, without much flattery, that my prospects are better than yours."[4]

Wilson's remarks were unsettling and, in some ways, prophetic. As he predicted, Wilson did become disgusted with the backwoods, and within four months he was back in England. In the interval he had been stricken with ague, abused by his rough colonial neighbours, and cheated out of several hundred pounds. The Moodies had similar experiences, and there were many times when they, too, were sorely tempted to return to England. But unlike Wilson, whom they met briefly in Canada, the Moodies managed to resign themselves to their many disappointments, and they remained in the colony for the rest of their lives.

Tom Wilson's gloomy pronouncements were, in any event, all but forgotten when Moodie received the happy news that a brother officer, Lt. Thomas Traill, planned to marry Susanna's older sister, Catharine. Happier still was the news that the Traills were also intent on emigrating. They were sailing only a week after the Moodies and were planning to settle in the same part of Upper Canada.

Thomas Traill's background was very similar to that of his friend, Dunbar Moodie, for he was also the younger son of a distinguished Orkney family. After taking a degree at Oxford, he had been gazetted second lieutenant in the 21st Fusiliers. In 1816 he retired from the regiment on half-pay and shortly after married a woman who bore him two sons. When his first wife died, his sons were taken in by one of his brothers, leaving Traill free to devote himself to travel and literature. But by 1832, when he married Catharine, he realized that he could no longer afford to lead the life of a dilettante, and like Dunbar, who was seven years his junior, he decided his best course was to begin a new career in the colonies. Thomas was more fortunate than Dunbar, however, in winning the hand of "Katie," the most cheerful, the most gregarious, and the most indomitable of the Strickland girls. Indeed, the wives of the two half-pay officers could not have been more different; and though they emigrated at the same time, settled in the same area, and both wrote books about their lives in Canada, the experiences of the two bore no resemblance. Katie Traill looked upon Canada as "the land of hope," and three years after she settled there, she declared that she was greatly satisfied with the move. Susanna Moodie for many years regarded Canada as the land of broken dreams and hardships. Both women also looked upon their husbands' decision to emigrate in totally different ways. In her first book, *The Backwoods of Canada* (1836), Mrs. Traill wrote about the strength and the virtues that men like Thomas Traill brought to the New World:

> ... the half-pay officer, by thus leading the advanced guard of civilization, and bringing into these rough districts gentle and well-educated females, who soften and improve all around them by *mental* refinements, is serving his country as much by founding villages and pleasant homesteads in the wilds as ever he did by personal courage or military stratagems in times of war.[5]

Susanna Moodie declared in her first book, *Roughing It In the Bush* (1852), that Canada was suited only for paupers who had large families and low expectations. "Higher class" emigrants, including "officers of the army and navy with their families," Mrs. Moodie wrote, were "perfectly unfitted by their previous habits and education for contending with the stern realities of emigrant life. The hand that has long held the sword, and been accustomed to receive implicit obedience from those under its control, is seldom adapted to wield the spade and guide the plough, or try its strength against the stubborn trees of the forest." Mrs. Moodie's intentions in writing her book was to dissuade Britons of her class from following the road that she and and Dunbar had been forced to take: "If these sketches should prove the means of deterring one family from sinking their property and shipwrecking all their hopes, by going to reside in the backwoods of Canada, I shall consider myself amply repaid for revealing the secrets of the prisonhouse, and feel that I have not toiled and suffered in the wilderness in vain."[6] Katie, needless to say, wrote for a very different purpose.

In fairness to Mrs. Moodie, the area in which she, her sister, and their husbands settled was largely undeveloped. The province of Upper Canada had been established only forty years earlier (1791), and although it had been settled by a large number of United Empire Loyalists, transplanted Americans, and land-hungry Britons, the province was still sparsely populated. The Back Townships, i.e., the surveyed tracts that lay to the north of the "Front" on Lake Ontario, were heavily wooded, and roads throughout the province were either nonexistent or virtually impassable. Furthermore, while retired officers like Moodie and Traill were entitled to several hundred acres of free-grant land, the implements and the labour necessary for clearing the land were costly and in short supply. Luxury goods were almost unattainable and of the staples, only flour, whiskey, and salt pork were cheaply and readily available. All in all, the backwoods were a far cry from the manicured fields of Norfolk.

On the other hand, the Moodies and the Traills were not going to a totally alien land, for the province rested firmly on British laws and traditions. Nor were the gentle pioneers without company or compatriots, for in 1832 upwards of 40,000 British immigrants poured into the province. To be sure, few of the immigrants were of the class which Mrs. Moodie would have had to tea at Reydon Hall; however, the Newcastle District (now a part of Peterborough County) did boast a large number of emigrants from the British upper classes, and it was there that the Moodies and Traills settled. Moreover, the two families had a small amount of capital, and they had connections. Among the most valuable of their connections was Susanna and Katie's brother, Samuel, who had come to Upper Canada seven years earlier and who, by the time his sisters arrived, was an experienced backwoodsman and a man of property.

Samuel Strickland, though younger than his sisters, was Thomas Strickland's eldest son. He had been educated in a private academy at Norwich but was not a particularly scholarly boy. Like his younger brother, who made a career for himself in India, Samuel was more interested in manual work and mechanical contrivances. He was also interested in athletics, in wildlife and—most of all—in adventure. His taste for adventure and in particular his anticipation of finding it in Canada may have been sparked by General Wolfe's writing desk and other memorabilia of the hero of Quebec which reposed in the drawing room at Reydon Hall. Or his interest in Canada may have originated with his father's gardener, who had relatives in British North America. Whatever the cause, Samuel decided to pursue "an active, rather than a professional life," and in 1824 he decided to accept an invitation to join a family friend in Upper Canada. He was twenty years old when he emigrated.

The friend, Col. H.B. Black, owned a 200-acre "estate" near the village of Whitby. As Strickland discovered, however, the colonel's "literary tastes and sedentary life had ill-fitted him for the rough customs of the colony." The estate which Strickland had come to manage had "scarcely seen a grain of corn"; the Irish labourers whom the colonel had contracted to work the farm had little knowledge of agriculture, and Yankee sharpsters had duped the colonel out of most of his capital.[7] Putting the estate to rights was no easy task, for Strickland was as ignorant of colonial ways as the colonel, and not long after he arrived his ignorance resulted in the death of the colonel's only team of oxen. But the colonel was a forgiving soul, and Strickland, who was conscientious, soon made amends. In so doing, he not only gained a knowledge of colonial farming but he also won the hand of the colonel's daughter. The marriage was a happy one but tragically short, for Strickland's wife died a year after their wedding while giving birth to their first child.

Following his wife's death in 1827, Strickland purchased a

partially cleared farm near Peterborough. On it he erected a
small, one-room log cabin, which he furnished with a hand-
hewn table and stools. Its only luxury, he recalled later, was a
bed he contrived by stretching strips of elm bark across iron-
wood poles. He was not long in the cabin, however, for later in
1827 he remarried. His second wife, Mary, bore him fourteen
children, and for many years Samuel was busy building larger
and larger dwellings.

For several years he was also kept busy as paymaster and
overseer for the Canada Company, a London-based land and
colonization company which was chartered in 1826. Formed at
the instigation of the Scottish novelist John Galt, the company
had acquired over two million acres of Crown land which it endeavoured to sell to incoming settlers. A large portion of the
company's lands lay in the heavily timbered region between Lake
Ontario and Lake Huron known as the Huron Tract. Strickland, who was retained personally by Galt in 1828, was hired to
help with the construction through the tract of a road which
linked the new towns of Guelph, fifty miles southwest of York
(Toronto), and Goderich, on the shore of Lake Huron. The experience he gained during his three years with the company
proved invaluable when Strickland later re-established himself in
the backwoods of Otonabee Township. His years in the Huron
Tract also brought him into contact with some of the leading
men in British North America. One of the most colourful and
dynamic of these men was Dr. William "Tiger" Dunlop, warden
of the woods and forests of the Canada Company.

Dunlop, who was born in 1792, was the son of a wealthy
Greenock banker. After taking a medical degree at the University of Glasgow, he was gazetted assistant surgeon in the 89th
Foot and sent to Canada during the last stages of the War of
1812. Following a brief but adventurous sojourn in India—
where he earned the sobriquet "Tiger" in consequence of his
hunting prowess—he returned to North America in the service
of the Canada Company.

Tiger Dunlop was a high-spirited, hard-drinking character
who revelled in the raucous and sometimes riotous life of the
frontier. He was a great joker, who delighted in such pranks as

hiding a live porcupine in a nail keg and inviting neighbours to help themselves to a handful of nails. The Tiger was, nonetheless, an aesthete who wrote essays which were both erudite and entertaining. A friend of Carlyle and an intimate of such luminaries as John Wilson and J.G. Lockhart, Dunlop was responsible for founding the Toronto Literary Society in 1836. The multifaceted Tiger was also responsible for the genteel, aesthetic circle that formed in the vicinity of Gairbraid, the home he shared with his brother, a half-pay naval officer, near Goderich. The house was located in Colbourne Township and for this reason Dunlop's circle was known as the "Colbourne Clique." The clique included university men, retired bankers, and ex-army officers, a good many of whom had been enticed to the area by Dunlop's *Statistical Sketches of Upper Canada for the Use of Emigrants* (1832). The title of the book is misleading, for it has little to do with statistics; in fact, the whole work is misleading, since it paints such a rosy picture of backwoods life. Much of the book is devoted to field sports, and virtually nothing is said of the toil which was an inseparable part of pioneer life. As for the extreme climate of Upper Canada, Dunlop wrote: "In the summer it is the climate of Italy, in winter, that of Holland." The Tiger afterwards admitted that his *Sketches* were a trifle far-fetched but defended the work by stating that he was anxious to attract "good settlers of the better sort" to the tract. [8]

Dunlop left the Canada Company in 1838 to pursue other business interests. He was subsequently elected to the assembly of the provincial legislature where he promoted the establishment of a secular university, the use of scientific agricultural techniques, and the interests of the medical profession. Prior to his death in 1849, Dunlop also served as superintendent of the Lachine Canal, near Montreal. His friend Samuel Strickland was never as active in the affairs of the colony, though he, too, became a prominent figure in civil and military circles. He achieved the rank of colonel in the Peterborough Militia, served as commissioner of the Court of Requests for the townships of Douro and Dummer, and was appointed justice of the peace for Peterborough County. In every respect Strickland did very well for himself in Upper Canada, and by the time his sisters and

brothers-in-law arrived, he was admired and respected from Cobourg to Goderich.

Wisely, Lieutenant Traill and his wife secured a location
close to Strickland's home on the Otonabee River north of Peterborough when they arrived in the summer of 1833. Within a few
months they had made a start on clearing their land and had
erected a snug log house which bore the name Westove, in honour of Traill's Orkney estate. The Traills' presence added to the
tone of a district which came to be regarded as one of the most
respectable in the province. One traveller who visited the Peterborough area in 1835 reported that its residents were among
"the most polished and aristocratic in Canada."[9] To be sure, the
population of some of the communities in the vicinity was small,
but as Mrs. Traill said, even a handful of gentlefolk had an impact in an area which, for the most part, was settled by uneducated immigrants from Ireland and America. Such was the case
at Sturgeon Lake, a few miles north of the Traill/Strickland
locations, where John Langton settled in 1833. In April of that
year, Langton wrote to his father that while the population of
the lake was only six, four of the settlers were Oxbridge men,
and one was a graduate of the Royal Military Academy at Woolwich. "The sixth," Langton noted drolly, "though boasting no
such honours, has half a dozen silver spoons and a wife who
plays the guitar."[10]

Langton was himself a gentleman, having taken his degree at
Trinity College, Cambridge, in 1829. On completing his studies
in classics and theology, Langton and his brother had been associated briefly with their father's export business in Liverpool.
His brother subsequently moved on to Manchester, where he
founded the Manchester and Salford Bank and where he was involved with several early railway companies. John also had an
interest in finance and transportation but decided that the future
was brighter and life more varied in the backwoods of Upper
Canada. So it proved to be. He spent his early years working
Blythe Farm (named after his boyhood home near Ormskirk),
and by the early 1840s it was one of the most prosperous farms in
the Newcastle District. He then moved to Peterborough where
he had established a successful lumber mill. After serving as a

member of the Legislative Assembly, he was appointed auditor general and deputy minister of finance for Canada. For many years he was also vice-chancellor of the University of Toronto.

When Langton came to Sturgeon Lake, he had little idea that he would enjoy such a distinguished career; he was only twenty-five years old at the time and was completely unfamiliar with colonial life. But he quickly acquired the skills of the backwoodsman and learned to use his time and his energy to best advantage. Instead of giving way to loneliness or succumbing to the temptations of backwoods taverns, as many young bachelors did, he developed a daily routine. He arose early each morning, stoked his fire, and cleaned his small cabin while the kettle boiled. After breakfast he would have a cigar and read from one of the many books he had brought with him. The books ranged from agricultural works to classical texts and philological treatises. He devoted the remainder of the day to manual labour: clearing underbrush, chopping trees, pulling stumps, ploughing, and planting. An hour before sunset he would chop a supply of firewood and start his dinner. While it cooked, he made bread for the following day. His dinner and domestic chores were usually finished by the time it was dark. "Another cigar's time is then devoted to meditation and digestion, and after reading, writing, or sewing for half a candle, I go to bed."[11] Such a routine was vitally important to the independent settler in the backwoods, for it gave a sense of purpose and a semblance of order to the day. Langton's days were not entirely devoted to toil, though, for he still had time to enjoy the company of neighbours. The neighbours, who in fact lived many miles distant, included the colonel who had commanded Traill's regiment, an army officer who had fought with Abercromby's expedition at the Battle of the Nile, and a retired Royal Navy admiral. The neighbours who came together for barn-raising bees and other "socials" also included a retired clergyman whose daughter Langton married in 1845.

Dunbar Moodie and his wife did not join this select circle until 1834. After leaving the *Anne* in Montreal they made their way by coach and steamboat up the St. Lawrence to Cobourg, where they purchased a partially cleared farm, named Melsetter after

Moodie's home in the Orkneys. Here they spent the first of many unhappy years in Canada. Their troubles began within weeks of arriving in the country when Dunbar sold his commission and purchased stock in a steamboat company. The stock proved to be worthless, and for several years the Moodies lived in abject poverty. Until they moved to Douro Township, near the Traills and Stricklands, the Moodies were also cheated and abused by their neighbours—just as Tom Wilson had predicted. They had, consequently, no regrets when they abandoned Melsetter. Still, their troubles were far from being over. The bees they held to build their 36-foot by 32-foot log house and raise a barn were disastrous because a number of the men who had been invited to the bees became aggressively drunk. During their second year, their crops failed, and by 1836 they were heavily in debt. Only by selling his best cow and most of his clothes could Dunbar raise enough money to pay his servant. The following year the house burned down, the pigs and oxen were lost, and Moodie broke his leg. And so it went, as bad luck and poor judgement resulted in one misfortune after another. It was not until 1840, when Moodie was appointed sheriff of Hastings County, that life became halfway bearable.

Moodie owed his appointment as sheriff, as he owed his captaincy in the local militia, to his wife, who lobbied the lieutenant governor on his behalf. Holding the shrievalty meant that the Moodies were able to leave the "bush" and move to the small town of Belleville, where Susanna could devote herself to literary pursuits. The move was a godsend, as far as she was concerned: it was like being released from prison.[12] Dunbar was also pleased with their move to "the clearings," although even then his life was not easy. Local residents greatly resented his appointment, and the next twenty-three years were dogged by petty squabbles, bickerings, and vendettas.[13] Small wonder that Moodie's memoir, *Scenes and Adventures as a Soldier and a Settler During Half a Century* (1866), is such a plaintive tome, so different from the memoirs of Strickland, Dunlop, and Langton.

In one of his letters to his father, Langton remarked that "the art of managing servants is perhaps the most important one a new settler has to learn."[14] It was an absurd statement, hardly characteristic of Langton, who well knew that there were more important arts to be learned in the backwoods of Canada. For the Moodies, however, "the servant problem" was overwhelming and a cause of their chronic misery in the New World. Quite simply, they could not get any reliable help, and during their first year in the woods they went through no less than eight servants. The servants quit for a variety of reasons: some, like the nurse who accompanied them from England, left to marry local settlers; some left because their wages were too low; others left because the mistress of the house was so pompous and prickly. Susanna insisted that her servants act in a respectful, deferential manner and was appalled when her "girls" had the audacity to engage freely in conversation and sit at the Moodies' dinner table. Even in the small log cabin, Mrs. Moodie refused to compromise her standards.

Susanna's dislike of the lower classes, "with all their insolent airs of independence," was evident as soon as the *Anne* approached the quarantine station at Grosse Isle, downriver from Quebec City. "I was not a little amused at the extravagant expectations entertained by some of our steerage passengers," she wrote: "The sight of the Canadian shores had changed them into persons of great consequence. The poorest and the worst-dressed, the least deserving and the most repulsive in mind and morals exhibited the most disgusting traits of self-importance...." Her disdain soon changed to horror as she watched the destitute passengers, freed from the wretched confines of the steerage deck, wade ashore and begin dancing with glee. She cringed at the sight of an Irishman who, on setting foot on Canadian soil, flourished his shillelagh and shouted, "Whurrah! my boys! Shure we'll all be jintlemen!" She recoiled from the Scottish crofter who exclaimed, "Hout, man! hauld your clavers, we shall a' be lairds here...." How these "vicious, uneducated barbarians" could presume so much was more than Mrs. Moodie could fathom. But she found when she and Dunbar reached their location in Upper Canada that the pauper immigrants did indeed regard themselves as people of consequence, and because they did, the Moodies had to endure "the saucy familiarity of servants who, republican in spirit, think themselves as good as their employers." Only in later years, after she had settled in Belleville, did Susanna begin to understand why the uneducated British immigrants thought and acted the way they did. The "secret," as she called it, was simple. The obsequious treatment she had received from servants in the Old Country had not been heartfelt. The lower orders were deferential towards their masters because of economic necessity. In a country where opportunities for uneducated men and women were severely limited, those in service did everything within their power to remain employed. To be dismissed, without a "character," meant the workhouse. But in the colonies, where labour was scarce, land plentiful, and opportunities almost unlimited, the uneducated classes did not have to fawn and cringe. In Canada it was a seller's market, and after generations of humiliation, pauper Britons were not about to sell themselves short. [15]

John Langton could have told her as much. "The working classes here," he observed in one of his letters, "naturally feel an independence which you do not find at home." He added that well-born emigrants who treated their servants as inferiors would find themselves "cordially hated" and soon without servants. [16] Susanna's sister, Catharine, could also have told her much about the realities of class relationships. When they emigrated, the Traills paid £30 for a private stateroom on a cargo ship so as to avoid travelling with pauper Highlanders, but they experienced very little trouble with the poorer classes in the New World. In fact, only once were they involved in a situation which, for the Moodies, was almost a daily occurrence. On that occasion the Traills were engaged in a disagreement with a Scottish steamboat engineer who was conveying them to Peterborough. The engineer, who had recently immigrated, was overly familiar with Catharine and ill-mannered towards Thomas. When the Scot declared that he considered himself a gentleman, Traill dryly commented that he did not hold the same opinion. "Pray, what makes a gentleman, I'll thank you to answer me that?" the Highlander demanded. "Good manners and good education," the lieutenant replied. "A rich man or a high-born man, if he is rude, ill-mannered, and ignorant, is no more a gentleman than yourself." Aside from that exchange—which ended amicably when Traill politely asked the engineer to explain the mysteries of the steam engine—the Traills got on easily with their neighbours and countrymen. At the roadside inns, Katie reported, servants "seemed to vie with each other in attention to us." The Moodies, who stayed in many of the same inns, found the staff uniformly rude. Whereas the Traills declared that most of their American-born neighbours were cordial and polite, the Moodies spoke only of "coarse, . . . vulgar Yankees." As for the Irish, whom Mrs. Moodie manifestly disliked, they provided Katie Traill with valuable advice in matters relating to cooking and household economy. [17]

How was it that these two couples, who had almost identical backgrounds and who settled in similar areas, had such different experiences? How was it that the Moodies were so dependent on hired help, while the Traills—husband and wife—rolled up their sleeves and pitched into manual labour? Why were the Traills generally buoyant and the Moodies depressed? The answer has much to do with the settlers' attitudes towards themselves and towards their circumstances. The Moodies felt abused and threatened at every turn and were constantly attempting to demmonstrate that they were gentlefolk. The Traills, in contrast, were confident and adaptable and so felt no need to maintain the rituals, mannerisms, and idiosyncracies which outwardly denoted good breeding. "We pride ourselves on conforming to circumstances," Mrs. Traill wrote, "and as a British officer must needs be a gentleman and his wife a lady, perhaps we repose quietly on that incontestable proof of our gentility, and can afford to be useful without ignoring it." [18]

Mrs. Traill, it must be owned, was a remarkable woman. Mrs. Moodie, unhappily, was more representative of the English gentlewomen who were forced to begin anew in the backwoods. Many of these women succumbed to the isolation, the climate, and the rough manners of their colonial neighbours. Like Susanna, they would give in to fits of despair, throw themselves onto their beds, and cry out, "Dear, dear England! Why was I forced by necessity to leave you? What heinous crime [have] I committed that I, who adore you, should be torn from your sacred bosom, to pine out my joyless existence in a foreign clime?" After spending eight months in the province, Anna Jameson, the estranged wife of Canada's attorney general, reported that such outbursts and emotions were common. In 1838 the inveterate lady traveller noted that she had "never met so many repining and discontented women as in Canada." "I never met *one* woman recently settled here who considered herself happy in her new home and country: I *heard* of one, and doubtless there are others, but they are exceptions to the general rule." [19] John Langton's spinster sister, who kept house for him for many years, formed a similar opinion. "I am afraid women deteriorate in this country more than the other sex," she wrote in 1840. [20] She also noted, as did several other commentators, that many English gentlemen had given up their farms and returned to the Old Country because their wives were so unhappy. A number of these commentators concluded that bachelorhood was, therefore, the best state for a gentleman emigrant, at least during the emigrant's first few years in the colony.

Life in the backwoods was, understandably, an ordeal for most delicately bred women, particularly when they found that they had to endure hard physical labour on top of all the other difficulties and inconveniences which were a part of pioneer settlers' lives. The extent of their labour and the mental adjustments they had to make are evident from the letters of an emigrant lady who settled with her family some years later in the Muskoka district:

> It is one thing to sit in a pretty drawing-room, to play, to sing, to study, to embroider, and to enjoy social and intellectual converse with a select circle of kind friends, and it is quite another to slave and toil in a log-house, no better than a kitchen, from morning till night, at cleaning, washing, baking, preparing meals for hungry men (not always of one's own family) and drying incessant changes of wet clothes. [22]

This unhappy lady wept frequently and took to falling off her chair "in fits of giddiness" as a result of the heat, the cold and the hard work. On such occasions she usually managed to regain her composure with the help of a bottle of "Oxley's Essence of Ginger," but eventually even Oxley's proved ineffective. After a two-year struggle she left the forest, broken in spirit and in health. That Mrs. Moodie did not suffer a similar breakdown may be attributed to a strong character, although her character was but a shadow of her sister's. Katie Traill went from strength to strength, overcoming misfortunes and encouraging her husband when his spirits seemed to flag. Perhaps she was the lady Anna Jameson heard of during her travels in Upper Canada.

In 1837 Lieutenant Traill and his brothers-in-law were among the "noble-minded Britons" who answered Sir Francis Bond Head's call to oppose the forces of "ruffianism and radicalism."[23] Sir Francis, the lieutenant governor of Upper Canada, issued the call just before radicals and liberal reformers attempted to dislodge the Tory oligarchies in Upper and Lower Canada. The Rebellions of '37 lasted less than a week in both colonies and were easily suppressed. They did, however, lead to the union of Upper and Lower Canada (which, after 1841, were styled Canada West and Canada East respectively) and to the granting of responsible government in the United Province of Canada.

Immediately after the rebellions, immigration to British North America declined: whereas the number of British immigrants in 1836 had been approximately 34,000, in 1838 less than 5,000 passed through colonial ports. But the decline was temporary, and by 1841 the number of immigrants exceeded 38,000. The Eastern Townships of Canada East received many of these immigrants, and some areas, notably Compton, Brome, and Sherbrooke counties, enjoyed a considerable boom. However, relatively few gentlemen were among the Britons who settled in the Eastern Townships. The British American Land Company, which from 1833 to 1850 was largely responsible for developing the townships, was held in low regard by independent migrants; furthermore, the British gentleman emigrant was not overly disposed towards French Canadians who, by the middle of the century, were beginning to move south from the seigneuries along the St. Lawrence into the fifteen counties that comprised the townships. Consequently, with the exception of the rivulets that trickled into Nova Scotia, New Brunswick, and Prince Edward Island, the tide of English-speaking gentlemen continued to flow principally to Canada West.

In the 1790s, when the province was founded, there had been

talk of creating a peerage in British North America as a means of inhibiting republican influences. The lieutenant governor, John Graves Simcoe, and some of the Loyalist leaders had been particularly keen on the idea. In the aftermath of the 1837 rebellions, when Tory patriarchs were again haunted by the spectre of godless republicanism, a call for a colonial baronage went up once more. As had been the case in Simcoe's time, the advocates of a special aristocracy were disappointed. [24] Efforts were made, nevertheless, to protect the English church and the monarchy in the colony, and there were many who looked upon the gentleman emigrant as a valuable ally in this regard. The Reverend A.W.H. Rose, for example, an Anglican clergyman who feared that English institutions were being undermined by Methodist preachers and Yankee settlers, appealed directly to gentlemen emigrants to help him fight the "good fight." Writing under the pseudonym "Pioneer of the Wilderness," he urged emigrants to include in their luggage paintings of village churches, prints of English cathedrals, and other pictures that would inspire loyalty:

> Portraits of Her Majesty, Prince Albert and the royal children, Wellington and Nelson, views of Windsor Castle, the Houses of Parliament, . . . our wooden walls and such like, are greatly wanted to be disseminated in Canada, to supplant, as far as possible, the influx of tawdry sheets protraying "The Signing of the Declaration of Independence," [President] Washington, General Taylor, the Capitol, the Mexican battles, etc. . . . [25]

Just how effective these talismans were in the scattered backwoods communities is a matter for speculation, although certainly Canadian government officials welcomed the emigrants who bore them. The authorities recognized that well-born emigrants had rendered valuable service, not only in the militia regiments which had been called out at the time of the rebellion but also in the day-to-day running of the colony. Accordingly, when the Bureau of Agriculture stepped up its drive for British settlers in the 1850s, part of the campaign was aimed directly at the gentleman emigrant. Opportunities in Canada were advertised in quality newspapers such as *The Times* and in periodicals such as the *Field*, which were read almost exclusively by the middle and upper classes. The bureau also issued a number of new publications, including reprints of some of Mrs. Traill's cheerful hints for settlers, in its campaign for well-bred emigrants. [26]

The campaign was facilitated by the Crimean War, which led to a new corps of half-pay officers. The Crimean veterans, along with other gentlemen who were either reduced in circumstances or simply adventurous, began to make their mark in Canada in the years immediately prior to Confederation. Some of these emigrants bought improved farms along "the Front," while others received free-grant lands in the Ottawa Valley. A large number took up homesteads in the Muskoka district, which was surveyed and opened for settlement in the 1860s. And, as ever, many of the gentlemen emigrants and their families settled in larger, established communities such as Toronto. Although a few—Anna Jameson included—found society in Toronto pretentious, most English travellers and settlers endorsed their compatriot W.H.G. Kingston's view of the city. "Toronto," he wrote, after his wanderings in 1856, "is a thoroughly English place, in its appearance, and in the habits and manners of the inhabitants. They are in all respects a loyal, honest, straight-forward, right-thinking class of people, and nowhere in the New World will a person from the Old Country find himself so perfectly *at home*." [27] True enough, for the city contained most, if not all, of the amenities beloved by the discriminating gentleman. But Toronto the Good was not the only community to claim the affections of English gentlefolk; soon after Kingston wrote those words, a growing number of gentlemen began turning their attention to the other side of the continent towards the new colonies of Vancouver Island and British Columbia. Indeed, within a few years of Kingston's visit to Canada West and Toronto, a correspondent in one of Kingston's periodicals was extolling opportunities and resources in the Pacific colonies. "There is not a portion of the world's surface which possesses greater natural advantages, or a field more suited for the employment of the energies, industry, and capital of the British Colonist...than...British Columbia." As for Vancouver Island, it was, Kingston's correspondent said, "England all over again, and with many additional advantages.... "[28]

CHAPTER II

GENTLEMEN ADVENTURERS

In 1843 James Douglas, one of the Hudson's Bay Company's chief traders in the Pacific Northwest, sent a report to his superiors in London, describing the site of a new fort they had ordered him to construct on Vancouver Island: "The place itself appears to be a perfect 'Eden' in the midst of the dreary wilderness of the North west coast, and so different is its general aspect from the wooded, rugged regions around, that one might be pardoned for supposing it had dropped from the clouds into its present position." A year later another Hudson's Bay Company (HBC) official described the location in similar terms. It was, he wrote, "a very Elysium in point of scenery and climate."[1]

The area around Victoria, as the company post was named, had much to commend it. Situated on the southern tip of Vancouver Island, it boasted a number of fine harbours, good agricultural land, and a plentiful supply of timber and fresh water. Thanks to the offshore currents, prevailing winds, and the nearby Coast Mountains, it was blessed with warm summers, mild winters, and abundant but not excessive rainfall. In 1849 this Eden of the Far West was named capital of the new Crown Colony of Vancouver Island. The colony was established for strategic purposes following the loss of the Oregon Territory to the United States three years earlier. Yet though the British government was anxious to reaffirm its presence on the northwest coast of America it did not wish to bear the cost of a new colony. The HBC, therefore, was designated as the Crown's "sponsoring agent" for a period of ten years.

By the terms of the 1849 charter the HBC was able to retain its property and trading privileges on the Island for a nominal fee of seven shillings per year. In exchange, the Company was to survey the island, promote immigration, regulate local commerce and industry, and provide roads, churches, schools, and other amenities for the settlers. The company was not, however, to provide land cheaply and indiscriminately to all comers, for the Colonial Office wished to implement some of the colonization theories of the radical imperialist, Gibbon Wakefield. Accordingly, instead of making free land grants, as was the practice in the Canadas, the Crown set the price of land on Vancouver Island at £1 per acre and the minimum lot size at twenty acres. In addition, for every hundred acres that he bought, the purchaser had to bring out at his own expense three married couples or five single men. By establishing these regulations the Colonial Office and its agent, the HBC, sought to discourage squatters, speculators, and absentee landlords. They also wished to transplant some of the institutions of the Old Country—especially the yeomanry and the squirearchy—in the hope of avoiding the agitations that had erupted in the Canadas in 1837. As an HBC official in London explained to Douglas (who was later appointed governor of the colony),

> The object of every sound system of colonization should be, not to reorganize Society on a new basis, which is simply absurd, but to transfer to the new country whatever is most valuable and most approved in the institutions of the old, so that Society may, as far as possible consist of the same classes, united together by the same ties, and having the same relative duties to perform in the one country as in the other.[2]

In theory, the Wakefield system had much to commend it, for absentee landlords and squatters had caused problems in a number of colonies, particularly in Prince Edward Island and Nova Scotia. In practice, however, there were many weaknesses which were soon apparent when the system was introduced to

Vancouver Island. Regulations that discouraged speculation, for example, also tended to inhibit investment, and as a result the colony experienced little economic growth during its first decade. Similarly, the system did not provide much inducement for independent farmers, artisans, and tradesmen, and until the Colonial Office relaxed the regulations governing the price and allocation of land in the 1860s, many of these valuable settlers were lost to the Canadas or to the United States. The system did, nevertheless, appeal to gentlemen like twenty-seven-year-old Walter Colquhoun Grant, who had the inclinations but not the financial resources of the landed gentry. By expending a relatively modest amount of capital, such gentlemen could expect to establish themselves as country squires in one of the most salubrious parts of the British Empire.

Grant, who was the first colonist to settle on the island independently of the Hudson's Bay Company, came from a distinguished Scottish family. His father, Lt. Col. Colquhoun Grant, had been Wellington's chief intelligence officer at Waterloo; his uncle and mentor, Gen. Sir Lewis Grant, was colonel of the 96th Foot and sometime governor of Trinidad and the Bahamas. Grant himself held a captaincy in the elite 2nd Dragoon Guards (Royal Scots Greys), and had it not been for a bank failure, he would doubtless have pursued a military career. The bank failure—which involved a loss of some £75,000—reduced his income drastically, and since he had a great many debts he was compelled to sell his commission and look for civilian employment. Fortunately, his uncle had contacts in Whitehall who arranged for Grant to be appointed chief surveyor of Vancouver Island. With Sir Lewis's help, Grant was also able to raise sufficient money and recruit enough men to reserve one hundred acres of land in the new colony. [3]

Grant's men—a carpenter, a blacksmith, and a half-dozen labourers—left England in November 1848. They travelled to the colony via Cape Horn, an arduous 14,000-mile journey which in the sailing ships of the day took upwards of five months to complete. Captain Grant—he retained the courtesy title even though he had resigned his commission—followed in March 1849, travelling by the faster but more expensive "Panama

Route." This route entailed a sixteen-day crossing from Southampton to St. Thomas in the Virgin Islands aboard a Royal West Indian steam packet. At St. Thomas, travellers caught an intercolonial steamer to Aspinwall (Colon) on the Caribbean side of the Isthmus of Panama. Until the Panama Railway was built in 1855, they were obliged to make their way by mule train or wagon through feverish jungles and swamps to Panama City on the Pacific side of the isthmus. There they would board a Pacific Mail Company steamer for San Francisco, whence they would proceed in another vessel—usually a barque—to Vancouver Island. This 8,500-mile journey normally took from two to three months to complete, but because of delays in Panama and San Francisco it took the captain almost six months to reach his destination.

Grant chose property at Sooke, twenty-five miles from Victoria. The location was a good one, despite its distance from the capital, for much of the property was open "prairie land" which did not require extensive clearing. The captain named the property Mullachard, in honour of his ancestral home in Scotland, and within a few months of arriving in the colony he had made a good start on developing his farm. He imported a small herd of dairy cattle from Oregon, planted a vegetable garden, and sowed several acres in oats and barley. He also constructed a small sawmill at the mouth of a stream that ran across his property. But while Grant became a reasonably competent farmer and sawyer, he considered himself first and foremost an officer and a gentleman. Mullachard reflected the fact. The estate was approached by a long, serpentine drive which was intended to remind visitors of the carriageways that led to some of the stately homes of Britain. At the end of the drive was a stoutly built, whitewashed farmhouse filled to overflowing with books, sporting rifles, and expensive furniture. Outside the farmhouse were a tall flagpole and a pair of highly polished brass cannon.[4]

The cannon were placed in case of Indian attack, although happily the Native people never beseiged or even threatened the farm. In fact, the only altercations that took place at Mullachard were between the captain and his labourers. The quarrels, which arose because of workers' wages and living quarters, were never violent; however, they did lead to desertions and dismissals, and as a result Grant was unable to realize some of the grandiose plans he had for his estate.

Master-servant problems were by no means uncommon in the New World, as Dunbar Moodie and his wife well knew. But Captain Grant was also involved in disputes with the Hudson's Bay Company over the slow rate of growth and the high cost of living in the colony. His disputes with the HBC, the wrangles he had with his "rascally" labourers, and the debts he accumulated while trying to develop Mullachard eventually led to his disenchantment with the colony he had initially regarded as "a grand field for fresh and vigorous enterprise." As his disenchantment increased, he became uncharacteristically morose and, as he informed a cousin in Scotland, had it not been for a two-month holiday in the Sandwich Islands (Hawaii), "I really believe I sd. have committed Suicide by hanging, drowning, or otherwise."[5] The sojourn to Hawaii revived the captain's spirits, but unfortunately it did not resolve his problems, for in 1853 he disposed of his property—cannon and all—and returned to Britain.

Viewed objectively, Captain Grant's migration to Vancouver Island could not be adjudged a success, despite the fact that he and the colony seemed so well suited for each other. There was, therefore, a certain irony to the whole episode—an irony that was not lost on those who were critical of the Wakefield system of colonial settlement. Vancouver Island's first independent colonist did, nevertheless, contribute to the development of the colony. He did so not only through his pioneering efforts in agriculture and sawmilling, but also through the descriptive papers he presented to the Royal Geographical Society in 1857 and 1859. His papers dealt with the physical geography and resources of the island and helped to attract other emigrants.[6] Although he resided in the colony for only a short time, the captain also left an enduring legacy, in the form of yellow-flowering broom. The broom—which Grant planted at Mullachard to remind him of Scotland—is now found throughout the island. And then there is cricket, a sport the captain introduced when he presented a set of bats and wickets to the boys of the HBC school at Fort Victoria in 1849. Like the flowering shrub, the gentlemanly game of cricket took firm root on the island and has flourished there ever since.

When Captain Grant returned to Britain, he left a small, isolated colony with a white population of less than 450. The only settlement of consequence, Victoria, consisted of a stockaded fort, a handful of warehouses, and a few dozen farmhouses. Occasionally a trading vessel would call from San Francisco; sometimes a Royal Navy warship would put in to nearby Esquimalt harbour. Otherwise, the 250 colonists who lived near the fort led quiet, uneventful lives until 1858. In the spring of that year, their reverie was shattered when gold was discovered on the Fraser River across the Strait of Georgia. Victoria became the main provisioning centre for the gold fields, and by Christmas of that year the town had a "floating" population of almost 2,000. No sooner had the Fraser River gold rush subsided when word was received in 1861 of new gold discoveries near Williams Creek in the Cariboo. The rush to the Cariboo led to a further round of excitement and activity in the once-sleepy HBC post, as several thousand more miners descended on Victoria in search of supplies, prospectors' licences, and transportation to the mainland. In the midst of this second bonanza, the old warehouses and the stockaded fort were demolished to make way for new buildings of stone, brick, and ornamental iron. Incorporated as a city in 1862, Victoria took on a permanent, prosperous appearance. Captain Grant would scarcely have recognized the place.

The gold rushes of 1858 and 1861 were important to the development of Victoria, but they had an even greater impact on the mainland where the gold fields were located. The first led to the creation of the new colony of British Columbia which, until 1866, was administered separately from the colony of Vancouver Island. The second led to the growth of the mainland city of New Westminster, to the building of roads, and to the opening of British Columbia's interior valleys. There were, however, important differences between the two gold rushes. The bonanza of '58 was a short-lived, raucous affair, dominated by California miners who had little respect for British institutions. Most of those who swarmed over the sandbars of the lower Fraser were transients, and when the rush ended in 1859, the American miners disappeared as suddenly as they had arrived. In comparison, the Cariboo gold rush, which did not abate until 1865, was well-organized and peaceful. Because it was more orderly and because it was of a longer duration, it also attracted a better class of prospector. As British Columbia's chief justice, Matthew (later Sir Matthew) Baillie Begbie observed, it seemed "as though every good family of [eastern Canada] and Great Britain had sent the best son they possessed for the development of the gold mines of the Cariboo."[7]

Gold fever is a kind of disease. It strikes suddenly, without warning, and takes as its victims not only the idle dreamers and rolling stones of the world but also sensible, serious-minded men who, had they not been stricken with the fever, would have devoted themselves to orthodox trades and professions. Sometimes gold fever is brought on by greed, but as often as not it arises simply from a desire for change, adventure, and excitement. It was this romantic strain of the fever that gripped nineteen-year-old John Clapperton and his friends and prompted them to abandon comfortable homes and promising careers in England in favour of a rough-and-tumble life in the gold fields of far-off British Columbia.[8]

Clapperton and his companions reached Victoria by way of Panama after an exhausting three-month journey on 2 June 1862. They were met by an English clergyman who advised them to remain in the capital for a while in order to "find their feet." Although a few of the youths followed the vicar's advice, most of the party were impatient to get started. Indeed, within hours of arriving in the city they had outfitted themselves in "the highest style" of miners' fashion: red flannel shirts, blue denim trousers, and broad-brimmed felt hats. They also scurried to buy necessary hardware, such as picks and gold pans, as well as glamourous but unnecessary items such as bowie knives and revolvers. A waterproof blanket, a frying pan, kettle and oil can completed their outfit.

Two days later Clapperton and his jauntily attired pals were aboard the steamer *Enterprise*, headed for New Westminster and the new El Dorado. "We felt wild and free as the waves,"

Clapperton recalled, "now cracking a pleasant joke with each other, anon., admiring the beautiful scenery of the Straits [of Georgia], and expressing half sympathy, half contempt, for those of our shipmates who [had] resolved to remain in Victoria."9 At New Westminster they caught a riverboat to Hope, then trekked north along one of the main gold trails to the town of Lillooet, on the banks of the Fraser. They pitched up outside the town and spent the next few months fighting blackflies, nursing blisters, and looking for gold. Each day, irrespective of the weather, they scoured the sandbars of the river; each day they methodically sluiced and sifted what seemed to be tons of gravel. Each day they came away empty handed, or almost so, for the few ounces of gold they recovered did not nearly cover their expenses. Eventually, they decided to withdraw downstream to Yale where they found work on one of the roads which the Royal Engineers and private subcontractors were building. They worked with the road gangs just long enough to replenish their bankrolls, then proceeded north to join the thousands of sourdoughs who were working the creeks and hillsides around Barkerville, the unofficial capital of the Cariboo.

Barkerville was a boom town which, for a brief time, was the largest community north of San Francisco. There Clapperton experienced "fully the strange infatuation that seems to possess every man who follows the adventurous, exciting, hard life of a gold miner." But he realized that, despite the skills involved, "gold mining is a kind of gambling or, rather, a lottery."10 There was no shortage of players, but very few winners. Unfortunately, Clapperton and company were among the losers in the Cariboo stakes, and in 1864, as winter approached, they quit the diggings and trudged wearily down to New Westminster. They caught the first boat to Victoria, and although the voyage was as scenic as ever, the young adventurers were much less jovial than when they had first made the crossing. They were not the only ones, for when they arrived in Victoria they found the city full of disappointed men.

Richard Byron Johnson also found the city overflowing with down-and-out miners when he arrived that year. Like Clapperton, he was struck by the fact that many of those who languished in tents and makeshift shanties along the waterfront had, in happier times, been respected professional men, army officers, and merchants. Gold fever had made idlers and scroungers of many of them. Johnson, an English public school man, was determined that he would not suffer a similar fate, particularly as he had a letter of introduction to Gov. James Douglas. Accordingly, soon after he arrived in the city he made his way to the governor's residence. There he was received courteously, if guardedly. "I had some dim notion of the possibility of a snug government berth . . . with nothing to do and plenty of pay, and hinted this misty idea in a subdued way to my friend the governor." Douglas nodded sympathetically, smiled, then motioned Johnson towards a large drawer in one of the desks he kept in his study. Johnson peered into the drawer and was appalled to find that it contained "a thousand or more 'letters of introduction.'" Douglas then told him that if he wanted a job he should make his way to the mainland, where there was plenty of work on the road gangs.[11]

Reluctantly Johnson followed Douglas's advice, though first he decided he would try his luck with a few other letters of introduction in New Westminster. But things were much the same there as they were in Victoria. Arthur Birch, the colonial secretary at New Westminster, reported in a letter to his brother that the city was "over-run" with well-connected young Englishmen, many of whom were working at jobs which, under normal circumstances, they would have shunned. "The 'boots' at the hotel is the son of a doctor in Harley Street and has met me in 'society'. . . ," Birch wrote, "the son of a clergyman in Somersetshire is chopping wood for the Public Office, [while] half the stokers on the river steamers are decayed Gentlemen. . . ."[12] After working with some of these gentlemen on the riverboats, Johnson headed north where, as Douglas had predicted, he had no trouble signing on with a road construction crew. Yet although the work was steady, it involved long hours of exceedingly hard physical labour. The wages were also nothing to write home about. He consequently decided to try his hand at prospecting, and after several false starts he struck pay dirt at Jack of Clubs Creek, near Quesnel. But as so often happened, he lost his "pile" as quickly as he made it, and soon he, too, was among the ranks of the sometime-sourdoughs in Victoria.

Back in the capital, Johnson worked as a brewery drayman and as a clerk in a dry goods store. He then fell into company with the influential but impulsive Victoria journalist and politician, Amor de Cosmos. De Cosmos encouraged Johnson to write for his newspaper, the *British Colonist*, and intimated that under his tutelage the young Englishman would enjoy a prosperous career in the colony. "This was the chance I wanted!" Johnson wrote afterwards. "Dreams of the magic letters M.L.A. (Member, Legislative Assembly) appended to my name... capital stock in mining companies and other happy tricks of fortune passed before my mental vision in pleasant array." Alas, although De Cosmos later became premier of the province of British Columbia, his patronage brought Johnson few rewards. So, after a brief but unsuccessful foray into the silver fields of Nevada, Johnson returned to England where, ironically, he achieved the kind of fame and fortune that had eluded him in North America. He made his fortune not by speculating in capital mining stock but by regaling the British reading public with tall tales of high adventure in the Far West.[13]

Unlike Johnson, John Clapperton had little faith in letters of introduction or influential acquaintances; moreover, despite his disappointments in the gold fields, he developed a genuine attachment to British Columbia. Realizing that his chances of securing a "plum" government job in Victoria were all but "invisible," he flogged his picks, pans, and shovels, along with his bowie knife and fancy revolver, and returned to the mainland. He pre-empted land near Merritt, in the Nicola Valley, and with the few dollars he had remaining purchased some sheep and farm equipment. It proved to be an inspired move, for the "Laird of Nicola," as Clapperton was subsequently known, enjoyed a long and prosperous career in agriculture.

As both Johnson and Clapperton made clear, competition for "snug government berths" was keen during the gold-rush years, and the fact that a number of colonial positions were filled in Britain led to feelings of resentment among some of the gentlemen who were stranded in British Columbia. Some disappointed

gold seekers and their sympathizers even accused Governor
Douglas of deliberately promoting outsiders over the heads of
residents.[14] Their charges were unfounded, for whenever possible Douglas appointed emigrant gentlemen to local offices. Inevitably, though, there were positions that could not be filled
from the pool of local aspirants, and in such cases the colonial
secretary, Sir Edward Bulwer Lytton, would despatch a candi-
date from London. Lytton's men usually had had military, legal,
or administrative experience elsewhere in the Empire, and
though a few of his appointees were disappointing, most carried
out their duties with efficiency and zeal.

One of the first gentlemen sent by Lytton to promote the
"social welfare and dignity" of British Columbia was Chartres
Brew, a thirty-two-year-old Anglo-Irish gentleman who arrived
in the colony during the Fraser River gold rush. Brew was a tall,
barrel-chested man who sported a bushy set of whiskers and
possessed what the Victorians called a frank, open, manly face.
Matthew Begbie, who came to know Brew well, described him
as a "man imperturbable in courage and temper, endowed with a
great and varied administrative capacity, most ready wit, most
pure integrity, and a most humane heart." A veteran of the Crimean War and a former police inspector in the city of Cork,
Brew had been sent to organize a force similar to the Royal Irish
Constabulary. As it was originally envisaged, the force proved to
be too expensive for the colony, though Brew was able to recruit
a smaller body which rendered valuable service on the mainland.
Indeed, it was thanks largely to Brew and his officers that order
was maintained in the town of Yale when it was threatened in
1859 by a band of American vigilantes. It was also thanks to
Brew—whom a later B.C. governor said was ever willing to undertake "disagreeable, dangerous, and unhealthy" duties—that
peace was maintained among the miners of the Cariboo and
among the Indians in the Chilcotin district farther north.[15]

In addition to his duties as chief inspector of the police force,
Brew served as stipendiary magistrate and gold commissioner at
New Westminster. He was appointed member of the British Columbia Legislative Council and, after the mainland and island
colonies were merged in 1866 to form the United Colony of Brit-

ish Columbia, he served as colonial treasurer and chief commissioner of lands and works. Until his untimely death at Barkerville in 1870, Brew also distinguished himself as a town planner, mining engineer, and county court judge. Without doubt, he was one of Lytton's most outstanding appointees.

During his tenure as police inspector, Brew was assisted by John Carmichael Haynes, another Anglo-Irish gentleman who came to British Columbia in 1858. Haynes, who was twenty-seven when he emigrated, spent a year as police constable at Yale before assuming the duties of revenue and customs officer in the Similkameen district, near the American border. Like Brew, Haynes was tall and muscular—"a picture of manly strength," as one newspaper described him.[16] Like Brew, he served as justice of the peace, county court judge, and member of the colonial legislative council. Haynes is best remembered, though, as a cattleman and for being one of the first settlers to recognize the agricultural potential of the Okanagan Valley. He began acquiring property south of Okanagan Lake, at Osoyoos, in 1866 and over the next two decades built up a 22,000-acre spread. The cattle he raised on the ranch found a ready market in nearby communities, and Haynes, who had come to the colony with only a few dollars, amassed a considerable fortune. Some of the money he spent on building a large, broad-verandahed ranch house. Some of the money he invested in thoroughbred horses, for which he had a passion. However, unlike some of the cattlemen who later settled in the area, Haynes was not one to appear in ordinary twill shirt, denim trousers, and stetson. He preferred a neatly buttoned tweed jacket, tailored riding breeches, and pith helmet. "On horseback," his daughter recalled, "he invariably appeared as if 'riding in the Row.'"[17]

"The judge," "the squire," or "the baron," as Haynes was variously known, shared his equestrian passions with several of the ex-army officers who settled in the interior in the 1860s. These gentlemen—notably Capt. Charles Houghton, late of the 20th Regiment of Foot, Capt. John Martley, a veteran of the Crimean War, and Lts. Charles and Forbes Vernon, formerly of the Lancashire Fusiliers—came to British Columbia to take advantage of the Military Settlers' Proclamation Act of 1861, under which commissioned officers were entitled to up to 1,400 acres of land. Unfortunately, by the time most of the officers reached the colony the act had been superseded by the less generous Military and Naval Settlers' Act (1863). This act, however, still allowed former officers in Her Majesty's service to claim between 200 and 600 acres of land, depending on their rank. Most of the officers made good use of these grants, invested their capital wisely, and eventually built up some of the most prosperous ranches in British Columbia. John Martley, for example, used his grant to establish a large ranch called The Grange atop Pavilion Mountain, near Lillooet. Captain Houghton and the Vernon brothers used their grants to form the nucleus of the Coldstream Ranch, which was located near present-day Vernon.[18] But perhaps the most successful of the British gentlemen who took up ranching during the gold rush years were the Cornwall brothers, Clement Francis and Henry Pennant. They were the younger sons of the Reverend A.G. Cornwall, a landed gentleman and chaplain-in-ordinary to Queen Victoria. Clement took his B.A. from Magdalene College, Cambridge, in 1858 and was called to the bar from the Inner Temple four years later. Henry took his degree in classics from Trinity College, Cambridge, in 1861.

At Trinity, Henry Cornwall was a student of Leslie Stephen, and like many of Stephen's protégés he was a hearty, athletic young man. He had always had a thirst for adventure and on coming down from Cambridge was greatly excited by reports of the B.C. gold fields. Clement was about to begin practice as a barrister in the metropolis and so was less interested in the reports. But his brother's enthusiasm was infectious — as indeed was gold fever — and in April 1862 he agreed to accompany Henry to the new El Dorado. Clement was then twenty-six years old; Henry was twenty-four. Both brothers were confident that they would make their fortunes, though when they left England they did not intend to make the colony their permanent home.

Since the Cornwalls came to British Columbia in search of gold, they took only a cursory look at Victoria before making their way to the Cariboo. They reached Lillooet in June 1862 and found it to be "a pretty and ... thriving place."[19] John Clapperton, who was there at the same time, would probably have challenged the description, for he and his companions did not think too highly of Lillooet. Nor did Viscount Milton and Dr. Walter Cheadle, who stopped there a year later after their celebrated overland trek from the prairies. The dusty little town was then full of rough-looking miners who used a constant string of oaths and slang expressions—such as "bully for you" and "you bet your life"—which the intrepid but cultured travellers found difficult to understand.[20] The Cornwalls did not have the same problem. They understood perfectly well what the miners in Lillooet meant when they said that most of the readily accessible diggings were "played out." So, instead of heading for Barkerville as planned, they turned east towards Kamloops. After a three-day ride, they found themselves in some of the finest ranching country in North America.

Judge Begbie had passed through the same area a few years earlier and had been much impressed with it. "The entire country," he wrote, "resembles a vast park attached to a nobleman's mansion in England—nothing but grass and ornamental clumps of trees."[21] Henry and Clement were similarly impressed, and in July 1862 they pre-empted 320 acres along the Thompson River, south of Cache Creek. Their first home was a rude shack—"a sort of shed," Clement called it—but by November they had built a spacious, well-insulated log house, complete with fireplace and formal sitting room. The latter contained a large bookshelf and was decorated with prints, hunting rifles, and fishing rods—all of which, as Clement said, made the room look "uncommonly smart and comfortable."[22] They christened the house Ashcroft Manor, in honour of their family home in Gloucestershire.

In the early sixties, few homes in the Thompson River valley sported such aristocratic names. Few settlers in the valley were as well off financially as the Cornwalls. Not long after they moved into their log house the two brothers received over $6,000 from their father in England. They used the money to build a livery stable and roadhouse to serve the sourdoughs who passed by Ashcroft en route to the Cariboo. The stables and the inn both showed a good profit, as did the sawmill and gristmill which the brothers built the following year. But cattle ranching had attracted the Cornwalls to the valley, and thanks to an additional $8,000 from their father, they were soon able to stock their ranch. They began cautiously with a small herd; however they quickly mastered the business and by the mid-sixties were running almost 400 head of cattle which they sold to the beef-hungry mining communities to the north. Since the herds grazed cheaply on the abundant bunch grass, the Cornwall brothers were usually assured of high profits.

Like Judge Haynes and the other gentlemen ranchers of British Columbia, the Cornwalls were avid equestrians. In 1865 they laid out a racetrack adjacent to their roadhouse, and in 1866 they held the Ashcroft Derby and the Lytton Steeplechase. Both events became annual fixtures. Three years later, the Duke of Beaufort, a relative, provided them with their first pack of hunting hounds. Thereafter, the Cornwalls' overriding passion was chasing coyotes—a common substitute for the fox in western Canada. "Oh! the thrill that went through one when that halloa or uplifted cap shewed that the varmint was at length found, and the ecstasy of the first few minutes which unmistakeably proved that there was a scent on which the hounds could race," Clement wrote after one of the hunts. Following another successful outing he confided to his journal:

> How I have always pitied poor devils whose want of sporting education or opportunity when young—they being Englishmen—has prevented them knowing the raptures of the Chace [sic].
>
> Nothing, nothing whatever even approaches to its intensity, and however attractive other pursuits and sports may be in their way, yet, if one compares at all, the case is essentially one in which *hunting* must be placed *first* and the rest NOWHERE! [23]

The Ashcroft hunts—which were reported in the *Field* and other British sporting magazines—attracted sportsmen from as far away as the Similkameen district and Vancouver Island. The hunts helped to unite the gentlemanly class of settlers in the colony, and the bonds formed over stirrup cups were often reinforced by marriage. Thus in 1871 Clement Cornwall married Charlotte Pemberton, cousin to J.D. Pemberton, the Trinity

College, Dublin, man who had taken Captain Grant's place as colonial surveyor in Victoria. Henry's bride, three years later, was Captain Martley's stepdaughter, Mary.

Most well-born emigrants subscribed to the aristocratic belief that private privilege meant public service, and for this reason almost all of the gentlemen who pioneered in British Columbia accepted responsible positions in the civil service or stood for public office. The Cornwalls were no exception. Henry served as Indian agent in the Thompson River valley and local justice of the peace. Brother Clement served as a colonial MLA, and, after British Columbia joined Confederation, as one of the province's senators. The Honourable Clement Cornwall, as he came to be known, also served as lieutenant governor of the province from 1881 to 1887.

While the Cornwalls, the Vernons, Houghton and Haynes were rising to eminence as a result of their activities on the mainland, other gentlemen emigrants were establishing themselves successfully on the island. The Vancouver Island gentry—too numerous to mention by name—oversaw Victoria's transformation from a gold-rush boom town to a city of stately homes and well-tended gardens. In company with the city's Anglican clergymen, its private school masters, and the naval officers from nearby Esquimalt, they helped to give Victoria that "good standard of civilisation & morals" which so impressed Lady Franklin, Viscount Milton, and a score of other aristocratic visitors.[24] More important, these men, and their counterparts in the eastern provinces, were in a position to receive the second and larger group of gentlemen emigrants who began pouring into Canada after Confederation. Many of those who came in this second wave were youthful adventurers like Samuel Strickland and John Clapperton. But the wave also included many well-born, well-educated young men who were forced to emigrate because they were unable to find suitable positions in the Old Country. These young men especially appreciated the welcome they received in centres like Peterborough, Toronto, and Victoria, where an earlier generation of emigrants had already established a society of gentlemen.

CHAPTER III

SUPERNUMERARY GENTLEMEN

The last quarter of the nineteenth century was marked by events and trends that had profound consequences for British gentlemen. For some, notably middle-class gentlemen whose fortunes were based on commerce, the changes were beneficial. Parliamentary and educational reforms, advances in science and technology, the growth of manufacturing and commerce, the expansion of the overseas empire — these and a host of other developments allowed the middle classes in Britain to improve their social, political, and economic position. But for members of the landed gentry, whose fortunes and philosophies originated in a preindustrial age, the period was anything but golden. It was a time when their investments and incomes declined, when their social and political privileges were challenged, when their long-held beliefs and assumptions were shaken. For many of these gentlemen, the late-Victorian years were marked by uncertainty and despair.

Many of the problems that beset the landed classes originated with the agricultural depression, which began in the mid-1870s and lasted until the end of the century. Brought about by inclement weather and an influx of inexpensive foodstuffs from North America, Australia, and Argentina, the depression involved a series of crop failures and a decline in the selling price of wheat. The depression also led to rising costs of labour, since much of the rural workforce fled to the industrial cities or to the colonies. Together, the high labour costs, the low prices, and poor harvests imposed considerable burdens on those who depended on revenue from their country estates. Worst hit were the lesser gentry, who relied on smaller margins of profit and who did not possess revenue properties in the cities which could offset losses sustained in the country. For members of this class, the agricultural depression resulted in as much as a 40 per cent loss of income.[1]

Of course, the gentry still possessed land, and that in itself guaranteed a certain amount of wealth and status. But relatively few members of the gentry realized a cash profit from their property, and because of the laws of primogeniture, only the eldest sons of landed gentlemen could inherit the family estates. In an age when large families were the norm, there were inevitably younger sons to settle. Traditionally, these sons had entered the liberal professions: that is, the church, the law, or medicine. Alternatively, younger sons were provided with places in the civil service or with commissions in the army. But like almost everything else during this period, the traditional professions underwent changes. Some became more specialized, others became more competitive. Few were reserved, as had once been the case, for the younger sons of the gentry.

Of the liberal professions, only the Church of England remained completely open. Yet while the church was able, and indeed eager, to accommodate new clergymen, it was not regarded as a compelling vocation by the scions of good Anglican families. In fact, the number of well-born public school boys entering the church declined steadily during the century. For example, of the boys who left Rugby School in the 1830s, almost 40 per cent took Holy Orders; by the 1860s the number had fallen to 14 per cent and by the 1880s it was down to 5 per cent. At Harrow, over 20 per cent of the class of 1835 had entered the church; by 1860 only 7 per cent were being ordained, and twenty years later a mere 3 per cent of the graduates were joining clerical ranks. Figures for graduates of Winchester, Shrewsbury, and the other Great Schools show a similar decline over the period.[2] This

decline may be attributed to the meagre stipends paid to Anglican curates and to the fact that the church offered limited prospects of promotion; the decline may also be attributed to the fact
that it was no longer necessary, during the last decades of the
century, for young men who wished to teach in elite schools and
colleges to be in Holy Orders. For the most part, though, the declining enrollment in the church must be attributed to the religious doubt and controversy that characterized the age.

The declining interest in the church affected many families
who wished to settle their younger sons in respectable callings
and, accordingly, a large number of youths were redirected towards law. The legal profession, as a result, soon became overcrowded. Furthermore, because of reforms made during the
1850s, the legal profession became increasingly difficult to enter.
The Inns of Court, which were responsible for barristers, and
the Law Society, which governed the less prestigious solicitors,
both instituted rigorous qualifying exams and imposed other
hurdles which excluded all but the most gifted aspirants. Even
then, those who were called to the bar were not assured of a
competence, for though young men who practised law enjoyed
high social status, only a few were able to depend upon lucrative
briefs.

The third of the liberal professions, medicine, also became
more competitive and selective, especially after the passing of the
Medical Act of 1858 which raised standards and increased discipline within the profession. As was the case with the legal profession, the advent of higher qualifications and stringent examinations kept out many younger sons who, in an earlier period,
might have slipped into the medical practitioners' ranks. Moreover, as scientific knowledge increased, the profession became
all the more demanding. Again, though, increased competition
and high standards did not guarantee financial success for those
who managed to enter the profession. The destitute doctor, like
the briefless barrister, was a common figure in late-Victorian
society.[3]

These developments were related to the "rise of meritocracy." The meritocracy arose as British society became more industrialized, as scientific knowledge increased, and as tech-

nology began to manifest itself in all walks of life. It arose, too, when Britons were forced to take account of German and American industrial rivals. In other words, the meritocracy arose as Victorian society became more complex and more competitive. At the same time, and for the same reasons, the patronage system declined, and young men who had hitherto been able to advance in the professions simply because they had good family connections—or "interest," as it was known—found themselves overshadowed by rivals who possessed greater intellectual skills and initiative. Increasingly, the most lucrative posts went to the latter, and by the 1870s a young man, however well-connected, had to be a "meritocrat" (or, in the equally unflattering phrase of the time, a "competition wallah") if he was to make his way in the world.[4]

The practice of recognizing and rewarding merit instead of interest became an important feature of the civil service. The practice began in 1853 when competitive entrance examinations were introduced to the India civil service; two years later, the principle of competitive entry was introduced to the Home civil service. Initially, only nominated candidates were permitted to sit the exams, but as the winds of reform stiffened, the number of appointments made through patronage and nomination declined. By 1870, almost all posts within the service were being filled by open competition.

During this period the officer corps in the army—the remaining avenue for younger sons seeking a competence and gentlemanly vocation—was reformed in a similar manner. For centuries prior to the rise of the meritocracy, it had been possible for well-born young men to secure commissions in cavalry and infantry regiments by influence or by purchase. Dunbar Moodie, Thomas Traill, Walter Colquhoun Grant, and many of the gentlemen ranchers of colonial British Columbia had secured commissions in this manner. But after the disastrous showing of the British army in the Crimea, and after the dazzling successes of the efficient, professionally led armies of Prussia, the Imperial army was subjected to a series of much needed reforms. One of the most important of the reforms came in 1871 when the practice of purchasing commissions was abolished. Other reforms followed, and by 1876 open competition provided the basis for the awarding of commissions in all infantry and cavalry regiments. As for the artillery and engineering corps, which had previously tolerated patronage but not purchase, they too were reformed, and by 1870 commissions were granted only to those who had completed a demanding curriculum at the Royal Military Academy at Woolwich. Even the Royal Navy, which did not change easily, became more professional with the introduction of limited entrance exams, higher standards on the officers' training ship, and the opening of the Royal Naval College at Greenwich in 1873.

The welter of reforms and new regulations created problems for many young gentlemen who sought places in professions which had once been open to and reserved for the "better classes." By the same token, the rise of the meritocracy added to the difficulties of fathers who were expected to maintain their sons until they could acquire a competence of their own. Some of the difficulties were alleviated as new professions—such as surveying, architecture, and civil engineering—came to be accepted as professions fit for gentlemen. The difficulties also eased somewhat as younger sons of landed families began to take an interest in commerce. But these alternatives were palliatives at best. The new professions, while providing a broader field for gentlemanly endeavour, were soon as rigidly controlled as the army, the civil service, law and medicine. As for the gentry's more accommodating attitude towards "trade," the new tolerance applied mainly to prestigious branches of commerce: high finance, the steel industry, railways, shipping, and the like. It did not apply to the retail trade, which was still regarded as infra dig. In any case, even the prestigious branches of commerce were hard hit in the economic recession of the late 1870s / early 1880s, and as a result many young gentlemen were dissuaded from entering the commercial arena. But whereas economic downturns and the tightening of the professions created problems for young gentlemen and their families, the public school system was the main source of difficulty. Specifically, the elite school system expanded, and as it did, the pool of competence-seeking gentlemen increased dramatically.

The expansion of the elite public schools was a consequence of the power, wealth, and ambition of the Victorian middle class. Thanks to a growth in commerce, trade, and industry during the first half of the century, the economic position of the middle classes had improved significantly. Their political position improved in a similar manner as a result of the Reform Act of 1832. Having attained political and economic parity with the gentry and the old aristocracy, the vast army of middle-class manufacturers, merchants, and financiers desired to be recognized as "gentlemen." They achieved that status, or at least their sons did, with the founding of new public schools which offered a type of education that had previously been the preserve of the upper classes. Among the most prestigious of the new foundations were Cheltenham (1841), Marlborough College (1843), Rossall (1844), Wellington College (1859), Clifton College (1861), Haileybury (1862), Malvern (1865), and Fettes (1870). Equally prestigious were a number of old grammar schools such as Sedbergh (1528) and Uppingham (1654) which, with the help of middle-class money and enthusiasm, were transformed during the mid-Victorian years into major public schools. All told, the number of recognized public schools rose from a few dozen in 1840 to almost one hundred in the 1870s. The number of scholars attending either public or grammar schools increased accordingly from about 9,000 in the early 1840s to approximately 30,000 in the 1870s.[5]

Most of the new schools were inspired by the spirit of Thomas Arnold, the reforming headmaster of Rugby: that is to say, they endeavoured to foster religious principles, gentlemanly attitudes, and intellectual abilities. Like the Great Schools such as Eton, Winchester, and Harrow, the new public schools offered a liberal curriculum designed to prepare students for Oxford and Cambridge. The new fee-paying academies and boarding schools also adopted, or replicated, many of the rituals and traditions associated with the Ancient Foundations: corporal punishment, spartan dormitories, the monitorial or fagging system, school ties and uniforms, Old Boys' associations, and public school jargon. As a result, a wealthy merchant's son who attended, say, Haileybury was not recognizably differ-

ent from a landed gentleman's son at, say, Harrow. Despite their
different backgrounds, the youths spoke with the same accent,
shared the same intellectual and recreational interests, and held
similar attitudes in matters of politics and religion. Both had
been imbued with the public schools' ethos: *ergo*, both were
gentlemen. With the abolition of purchase and patronage, both
were forced to compete for a limited number of places in the
gentlemanly professions.

The competition that resulted was in many ways a healthy
development, for it helped to maintain high standards within the
professions. The scramble for gentlemanly berths, however,
placed great pressures on gentlemanly competitors. These pressures increased annually during the last quarter of the century,
when it was evident that even the new professions were failing to
keep pace with the ever-expanding pool of middle- and upper-
middle-class gentlemen.[6] Because of the competition and
pressure, a large number of public school boys were compelled
to look beyond the established professions for respectable and
remunerative careers. Many of these young gentlemen then discovered that, despite the expensive education they had received,
they were unprepared for the demands of modern commerce, industry, and even agriculture. They found, in fact, that they were
ill-equipped for the demands and the complexities of a society
which they were expected to lead.

To appreciate the handicaps of public school alumni who
were excluded from the prestigious professions it is necessary to
understand something of the philosophy and curriculum of the
public schools. The schools, ancient or modern, endowed or
proprietory, were classical academies, not vocational institutions. They were not intended to provide practical training;
rather, they were founded to produce well-rounded, liberally
educated *gentlemen*. To meet their objectives, the schools devoted a great deal of time and attention to classical studies—to
Latin grammar, to Euclid's geometric theorems, to ancient history, and to Greek texts of the New Testament. Public school
programmes were weighted in this way because people believed
that students well trained in classical languages and traditions
would also learn intellectual discipline and mental agility. There
was much to be said for this philosophy, but the public schools

carried it to excess, and in many institutions the boys might spend as much as 80 per cent of their classroom time on the classics. Public schools virtually ignored other subjects—notably modern history, modern languages and literature (including English), applied mathematics, and geography—on the grounds that they were utilitarian and therefore vulgar. Most public schools regarded science, particularly chemistry and physics, with contempt. Eton, for example, did not introduce science courses to its curriculum until 1875 and even then the courses were not compulsory.[7]

The prejudice against scientific instruction, applied mathematics, and other "modern" subjects was rooted in an age when British society was insular and primarily agrarian, when interest and patronage governed the professions, when an affluent middle class had not successfully challenged aristocratic privileges. Such a prejudice was untenable in an age when Britain depended on technology, heavy industry, and international trade. Anachronistic attitudes continued in the Victorian public schools, nonetheless; in fact, despite the growing complexity of late nineteenth-century society, preindustrial prejudices actually became more widespread as new public schools slavishly followed the educational bias of the Ancient Foundations. This bias created a curious, often ludicrous, situation, since many of the young men who shunned modern subjects at school came from families whose fortunes rested on commercial, technical, and other allegedly vulgar pursuits. Such was the price of gentility.

Next to the classics, organized sports occupied the most important place in the public school curriculum. In some schools, games and organized sports even took precedence over academic studies. Games were regarded not as entertaining pastimes or recreational pursuits but as "character-building" exercises, wherein boys learned to develop the qualities of leadership, discipline, patience, sobriety, physical strength, and courage. This preoccupation with games derived in part from the Victorian cult of manliness, from contemporary ideas concerning militarism and imperialism, and from the faith euphemistically known as "muscular Christianity."

The importance of games is well illustrated in Thomas

Hughes's influential novel, *Tom Brown's Schooldays* (1857), where two long chapters are given over to the virtues of cricket and rugby football. The preoccupation with games—or, as critics termed it, the "athletic mania"—is also evident from the attitudes of the novel's hero, whom Hughes described as "the commonest type of English boy of the upper-middle-class." When asked by a friend what he hoped to accomplish at school, Tom unabashedly replies, "I want to be AI at cricket and football and all other games . . . and I want to carry away just as much Latin and Greek as will take me through Oxford respectably." By the 1870s games were compulsory in most public schools, and in the years that followed great pressures were put on boys like Tom Brown to excel in athletics. They learned from schoolmasters, clergymen, military officials, and politicians that manly sports and exercises were the symbol and guarantee of Britannic success; they were told that the boy who excelled at games was the boy who excelled in life. As one writer put it in 1872: "The playground shows what a man is capable of, and gives promise of what he can, may, and will do in the great world. The men who win boat-races and cricket matches are the men who win battles and change the fortunes of nations."[8]

Unfortunately, many youths who devoted their schooldays to sport and who had been lionized for their prowess on the playing field, cinder track, and river found that they were unable to pass the rigorous examinations that restricted entry to prestigious, gentlemanly professions. They discovered, too, that their athletic skills and their knowledge of the classics were of little account in the world of science, technology, and commerce. These were the youths whom S.H. Jeyes referred to in a widely noticed article which appeared in the 1890s: "Grown and growing up, we see them everywhere: bright-eyed, clean-limbed, high-minded, ready for anything and fit for nothing. . . ."[9]

Jeyes was a journalist, not a professional educator; however, he summed up neatly the problems that had arisen because of the schools' preoccupation with classics and athletics. He began by noting that in the middle years of the century most young men who left their schools with a tolerable but not distinguished academic record had been assured of decent berths in the army, the civil service, or in one of the professions. At that time, there was still a demand for "the Tom Brown-type." Then, "only a few hundred muscular Christians were turned out on the world each year," and these youths were easily absorbed into the respectable ranks of society. But those days had gone, Jeyes said, pointing to the dramatic increase in the numbers of public school graduates and to the tightening of the professional marketplace. "Lament it as we may, we must acknowledge the fact that the future is for one-sided men, those who have made the most of their special gift or, if endowed with several, have ruthlessly concentrated upon one." Jeyes then castigated the schools for continuing to churn out annually thousands of archaically educated all-rounders, the majority of whom stood little chance of finding employment to match their gentlemanly expectations. Jeyes called these graduates "gentlemanly failures." It was a descriptive term but unnecessarily disparaging, for the Tom Browns he referred to were the products rather than the failures of the elite education system. He might have better described those "bright-eyed, clean-limbed, high-minded" young fellows as superfluous or "supernumerary" gentlemen.

The advent of the supernumerary gentleman was a vexing problem for many British families. "The younger son question," as the Victorians called it, inspired almost as much debate as the Irish question, the Balkan question, and the other great "questions" of the day. The question was debated at meetings of the Headmasters' Conference, at religious and philanthropic gatherings, in Parliament, and in a great many books and periodicals. The question was even noted in the foreign press. "An anxious enquiry has lately been raised . . . in England . . . as to what is to become of the large class of penniless young men: the younger sons of the gentry, well-built, well-educated young fellows, whose fathers' moderate income goes to the elder son and as a dower to the daughters," an American newspaper commented in 1883. The editor of the newspaper waggishly suggested that the British government might accommodate these youths by creating a new army regiment in which the lower ranks would be made up entirely of younger sons.[10] The prospect of such a regiment clearly amused the editor, though the idea was not as far-fetched as he imagined, for the War Office was asked on several occasions if it would create just such a corps. On each occasion the request was politely refused. There were, however, other avenues which the supernumerary gentlemen could follow. T.H.S. Escott, another gifted journalist, pointed to some of these avenues in a book published in the early 1880s. Having discussed the competitive nature of modern English society, Escott warned that "the crowds of young men who now sigh for gentlemanlike employment, and despair querulously because it is not forthcoming, will have to reconcile themselves to a perceptible descent on the social scale." For these young men, whom Escott described as having "gone through an academic course without discredit but without lustre," there were three choices: they could become underpaid curates in dreary provincial parishes; they could become underpaid teachers in the recently created Board (state) Schools; or they could become emigrants.[11] Faced with these choices, a great many young men decided to become emigrants.

Since Malthus's time, emigration had been regarded as the great panacea for over-population, and people generally believed that overseas settlement could diffuse or overcome related problems such as overcrowding, unemployment, religious dissent, crime and political discontent. During the first half of the nineteenth century, most enthusiasts had the lower orders in mind when discussing the advantages of emigration, but from the 1870s on, emigration came to be regarded as a boon for the middle and upper-middle classes as well. In fact, although members of the upper classes had been emigrating from Britain in large numbers beforehand, it was not until the last quarter of the century that the "gentleman" and the "emigrant" were closely associated in the public mind. This phenomenon gave rise to a new genre of settlers' manuals, which included specialized works such as William Stamer's aptly titled book, *The Gentleman Emigrant* (1874). This same phenomenon also accounted for the pro-emigration articles that began appearing regularly in *Macmillan's Magazine*, the *Fortnightly Review*, and other prestigious periodicals. Two such essays written by Maj. Gen. the Honourable William-Henry-Adelbert Feilding were published in the *Nineteenth Century*, a respected and highly influential journal. The first essay, which appeared in April 1883, was entitled, "What Shall I Do With My Son?" The second, which appeared three months later, bore the title, "Whither Shall I Send My Son?"

Feilding wrote from the perspective of the worried Victorian father though he was a bachelor when his articles were published; and though he was able to articulate the concerns of many supernumerary gentlemen, he himself never had to worry about finding respectable employment. He was commissioned into the elite Coldstream Guards just before the Crimean War, and until his death in 1895 he enjoyed a distinguished military career. As the fifth son of the 7th Earl of Denbeigh, Feilding was, however, well aware of the problems facing large, upper-class families. These problems were especially evident to Feilding after he embarked on a tour of the Empire in the late 1870s. In Canada, in Australia, and at the Cape he met a great many well-born, well-educated young men. Initially, he was inclined to feel sorry for the young exiles, but his pity quickly changed to admiration. He admired their pluck, their mettle, and their energy; he admired the way they were "forging ahead" in the colonies; indeed, he came to look upon the youths not so much as casualties of the Old Country—as Jeyes and Escott tended to do—but as leaders of a "new order." They were colonizers and empire-builders, and these professions were every whit as noble and as important as any in the Old Country. He therefore concluded his essays on a positive, optimistic note by urging parents who were concerned for the futures of their sons to direct the lads to the empire overseas, where there was still a need for the public school all-rounder.[12]

We have no way of knowing how many fathers were heartened by Feilding's call; nor do we know how many youths left Britain solely because they were unable to secure places in the military or in the professions. It is apparent, nevertheless, that a growing number of public school boys were establishing themselves in careers overseas. At Harrow, for instance, less than 3 per cent of those who graduated in the 1840s settled overseas; in the 1870s that figure had risen to 10 per cent. At Rugby the number of emigrants increased from 6 per cent to 13 per cent over the same period. At the newer foundations, whose graduates were not regarded quite so highly in the professions as Old Boys from the Great Schools, the trend towards emigration was even more pronounced. The proportion of emigrants among Durham School students rose from 3 per cent in the early 1840s to 17 per cent in the early 1880s; at Marlborough the proportion of emigrants among graduates increased from 10 per cent in the 1840s to 18 per cent in the early 1890s; and at Clifton College the number of emigrant Old Boys rose from 11 per cent in the mid-1860s to just under 20 per cent in the late 1880s. At Uppingham, Haileybury, and several other new foundations the proportions of emigrants among graduates was, by the mid-1890s, as high as 30 per cent. The exodus of public school alumni continued throughout the Edwardian years.[13]

The lack of employment opportunities for professionally minded youths, the laws of primogeniture, the declining incomes of the landed gentry, and the overall rise of the meritocracy—these were the salient "push" factors in the emigration equation. But "pull" factors were also important, at least with regard to Canadian immigration. A number of factors made Canada attractive, not the least of which was its proximity to the Old Country. In the 1870s emigrants who booked passage on the new Allan Line or Dominion Line steamships could reach Montreal from Liverpool in just seven or eight days. Political stability was another point in the Dominion's favour. Canada had not been convulsed by a civil war; nor, with the exception of the short-lived Riel rebellions, had Canada experienced any serious insurrections or native uprisings. The civil service and the professions were expanding, too, as the population increased and new provinces—Manitoba (1870), British Columbia (1871), and Prince Edward Island (1873)—joined Confederation. The relatively low cost of living and the chances of favourable returns on invested capital were inducements, not only for the family man but also for young bachelors who received small annuities or modest allowances. On top of the economic advantages, there were social advantages, particularly for the emigrant who chose to begin his colonial career in centres like Toronto, Peterborough, or Victoria. There the gentleman emigrant could be assured of a warm welcome; there he would find an Anglican church, a cricket club, and other familiar institutions. There he could enjoy a society that had been nurtured by the gentlefolk who had settled in Canada a generation earlier.

A great many books of the day, including Harvey Philpot's widely read manual, *A Guide Book to the Canadian Dominion* (1871), commented on the social amenities. "In the small as well as the large towns of Canada," Philpot wrote, "the society is very 'good,' being composed in great measure of aristocratic families from the Old Country who migrated in years long gone by, and who have either entered business there, or are living in comparative comfort upon means too small to have allowed them to maintain their position at home." Philpot elaborated by noting that gentlemen who possessed a few hundred pounds a year could afford a comfortable home, a carriage, and, perhaps, one or two domestic servants. "What is more gratifying still," he said, "the broken-down gentleman will not find himself elbowed out of the society, with which he means to mingle on fair and even terms, by reasons of his poverty. Poverty in Canada, where everyone begins by being poor, is not made a disgrace, except it be brought about by idleness and dissipation." [14]

William Stamer made similar observations when he enumerated the pros and cons of emigration. He conceded that for the independently wealthy gentleman there was no place like England. But for less fortunate gentlemen, life in the Old Country could be purgatory. Young bachelors, Stamer said, might try to keep up appearances by economizing ruthlessly on their day-to-day expenses, but sooner or later they would find themselves in difficulties. They would be unable to reciprocate invitations to fashionable parties, they would be unable to pay their dues at the club, they would not be able to join their friends in equestrian sports or continental holidays. In short, they would be "elbowed out" of the kind of society they had been educated to appreciate. As for the family man with an income of a few hundred pounds a year, such gentlemen might conceivably be able to eke out an existence in places like Bath or Cheltenham, but even they would find their lives limited.

Their amusements would consist of a stroll in the park, a constitutional along the high road, and once or twice a year a flower show or archery meeting; for although there might be one continuous round of concerts, balls, and theatrical performances, their means would not permit of their assisting.[15]

Anyway, Stamer said, no right-thinking gentleman would want to endure the "dead and alive" routine of an English retirement town, not when he could immigrate to Canada.

Outside the towns and cities, opportunities for gentlemen were possibly greater. In Ontario, a province recommended as being particularly suited for British gentlemen, improved 200-acre farms near Lake Ontario could be purchased and stocked in the mid-1870s for approximately £1,500 ($7,500), or less than half the cost of a comparable property in England. These farms produced everything from prize-winning cereals to exotic fruits and thoroughbred livestock. "A man who owns a well-cultivated farm in Ontario," John Rowan declared in another widely read manual for emigrants, "is as comfortable and as independent as a farmer can be."[16] To the northwest, the Muskoka district, opened for settlement by the Ontario government in 1868, also offered opportunities, and though the quality of land was not nearly as good as it was along the "Front" or on the Niagara Peninsula, the free homesteads in the district attracted a great many land-hungry gentlemen. Many of these settlers located near new villages such as Hoodstown and Huntsville, both of which were established during the period by retired army officers. Other gentlefolk clustered around Bracebridge and Ilfracombe. In the 1870s the population of Ilfracombe was said to include a fair number of "gentlemen of good position and means from England"; Ilfracombe was also described as "the centre of an English colony of high county standing and much cultivation."[17] However, by far the most important area of new settlement was the North West Territories, which the Canadian government purchased from the Hudson's Bay Company in 1870. Here was a vast, virgin land, extending from Manitoba to the foothills of the Rocky Mountains. Here beneath that immense sky peculiar to the western prairies lay one of the most fertile areas in the world.

To promote and facilitate the settlement of the West, the government embarked upon an ambitious, innovative programme. A major part of the programme involved the chartering of the Canadian Pacific Railway (CPR), a transcontinental line which traversed the southern part of the prairie. Although financial crises and political scandals hindered construction of the line, the CPR was completed by 1885. Another part of the programme revolved around the Dominion Lands Act (1872), which provided male British subjects over eighteen years of age with 160-acre homesteads. In order to acquire patent to the land, settlers needed only to improve their homesteads over a period of three years and pay a $10 (£2) registration fee. Under the terms of the act, settlers could also pre-empt an adjoining quarter section (160 acres) for as little as a dollar per acre. Since the size of an average farm in England was less than 100 acres, and since prime agricultural land there was expensive, the homestead act was obviously very attractive to the gentleman emigrant as well as to the landless British labourer. To ensure that the advantages of the act and other opportunities in the West were fully known and appreciated in Britain, the Canadian Department of Agriculture also launched a $700,000 advertising campaign in the early 1870s. The campaign, which accelerated after the Department of the Interior became responsible for immigration in the 1890s, entailed the printing and distribution of literally millions of posters, pamphlets, and other inspirational literature; it involved the opening of new immigration offices in London and the provinces and the presentation of agricultural demonstrations and exhibitions throughout the United Kingdom. Although aimed principally at the labouring classes, the government's recruiting campaign also reached and inspired a good many gentlefolk.[18]

Daniel Gordon, the traveller and theologian, declared in 1880 that while the rich western plains offered advantages to "men of all nationalities, they offer special attractions to immigrants of the Mother Country, for there the shield of the Empire will still be around them."[19] A great many gentlemen emigrants were drawn to the Canadian rather than the American West for this very reason. By settling within the Dominion they could retain their citizenship, enjoy the protection of British laws and, of no small importance, avoid the anti-English sentiments that were rampant in many parts of the United States after the Civil War. Victorians also believed that the public school man was the kind of man who would eagerly uphold the "shield of Empire" in the West. The public school man had been reared in institutions that placed high premiums on such virtues as loyalty, discipline, and respect for tradition, and he was supposed to be an enterprising individual as well as a reliable team player. If anyone could further the imperial idea on the frontiers of the Empire, it was he. This idealized view of the public school man's role in the Empire was well expressed by the Reverend T.C. Papillon, an Old Marlburian, towards the end of the century. "Many a lad," Papillon said, "who leaves an English public school disgracefully ignorant of the rudiments of useful knowledge... and who has devoted a great part of time and nearly all his thoughts to athletic sports, yet brings away with him something beyond all price—a manly, straightforward character, a scorn of lying and meanness, habits of obedience and command, and fearless courage. Thus equipped, he goes out into the world and bears a man's part in subduing the earth, ruling its wild folk, and building up the Empire."[20]

For the young men the Reverend Papillon spoke of, no better opportunity could be found than the North West Mounted Police. Formed in 1873, the scarlet-clad Mounties marched west the following year. Their task: to drive out lawless American whiskey traders, to help locate the native Indians on government reserves and, generally, to ensure order and peaceful development in the newly opened settlement areas. The romantic exploits of the NWMP were celebrated in story and in song, and not surprisingly, the force captured the imaginations of many public school boys and university men. Indeed, the middle-class sons of Britannia regarded the force almost as a calling. They were excited at the prospect of galloping across the open prairie, carrying out patrols, chasing desperadoes, and rendering service to isolated homesteaders; they were impressed by the Mounties' integrity, their self-reliance, and their heroism; they were inspired by the way the "riders of the plains" upheld the majesty of the law and the ideals of the Empire across the vast frontier. The force, for its part, looked favourably upon the young public school men, most of whom were, as Papillon described, manly, courageous, energetic, and dependable. They were a class of immigrants well suited to upholding the NWMP's motto, *Maintiens le droit.*

Finally, the Dominion of Canada offered any number of opportunities to free-spirited gentlemen—to the rovers, the ramblers, and the emigrant sportsmen. Gentlemen of this stamp could find in Canada open spaces, natural beauty, and wild sport. John Rowan, who sometimes wrote under the pseudonym, "Cariboo," told readers of the *Field* that no other country in the world offered such opportunities to sportsmen as did Canada. Judging from the letters that appeared regularly in that august periodical, "Cariboo" was not exaggerating. "In a week's trip north-west of Qu'Appelle," one gentlemen reported, "I recently brought to bag the following: 154 duck, 78 teal, 120 widgeon and snipe, 48 partridge, 247 prairie chicken, and various, 23." The writer boasted, "I shot the above in six days clear, and had nothing but a cross-bred spaniel I brought out from England. . . . I could have doubled the result if I had had a setter and a good retriever."[21] Reports of this kind, along with highly acclaimed travel books such as Colonel William Butler's *The Great Lone Land* (1872) and the Earl of Southesk's *Saskatchewan and the Rocky Mountains* (1875), set the sportsmen aquiver and accounted for hundreds of the gentlemen who migrated to the Dominion during the period. Armed with their .450 Express rifles and their Castleconnell double-jointed fishing rods, and accompanied, mayhap, by faithful canine friends, they stalked, angled, bagged, and potted to their heart's content.

(*From* The Pioneer Farmer
and Backwoodsman,
estate of E.C. Guillet)

When Frederick DelaFosse left Wellington College in England (opposite, top) he emigrated to a farm in the Muskoka district of Ontario similar to that shown opposite. One can imagine the culture shock.

(*Saskatchewan Department of Culture and Youth: Historic Parks*)

"First day in the West." Cannington Manor bachelors, c. 1890

(Public Archives of Canada)

Gentlefolk playing croquet, Peterborough, Ontario, 1890s

(Glenbow-Alberta Institute)

Western Canada's first polo team, Fort Macleod, 1892

Cannington Manor Hunt Club outside Didsbury, early 1890s. The bachelors' wing known as the "Ram's Pasture" is visible on the extreme left.

CHAPTER IV

EMIGRANT SCHOOLBOYS

Most young British gentlemen who came to Canada during the late nineteenth and early part of the twentieth century had little idea of the conditions they would be facing. This is not to say that the youths were ignorant, for most of them had read books, articles, and brochures on the Dominion before they set out. But even the most accurate and objective of the publications could not give intending settlers a convincing picture of the country's size, its diverse geographical features, its vegetation, and the idiosyncracies of the people. Few emigrants actually concerned themselves with these matters, however, and those who did were comforted by the thought that they would be among friends. The Dominion was, after all, British-pink on the map, and in the minds of many of the emigrants, Canada was simply a remote, somewhat rugged, part of Great Britain. It was not an alien land by any means. Since most of the gentlemen emigrants had friends, relatives, or business contacts in the Dominion, they did not feel totally cut off from home. Moreover, many of the young gentlemen either brought a substantial amount of money with them, or were in receipt of regular allowances from their families in Britain.

The fact that the young gentlemen had some capital, had support from home, and had contacts in Canada gave them a decided advantage over a great many of their countrymen. Most of them appreciated their advantages and so began their colonial careers on a buoyant, confident note. Many were buoyed, too, by their public school education, which they had been taught to believe would help them immeasurably in whatever field they chose to enter. Being unmarried was also an advantage, in some ways at least, for the young bachelors enjoyed a flexibility and a mobility which was often denied to immigrants who had wives and children to settle. Finally, most of the public school boys and university men who came to the Dominion were blessed with good health and imbued with a spirit of adventure. They felt more than capable of meeting the challenges that lay before them. They saw themselves as part of a glorious crusade. They believed that by emigrating they were keeping an appointment with destiny. Like seventeen-year-old John Gwynn Swain, they fully expected to find fame and fortune on the other side of the pond.

Swain came from a respectable but modestly endowed Edinburgh family. His father was dead and his mother kept a small private hotel in the fashionable New Town district of Edinburgh. The hotel catered to lawyers and other professional gentlemen and provided Mrs. Swain with a steady income. Still, even with her pension, Mrs. Swain had little money for the luxuries she had enjoyed when her husband was alive. Master Swain found the situation unsatisfactory, and on leaving school he resolved to restore the family's fortunes. "My ambition soars high and I mean to show everyone what a boy can do if he has the brains and the will," he informed his mother and the world at large.[1] Johnnie, as he was known to his family, was a romantic of the first order; the young Scot was determined to blaze new trails— figuratively and literally— to undertake bold adventures, and to experience life to the full. He achieved most of these goals during his first two years in Canada.

Swain and a school chum, Hugh Gibson, left Greenock aboard the Allan Line steamer *St. George* in June 1867. The nine-day crossing was rough, and on occasion Swain and Gibson admitted to feeling a dull queasiness. But the two young gentlemen, comfortably housed in a private cabin, did not suffer nearly as much as their less affluent countrymen who were crowded in poorly ventilated quarters below decks. For the steerage passengers—"lying like pigs, vomiting in all directions"—the voyage was hellish. "Their retching was frightful," Swain recorded in his journal, "and the poor babies (of whom there are an immense number) were crying piteously [and] their mothers were too ill to attend them." During the second week of the crossing, two of the children, an infant girl and a boy of six, died from the effects of seasickness. Only then did Swain—who had spent most of the voyage exercising on gymnastic equipment and chatting with his fellow saloon passengers—apprehend that for many Britons emigration was a heartbreaking ordeal. "I felt very much for the poor mothers," he wrote after the two bairns were consigned to the sea, "and went to my room and thanked my Maker for preserving me."[2]

The weather improved as the *St. George* neared the Grand Banks, and after brief stops to disembark passengers in St. John's, Newfoundland, and Quebec City, the ship glided safely to its berth in Montreal. Swain was greatly impressed by the city with its palatial hotels, the imposing churches, and the recently completed Victoria Tubular Bridge. But despite the city's attractions, and invitations from friends to stop in Montreal, Swain and his partner decided to press on to Toronto. They arrived in time to take part in the first Dominion Day celebrations, marking the confederation of Canada.

Swain referred to 1 July 1867 as "a great day" and indeed it was, in more ways than one. In the morning, as he watched a colourful review of Volunteers and regular troops outside the lieutenant governor's residence, he realized that he was witnessing an event of historic importance. Later that evening, as he marvelled at the roman candles bursting over Lake Ontario, he was overcome by the feeling that his prospects, like those of the new Dominion, were exceedingly bright. He decided there and then to preserve his impressions and experiences for posterity. "Let Freddy [a cousin in Scotland] see this letter... also any of our friends you think proper," he instructed his mother, "but take great care and keep it *scrupulously clean.*" In another letter he drew attention to the fact that he was writing on expensive, high-quality bond paper. "The postage of this thick paper will cost me *more*, I know; but I don't mind, as I want you to keep all my letters perfectly clean, and get them neatly bound, as I am writing as nicely as possible for that purpose."[3]

Although he was eager to get on in Canada and make his fortune, young Johnnie was in no great hurry to find employment. He preferred instead to spy out the land while formulating a grandiose career strategy. His strategy was constantly changing, and though he did not realize it at the time, he passed up some very lucrative opportunities. In Montreal, for instance, he was introduced to R.B. Angus, a fellow Scotsman who had come to Canada ten years earlier. Angus was then manager of a branch of the Bank of Montreal. Two years after Swain met him, Angus became general manager of the bank; later he became bank president and one of the principal directors of the Canadian Pacific Railway. Swain, however, declined Angus's offer of employment in the mistaken belief that an association with the banker would not prove "advantageous." Similarly, he turned down several good posts in Toronto in the belief that something better would turn up. Yet the months Swain spent unemployed were by no means wasted. Anticipating more trouble from the Fenians, the Irish-American republicans who had attempted an invasion of Canada in 1866, Swain patriotically joined the militia. He was awarded a commission in the regiment and was invited by his fellow officers to join them in their social activities. Thanks to good food, fresh air, and plenty of exercise, he also gained weight, added over an inch to his height, and sprouted "a splendid set of whiskers." Thus, while he had yet to replenish his ever-dwindling bank account, he was well satisfied with his progress. "I shall never regret coming to Canada," he told his mother in a Christmas letter. "It is the best thing that ever could have happened to me."

Hugh Gibson, in contrast, found life a constant struggle. He had neither the patience nor the audacity his friend possessed. For example, Swain thought nothing of pawning his overcoat in order to attend a social function which he could not otherwise afford. To his way of thinking, keeping up appearances and mingling with the right sort of people was the best way of securing a competence. But Gibson was a rather timid soul who normally husbanded his scanty resources. Moreover, unlike the gregarious Johnnie, he craved security and routine, and within weeks of arriving in Canada, he took a clerk's position in a small country store. When he found that he was unsuited for the position, he accepted a job as a travelling salesman. The move was not successful, and over the next six months the unhappy Gibson drifted from job to job. He became scruffy and morose and, as often happened with British exiles, he took to drink.

Eventully Gibson turned up at Swain's boarding house in Toronto. Swain was appalled by his friend's appearance but agreed to take him in. He even allowed Gibson to share his bed. That was a mistake. A day or so after Gibson moved in, Swain reported, "I began to feel very itchy, and examined my flannels, when to my great *horror* and *disgust*, I found several LICE! I immediately made Gibson take off his shirt, and would you believe it, he was *literally crawling*. I never saw such a sight in my life!" Swain burned his flannel pyjamas and bed linen, fumigated the room, and expelled his friend from his lodgings. What became of Gibson is unknown, for Swain refused to have anything more to do with him. Writing some months after the event, he noted only that Gibson was "indeed a most consummate blackguard ... and is now doing God knows what."

The lice episode was an unsettling experience for Swain, but it reinforced his conviction that one had constantly to be on one's guard. One had to maintain one's standards. One had to remember that no matter how difficult the situation, one was still a gentlemen. In Swain's case the philosophy was expedient, for after spending a pleasant winter mingling with Toronto's elite, he was offered a position as cook and surveyor's assistant with a party of explorers who were planning an expedition to the western shores of Lake Superior. The position paid $50 a month plus expenses and provided Swain with the opportunity of satisfying his desire to "see the wild side of nature."[4]

The four-man expedition was led by Hugh Savigny, a provincial land surveyor. Like Swain, Savigny hailed from Edinburgh, although the two did not meet until Toronto. The deputy leader was Capt. James Strachan, son of the Bishop of Toronto.

Swain had met the captain in militia circles and through him was introduced to the upper echelons of Ontario society. Swain's friendship with the captain also accounted for his presence at the bishop's funeral in November 1867. The other member of the expedition was a magistrate and mining engineer from Sarnia, J.P. Donnally.

The expedition left Toronto in May 1868 and made its way via steamer to Fort William. The group then hiked inland and for the next few months scoured the area in search of gold, copper, and other valuable minerals. The terrain was rough and the mosquitoes and blackflies fearsome. Yet young Swain, who had hitherto been an urban dandy, positively revelled in the experience. "I am . . . *devotedly fond of the life with all its hardships*," he gushed in one of his backwoods epistles, "and I doubt if you will find many brought up in *such a home as I have* who could like a Canadian life." Johnnie was underestimating the mettle of gently reared emigrants, many of whom experienced greater difficulties and endured greater hardships than he did during the summer trek. Still, it was understandably an exhilarating moment for Swain, and to be fair, the young emigrant did undergo a few extraordinary experiences. "I have been stabbed by an Indian, nearly starved to death, upset in a canoe, wrecked on a steamer, and lots of minor things too numerous to mention, but which are always associated with camp life in the bush."[5]

Swain did not elaborate upon his more perilous adventures for fear of alarming his mother. Instead, he wrote animated, detailed letters describing his hunting expeditions, his fishing successes, and his newly acquired woodcraft skills. By the end of the summer, he could wield an axe, handle a canoe, and build a bough shanty with the best of them. Despite his stab wound, he delighted in the native Indians and was so taken by their culture that he began compiling an Ojibway-English dictionary. Most of all, Swain was impressed by the awesome grandeur of his surroundings, as is evident from the romantic verse that he wrote on birch-bark parchments: "Thou comest with a pleasant voice, O little stream to me / And softly spoken words are thine beneath the greenwood tree. . . . " His delight was equally apparent in the long letters that he composed during his solitary rambles. "Every day my love for [the country] gets *stronger* and *stronger*, and fresh beauties of nature appear to my eyes hourly . . . which serve to strengthen my love for the woods and my reverence for my Creator, who has made such a lovely world for man to live in. The aspect which is now spread before me . . . is past description. . . . My mind is almost incapable of appreciating it." [6]

Swain might have been satisfied had he experienced only adventure and beauty during his visit to Lake Superior. However, he decided to remain in the woods with Donnally after Savigny and Strachan returned to Toronto. It was fortunate that he did so, for while wandering along the shore of Black Bay, fifty miles north of Fort William, he stumbled across a very promising vein of silver. The vein was over 150 feet wide, and ore samples, which Swain had assayed in Sault Ste. Marie, indicated the presence of high-grade silver lead. The land on which the vein was located had been staked earlier by local prospectors, but after lobbying his family and friends in Scotland, Swain was able to raise enough money to buy up the claim. With Donnally's assistance, he also interested several American investors in the property. "The Happy Home Location," as Swain dubbed his discovery, was resurveyed and a new mining company duly registered in the autumn of 1868. Swain retained a one-fifth share in the company, though it is unclear whether the company actually developed the property or whether the shareholders merely speculated in mining stock. Whatever the case, Johnnie made money on the venture and in October was able to report that he was a "man of some standing in the world." "My prospects," he wrote, "are excellent in every way." [7]

In his last letters, Swain noted that he was hoping to visit Scotland, pay off the family debts and enjoy a festive Christmas with his mother. The letters also indicate that he planned to transact some business in Edinburgh and Glasgow, possibly with a view of raising more money for his Canadian investment. Whether he succeeded is not recorded, but John Gwynn Swain had reason to be pleased with himself, for he had realized most of the goals he had set when he emigrated. He had faced new challenges, had enjoyed unimagined beauties, and had signi-

ficantly improved his financial position. As he had intended, he
had shown "what a boy can do if he has the brains and the will."
He had shown, too, what a gentleman could do, given confidence, capital, and good connections.

James Seton Cockburn, a Scottish-born gentleman who immigrated to the province of Quebec, was also well connected. Indeed, his monogrammed portmanteau literally bulged with
letters of introduction. He also possessed a fair amount of capital and was completely self-assured. But Cockburn's experiences—which were recorded in a collection of letters entitled
Canada for Gentlemen (1885)—were tame compared to Swain's.
This witty, articulate, insouciant young man was curious, rather
than adventurous. He was under no delusion that he would
shake the world by emigrating. In many respects, he typified the
urbane young gentlemen who made up Canada's minor bureau-
cracy during the last quarter of the nineteenth century.

Although he was born north of the Tweed, Cockburn was
raised and educated in England. His father was a retired army
officer and his mother was a hostess of some standing in the West
Country. His sisters had married well, and his older brothers
were successful barristers and physicians. He hailed, in short,
from a respectable middle-class family. Yet despite his family
background and despite the training he had received as a
surveyor, James had been unable to find a satisfactory vocation
in Britain. He decided, therefore, to team up with his younger
brother, Henry, and explore opportunities in Canada. Mr.
Cockburn, who naturally worried about his sons' future, approved of their decision. He offered them words of encouragement, promised to assist them if they encountered any difficulties, and provided each of them with approximately £500 in
capital. Thus endowed, twenty-four-year-old James and his
eighteen-year-old brother clambered aboard a train for Liverpool in August 1884.

The port of Liverpool was particularly busy that summer.
The transit hotels were crowded with emigrants; colonial outfitters were doing a brisk trade, and the quays and warehouses
were piled high with emigrants' effects and other outbound
cargo. As usual, the port city also swarmed with touts, runners,

and disreputable hotel agents who preyed on unwary emigrants from the provinces. As the brothers Cockburn emerged from Lime Street railway station, carting their bags and clutching their pound notes, they were immediately collared by one of these agents, an unctuous character who reeked of whiskey and cheap cigars. The agent magnanimously offered to take the bewildered transients to a nearly "temperance" hotel and volunteered to see their luggage safely on board their vessel. It was an old ruse and had the Cockburns accepted his offer they would certainly have been robbed and possibly beaten in some dockside flophouse. Fortunately, before they could reply, an honest street-wise cabby intervened, drove off the agent with a few well-chosen profanities, and conducted the youths to a respectable hotel. There the two innocents were able to rest, bid farewell to friends, and prepare themselves for the rigours that lay ahead.

The Cockburns booked passage on the S.S. *Montreal* (Dominion Line) and like most emigrants of their social standing they travelled as saloon passengers. Their cabin, which they shared with another young gentleman, was graciously appointed and well ventilated. Even so, the saloon-class travellers were not immune from that great leveller, seasickness. First to succumb was the brothers' new-found companion, a soft-spoken Londoner who, James recalled, "frankly avowed himself 'awfully squashy inside' and proceeded practically to demonstrate the truth of his assertion." No sooner had the 3,300-ton liner left the mouth of the Mersey than Henry also "embraced the opportunity of confession and . . . became equally demonstrative."[8] Their "demonstrations" continued with depressing regularity during the days and nights that followed. James, older and more of a stoic, managed to contain his nausea but only by lying rigidly in his berth and abstaining from most of the meals. Since he was a gourmand and a wine lover, his stoicism made for a long and tedious crossing.

After spending a few days recuperating in Montreal, the Cockburns made their way to the city of Sherbrooke in the anglophile Eastern Townships where they endeavoured to find work. Their search lasted several weeks, for Sherbrooke, a sedate community of less than 10,000, offered few employment opportunities. Eventually, though, Henry was settled with a farmer in the district. He was to receive his room and board and, if he proved satisfactory, a small wage. It was scarcely a lucrative position, though James thought that it would prove to be a "character-building" experience. "Henry," he declared in one of his letters, "is at present very young for his years, and has a good many ways and ideas which time will moderate." James felt that working as a chore boy for a "fairly civilized" rural family would help his brother mature: the younger Cockburn would learn to be independent, would develop confidence, and would add muscle to his spare schoolboy frame. If all went well, Henry would also acquire skills which would allow him to take "root in the soil of the new country." [9] But what was sauce for the goose was not sauce for the gander, for while he extolled the advantages of Henry's situation, James had no desire to follow suit. Nor did he fancy working for his room and board as a blacksmith's assistant, which was the only job offer he received in Sherbrooke. Instead, James parcelled up his letters of introduction and returned to Montreal where life was gayer and the future brighter.

James's letters provided him with an entrée into Montreal society. He was introduced to the city's leading clubs and in one of these spent a happy few hours discussing big game hunting with Chester Arthur, son of the American president. But the letters did not provide Cockburn with employment. The harbour master in Montreal regretted that his department had no vacancies, and the Grand Truck Railway people were unable to provide him with a berth in their marshalling yards. Cockburn was not worried. He had several hundred dollars in his pocket and so was in no danger of starving. His confidence was unshaken, for he simply attributed his difficulties to an overcrowded job market. "There has been a great 'boom' on Canada as a field for labour," he informed his father. "Thousands and thousands of people have come and been sent by colonization societies, etc., and the consequence is, there are more people than there is work for, even in the agricultural line." [10] True enough, immigration was on the rise in the 1880s, and some occupations, particularly in the cities of eastern Canada, were overcrowded. But some of Cockburn's disappointments were undoubtedly due to the fact that he was looking in the wrong quarters. Aside from the snippets of information he had picked up on board the *Montreal*, he had little knowledge of steamships or harbour regulations. He knew even less about steam loco-motives. Furthermore, like John Gwynn Swain before him, young Cockburn often did not recognize the importance of the men he met. In September 1884, for instance, he called upon William (later Sir William) Van Horne, vice-president of the CPR. Energetic and exceedingly wealthy, Van Horne was ar-guably one of the most influential men in Canada. Cockburn—who flippantly referred to the magnate as "some sort of boss on the railway"—failed to appreciate Van Horne's position, and not surprisingly he came away from the meeting empty-handed. Still Cockburn was unconcerned, and for several weeks he re-mained contentedly in Montreal, enjoying the city's clubs, res-taurants, and theatres. He then rooted through his portman-teau, extracted a letter addressed to Sir David Macpherson, Canada's minister of the interior, and boarded a train for the nation's capital.

His first impressions of Ottawa were not encouraging. He re-garded the city as a "dead and alive hole," a "miserable little place." The railway station—"little better than a shed in a field" —was dirty, and the roads downtown were deplorable. "I came up in the hotel 'bus, and though I tried all I knew to sit firm and not let daylight be seen betwixt me and my saddle, I was jumped about like a dancing master, and I hammered those cushions till I thought of claiming a week's pay from the hotel for beating the dust out of them."[11] Sparks Street, one of Ottawa's principal thoroughfares, was covered "from one end to the other with three inches of liquid mud": it looked like "a canal of pea soup." The Parliament Buildings grounds were devoid of ornamental landscaping, and the lumber mills and log booms, crowded along the banks of the Ottawa River, gave an untidy aspect to the whole area. As far as Cockburn was concerned, the city's only redeeming features were its confectioners' shops, which dis-pensed large and inexpensive portions of ice cream. Neverthe-less, since winter was approaching and his funds were running low, Cockburn decided to remain in the capital. He took a room in a sparsely furnished five-dollar-a-month boarding house, unpacked his best suit, and called upon Sir David.

Macpherson managed to find Cockburn work as a draughtsman for Adam Harvey, one of Canada's leading patent solicitors. The salary was only ten dollars a month, but the office was warm, the position was secure, and the work was not taxing. Besides, Harvey was a congenial fellow who did not object if his clerks whistled or smoked their pipes in the office. Most young men would probably have attached little importance to these perks, but since Cockburn had previously worked in a similar capacity for a rather dour firm in England, he felt especially pleased with his new position. Perched on a high stool before a large drawing board, he puffed contentedly and whistled cheerfully as the days grew shorter and colder.

The winter of 1884–85 was unusually cold. Snow fell early and the temperature dropped to ten degrees below zero. James managed to insulate himself to some extent by fastening a six-inch beaver collar onto his woollen jacket. But what he really needed was a complete set of winter furs: mitts, hat, and long buffalo overcoat. Just before Christmas, to his great surprise and delight, he received the money to purchase such an outfit from his father. The money had been raised in a rather novel manner. Instead of dipping into his own pocket, James's father had his son's letters printed and bound by the Army and Navy Co-operative Society in London. The collected letters were then sold at 1s. 6d. to James's friends. "It may seem a paradox that a price should be attached to letters intended only for private circulation," the elder Cockburn noted in his preface to *Canada For Gentlemen*. He then explained that just as readers derived pleasure and information from the letters so would their correspondent derive pleasure and warmth from a fur overcoat.

Despite his initial reactions to the city, James settled comfortably in Ottawa. For social, rather than charitable, reasons he joined a local branch of the St. Andrew's Society and soon had a large circle of friends. In one of his last letters, he mentioned that he was planning to leave his lodgings and take a house on the outskirts of the capital.

Henry, when last heard of, was thinking of leaving the Eastern Townships and taking up a homestead in the prairie West. Since he seemed to enjoy rural life he may well have done so, though it is unlikely that he induced his brother to accompany him. Quite clearly, James was a man of the city, not the frontier. He was a gregarious soul, fond of theatres, clubs, and good restaurants. His interests lay not in some dreary western town, but in cities like Toronto, Montreal, and even muddy Ottawa. For James Seton Cockburn, and for hundreds of Englishmen like him, the older established communities provided social diversion, financial security, and enough novelty to keep life interesting. In return, gentlemen like Cockburn provided Canada with a cultured white-collar labour force which may have lacked glamour but which was, nevertheless, vital in turning the cogs of the nation's commercial and administrative machinery.

The prospect of a comfortable office, evenings at the club, and a snug suburban home was not everyone's idea of happiness. Nor, for that matter, was it every emigrant's idea of Canada. For most of the youths who emerged from public schools and Oxbridge colleges during the last quarter of the century, emigration meant wild sport and high adventure in the Canadian West. It meant wide-open spaces and a life free of the crowds and social constraints of the Old Country. It meant subduing the wilderness and, perhaps, a few wild Indians. It meant demonstrating grit, pluck, and other manly virtues. It meant all of this and more to Frederick Montague DelaFosse, a seventeen-year-old Englishman who sailed for Canada aboard the Allan Line steamship *Scandinavian* in the summer of 1878.

DelaFosse came from a military family. His father, who died in India when Frederick was eight, had been a captain in the artillery; his mother, who left him an orphan in 1872, was the daughter of a cavalry officer. Frederick's uncle and guardian, H.G. DelaFosse, was a much-decorated lieutenant colonel in the 101st Foot (Royal Bengal Fusiliers). As befitted a boy with these connections, Frederick was sent to Wellington College in Berkshire. The prestigious school, founded in 1859 as a memorial to the Iron Duke, catered to the sons of army officers; it had a large cadet corps and a curriculum which was tailored towards the

army entrance examinations. Given his background and schooling, DelaFosse's relatives assumed that he would pass the qualifying papers, complete a course at Sandhurst, and pursue a military career. His relatives were disappointed, for Frederick was
not a conscientious student. He was much more interested in
cricket, with the result that during his last term at Wellington he
placed twenty-sixth out of a class of twenty-seven in classics,
divinity, and history; ninth out of eighteen in French, and twentieth in a class of twenty in mathematics. These were not the
kinds of grades that led to Sandhurst.[12]

When it became clear that Frederick would not pass the army
exam, his uncle decided that the boy's best course was to emigrate. "The outlying portions of the Empire are calling for men,"
the colonel announced one day when Frederick was home for
the school holidays, "and Canada seems to be the place that
offers the most remarkable opportunities at the present time."
Frederick was surprised by his uncle's decision, and initially he
did not relish the idea of being exiled to the colonial backwoods.
But after studying various pamphlets, maps, and illustrated brochures which his uncle provided, Frederick began to warm to the
idea. "I discovered that Canada possessed boundless resources,
and when I read of its wonderful prairies and magnificent forests, of its splendid lakes and rivers, of the fishing and the hunting, of its glorious summers and bright cheery winters, the sporting heart within me leapt, and I was almost reconciled to the
abandoning of my summer's cricketing."[13]

Before leaving for Canada, DelaFosse was taken on a kind of
triumphal progress to the homes of relatives and friends, all of
whom were eager to wish him well. "I received many encomiums
on my pluck," he recalled, "and heaps of advice from everyone."
He also received a great many farewell gifts, including an English saddle, an expensive pair of riding boots, and a large supply of Cockle's Antibilious Pills. The latter he received from an
elderly soldier, who pronounced the pills an indispensable part
of every adventurer's kit.[14]

Like many young English gentlemen, DelaFosse began his
colonial career as a farm pupil in Ontario, the idea being that he
would acquire a knowledge of agriculture in a settled area before

striking out for the frontier; but his apprenticeship was not a
good one. His tutor, a retired British army captain, knew little
about productive farming techniques, and the Muskoka district, where DelaFosse undertook his apprenticeship, was not
suited for agriculture. He consequently quit Muskoka as soon as
he was able and in the summer of 1883 headed west to Winnipeg,
where he expected to find adventure, excitement, and a high-
paying job. Unfortunately, he was rebuffed at every turn. The
first job he found, with a survey crew bound for Alberta, ended
when the leader of the party absconded with the crew's wages.
His next job, bucking cordwood in Winnipeg's North End,
provided him with room and board but no income. He then
found work as a navvy on the CPR mainline. "That was really
my first introduction to the truly seamy side of life," he wrote
years later. The beds in the railway camp bunkhouse were alive
with vermin, and his co-workers—"an agglomeration of
Swedes, Russians, Negroes, Dagoes, and out-of-elbows Englishmen"—were brutal and dissipated.[15] Having made his way to the
Lakehead, he then spent a disheartening year shovelling coal,
working a survey line, and delivering newspapers in Port Arthur.
After a further stint bucking cordwood, DelaFosse decided that
he had had his "fill of adventure and hardship," and in 1885 he
retreated to the more civilized parts of the East. He subsequently
settled in Peterborough, where he was appointed chief librarian.

DelaFosse realized afterwards that he should have steered
clear of Winnipeg, for the city was in the grip of a recession
following its "boom" in 1881. The recession, which resulted in
high unemployment, accounted for the difficulties he experienced finding work in the city. He realized, too, that at 5′ 6″ and
110 lbs. he was not cut out to be a railway navvy. But would he
have been better off on a wheat farm, as government immigration agents advised? Possibly, although it should be noted that it
took a special breed of gentleman emigrant to succeed in cereal
agriculture. Those who did succeed usually had large families
who could assist with day-to-day chores and with ploughing,
sowing, and harvesting. Those who were unaccompanied by
family or friends required capital, so that they could hire experienced farm hands and purchase labour-saving equipment. Rich

or poor, married or single, the gentleman emigrant had to possess the temperament that would allow him to adjust to the monotonous landscape, the immense sky, the cold winters, and the long hours which were an inseparable part of the wheat farmer's life. The successful wheat farmer also had to possess a certain abstract quality which can only be described as a feeling for the soil. Despite a genuine interest in the West, DelaFosse did not possess these requisites. The money he had had when he emigrated he had squandered in the swamps of Muskoka, and because of his pride he was reluctant to call upon his uncle for additional funds. Anyway, although he was fond of nature, his unhappy experience as a farm pupil had rather soured him on agriculture.

Other young men who, like Frederick DelaFosse, came from comfortable homes and prestigious public schools, did, however, possess the personal qualities and resources necessary for "making good" in the wheat lands of the West. Edward George Everard ffolkes, a nineteen-year-old Haileyburian who settled in Manitoba in 1881, was one of them. ffolkes—he was most particular about the spelling of his name—was a member of a distinguished Norfolk family. His uncle, Sir William ffolkes, 3rd baronet, owned an 8,000-acre estate, a London townhouse, two country lodges, and some of the best shooting covers in East Anglia. His father, the Reverend Henry ffolkes, had the living in Hillington, King's Lynn. Edward's eldest brother, William Everard Browne, inherited the baronetcy, and his other brothers kept up a family tradition by entering the church and the army. But Edward did not fit comfortably into the established order of the landed gentry. Indeed, he found it difficult, as many younger sons so often did, to find a niche at all. His problems were compounded by the fact that he was not academically inclined, and as a result he entered Haileybury's modern rather than its classical side. In most public schools—Haileybury included—modern sides were generally considered less demanding than classical sides, but this was little comfort to ffolkes, who found it difficult to master modern languages, mathematics, and the other subjects that comprised the college curriculum.[16] He was, however, gifted with his hands and at an early age demonstrated an aptitude for woodworking and an interest in agriculture. Recognizing this, his parents decided that young Edward might find a better outlet for his talents and interests in Canada.

ffolkes began his colonial career at the Agricultural College in Guelph, Ontario. The college offered a comprehensive programme which included courses in trigonometry, surveying, zoology, and soil chemistry. Not surprisingly, ffolkes failed to enjoy the academic aspects of the programme; he found the lectures tedious, the assignments onerous, and the examinations "horrid." But he delighted in the fieldwork, and when he completed his year at Guelph in 1881, he had a thorough grounding in the practical aspects of agriculture and stock breeding.

Soon after he left the Agricultural College, ffolkes joined the westward trek to Manitoba. He spent his first few months in the province at Beaconsfield, northwest of Morden, with an Ontario-born farmer who showed him how to adapt the techniques he had learned at Guelph to prairie soil and climatic conditions. From the farmer's mother and housekeeper, ffolkes learned how to bake bread, mend clothes, and transform salt pork and beans into a reasonably appetizing dish. Having mastered these essentials, he purchased one and a half sections of tableland south of Portage la Prairie. The first year was a struggle, for the vicar's son had to endure a number of setbacks and inconveniences—including an exceedingly painful boil on his bottom caused by riding his horse bareback in cold weather. He persevered, however, and by the spring of 1883 he had built up a profitable farm with an inventory which included two teams of horses, a small herd of dairy cows, a binder, a reaper, and a small grist-cum-sawmill. Since he did not employ any labourers except at harvest time, his daily routine entailed long hours of hard, physical labour. But this he found rewarding. "My arms ache, and my back aches, and my eyes ache," he wrote, after describing a day on his farm, "and yet I say, what a glorious life this is." [17]

Although ffolkes enjoyed the solitude of the soil, he had always enjoyed team sports, parties, dances, and picnics as well. He was therefore pleased when he found that he could enjoy the same pastimes on the prairie. In a letter signed "Westward Ho!," which appeared in the *Haileyburian* (October 1883), ffolkes reported that the society around Portage la Prairie was "really first rate." His neighbours included several Old Country families who regularly held dances, picnics, and garden parties. He also met several public school boys and university men who were working on farms in the district and so had no trouble fielding an eleven or finding a tennis partner. He noted that both cricket and lawn tennis had a large following in the area and predicted that they would "soon be as popular here as in England."

The society ffolkes described in his letter to the *Haileyburian* was not limited to Portage la Prairie. Stonewall, Gladstone, Shoal Lake, and Birtle also boasted cricket clubs, and the towns of Morris and Souris, plus several hamlets near Turtle Mountain, took pride in the fact that they had been settled by "people of culture." Brandon had a very active Lawn Tennis Association, as well as a "gentleman's club," and neighbouring Rapid City and Minnedosa both supported amateur theatrical guilds. Farther west, in the district of Assiniboia, the town of Qu'Appelle had a well-established hunt club. Indeed, there were scores of small communities in the wheat belts of Manitoba and Assiniboia where the institutions and pastimes of Old Country gentlefolk were lovingly maintained.[18]

Henry McGusty, a young Rugbeian, was struck by this fact when he ventured west in 1889. At Oak Lake, a small town in western Manitoba near the Saskatchewan border, he found that the residents took their hunting, shooting, and tennis very seriously. He found, too, that formal balls could be staged even under the most primitive conditions. He gave one of these balls himself while staying with a fellow bachelor in a 20-foot by 16-foot cabin. Invitations to "McGusty Castle" and dance programmes (which listed a Military Schottische, a Saratoga Lancers, and a Sir Roger de Coverly) were sent out a few weeks ahead of time to the leading families in the area. The thirty guests who squeezed into the Castle were then treated to musical entertainment and a buffet supper of wild fowl. "Altogether we had a very good time," McGusty recalled, "though the contrast between a log-house and evening dress was rather striking."[19]

Capt. Richard E. Goodridge, formerly of the Royal Artillery, was similarly impressed by the "tone" of society in the western wheat lands. Goodridge had come to Manitoba in 1880 to help settle his three adolescent sons on a farm he had purchased near Headingly, ten miles west of Winnipeg. Once the boys were comfortably established, he and his wife had intended to return to their home in Devonshire. The captain found the prairie climate so "vitalising," however, that he remained in the West for almost ten years. The investment climate was also to his liking, and in 1882 he purchased a second farm near Qu'Appelle.

Goodridge had not expected to find many people of education and refinement in the "remote West." But as he noted in his first book, *A Year in Manitoba* (1882), one often encountered well-bred settlers—many of whom were "descendants or relations of well-known naval and military officers"—in isolated, unprepossessing rural communities. Unfortunately for the captain, one also encountered a good many Ontario-born homesteaders who did not share his sense of decorum or propriety. These homesteaders, Goodridge complained, in terms reminiscent of Mrs. Moodie,

> assume the most perfect equality and do not hesitate to intrude themselves on any occasion that offers. In fact, this familiarity is what shocks the senses of those who have been accustomed to the more reserved proprieties of European society. One meets it continually—a species of fraternity that, theoretically, may appear desirable but, in practice, is very much the reverse.[20]

After a few years in the West, the captain learned to take this "familiarity" in his stride, for he made no mention of it in his second book, *The Colonist At Home Again* (1889). In this book—subtitled *Emigration* NOT *Expatriation*—he wrote glowingly of the progress he had witnessed during his years in Manitoba. He referred to the new railways which had been built or chartered, to the handsome buildings which had been erected in Winnipeg, to the investment opportunities, and to the abundant and inexpensive educational facilities in the province. Goodridge, who came to regard himself as an unofficial emigration agent, also extolled the salubrious climate. "A winter spent in Manitoba ... would prove life from the dead to many overworked professional, commercial, official, and other brain-toilers, whose nervous systems have become unstrung and who can nowhere, I maintain, find equally accessible recuperative influences as in this country." [21]

Certainly there was much to be said for Manitoba, and for the neighbouring district of Assiniboia. Yet while extolling the advantages of these regions, the captain had to admit that a growing number of well-bred Englishmen were leaving, or simply by-passing, the prairie wheat lands in favour of the ranching districts of Alberta. The captain found this phenomenon perplexing, and not altogether pleasing. "It is astonishing," he wrote, "how singularly fascinating the wild, lawless life of a 'Cowboy' seems to prove to so many young and adventurous spirits of good education and connections." [22] Goodridge was mistaken in his belief that the ranching frontier was a "wild, lawless" place, but he was right in imagining that there was "an element of excitement" on the western rangelands. Indeed, from the mid-1880s on, the "excitement" of the Alberta ranching communities proved to be an irresistible lure for hundreds of gentlemen emigrants.

(Glenbow-Alberta Institute)

Herbert Church, aged 23, 1891

(Provincial Archives of British Columbia)

Warburton Mayer Pike, c. 1886

(Provincial Archives of British Columbia)

Henry Wright Bullock, c. 1900

(Provincial Archives of British Columbia)

Clive Phillipps-Wolley, 1909

Cannington Manor's main street, 1890s.

"Dudes" outside the Mitre Hotel, Cannington Manor, c. 1892

Shooting party at Sir John Lister-Kaye's ranch near Swift Current, Saskatchewan, 1895

A "fallen villain," staged by young English cowboys for Old Country relatives, c. 1886

Bradfield College Ranch, near Calgary, 1913

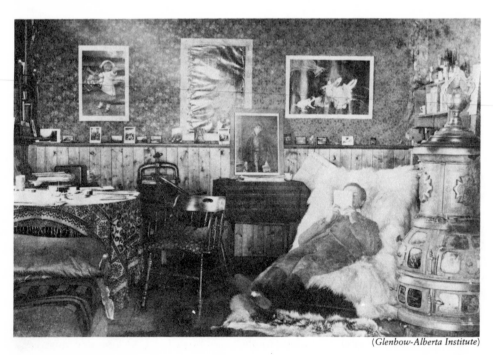

British-American Ranche, living quarters, c. 1886

(Barton Collection, Provincial Museum, Victoria, B.C.)

Townsite of Walhachin, B.C., 1913

(Provincial Archives of British Columbia)

"Longstockings" at a Cowichan and District Lawn Tennis Club party, Duncan's, Vancouver Island, 1888

Bachelors' party near Chemainus, Vancouver Island, New Year's Eve, 1892

CHAPTER V

HIGH-CLASS COWBOYS

During the quarter century prior to the Great War, southern Alberta was often described as "the paradise of the younger son."[1] It was an apt description, for in few parts of Canada could well-born young Englishmen find so agreeable a way of life. In southern Alberta they could enjoy a dry climate and a winter that, thanks to the warm chinook winds, was milder than it was elsewhere in the prairie West. Here, those sensitive to natural beauty could enjoy broad rangelands luxuriantly carpeted with bunch grass; meadows bright with wildflowers; spruce groves and aspen woodlands; rolling hills and valleys which sheltered tall willows and clear streams. Here, against the spectacular backdrop of the Rocky Mountains, gentlemen emigrants could combine the excitement of a frontier, the romance of the West, and the comforts of civilized society. Here, also, they could engage in ranching, an industry that most well-bred Britons much preferred to cereal agriculture.

The Alberta ranching industry began in the mid-1870s near the North West Mounted Police post at Fort Macleod. The police and the native Indians, who were settled on nearby reserves, provided the earliest cattlemen with a small but lucrative market. The industry expanded dramatically a few years later as a result of the "beef bonanza" that swept the western United States. This bonanza—a kind of ranching mania—developed when American stock growers, aided by new American railways, were able to take advantage of the vast beef markets that existed in the large cities of the eastern seaboard and Europe. The bonanza fever, which spread north of the border in 1879, gave a tremendous fillip to the fledgling Alberta industry.

With the coming of the CPR in 1883, Calgary became a major distribution centre and the focal point of the cattle industry. By Christmas 1884 the once tiny North West Mounted Police outpost had a population of over a thousand and all the trappings of a booming cowtown. Herds of cattle and teamsters' wagons rumbled through streets lined with hastily erected hotels and hardware shops; drovers, speculators and tradesmen jostled along the narrow boardwalks. Yet despite its buoyant atmosphere and boisterous face, Calgary was not a rough and violent frontier town. As a local newspaper put it a year after the railway arrived, "Calgary is a western town, but is not a western town in the ancient use of the word. It is peopled by native Canadians and Englishmen . . . citizens who own religion and respect law. The rough and festive cowboy of Texas . . . has no counterpart here."[2] Nor were the communities which sprang up in the ranching districts of southwestern Assiniboia the wild and woolly places of Captain Goodridge's imagination. Aside from a few altercations between cattlemen and farmers, the ranching districts of western Canada were peaceful and orderly.

The peaceful nature of the Canadian ranching frontier was partly due to the fact that the native Indians had been settled on government reserves before most of the cattlemen arrived. The treaty concluded with the Blackfoot Indians in 1877 was particularly important in this regard, for it allowed ranchers to settle safely beyond the immediate environs of NWMP forts and outposts. The close relationship which developed between the Mounties and local cattlemen was also important. Members of the two groups shared many interests, and on leaving the force a number of ex-Mounties took up ranching in districts that they had formerly patrolled. As a result, the antipathy that existed between stock growers and law enforcement officers in some parts of the American West was absent in Alberta and Assiniboia. Finally, because of government land surveys, homestead regulations, and leasing agreements, the Canadian West did not experience the chaotic "land rushes" or endure the "range wars" that took place in some of the American states and territories. Instead, the ranching frontier in western Canada developed in an orderly, almost bureaucratic fashion.[3]

The leasing arrangements introduced by the federal government in 1881 were of prime importance in developing the distinctive character of the Canadian cattle industry. The legislation allowed cattlemen to lease up to 100,000 acres of rangeland at the cost of a penny an acre for a period of twenty-one years. Cattlemen could also purchase acreage within their leased tract for use as a home ranch and corral for $2 an acre. In return, ranchers had to acquire ten head of cattle for every hundred leased acres within three years of taking out their lease. By offering such generous terms, the federal government sought to encourage the ranching industry and, more important, to attract large investors who could afford to run large herds of cattle on the leased tracts. The policy was successful inasmuch as it led to the creation of huge cattle empires, the czars of which co-operated with each other and with the Conservative government which had so favoured them. Although the legislation frustrated a number of smaller stock growers who could not afford to take up the large leases, it did help to establish the Canadian ranching industry on a stable foundation.

British investors, suffering from the agricultural depression in the United Kingdom, were among the first to take advantage of the new legislation, and by the mid-1880s several London-based consortiums had established cattle ranches in southern Alberta. The syndicates included Lord Castletown's Mont Head Ranche Company; the Earl of Lathom's Oxley Ranche Company; the Walrond Cattle Ranche Ltd. (Sir John Walrond-Walrond, Bart., director); Sir Francis de Winton's Alberta Ranche Company; and Sir John Lister-Kaye's Canadian Agricultural, Coal, and Colonization Company.[4] The directors, shareholders, and managers of these syndicates—along with the owners and managers of eastern Canadian outfits like the giant Cochrane

Ranch Company and the North West Cattle Company—comprised a small, but influential lobby which in recent years has been termed the "cattle compact." The members of this compact wielded considerable power, and until the closing years of the century they were able to achieve most of their political and economic demands. Members of this group also had a pronounced impact on local society and were largely responsible for the milieu of gentility that characterized many of the ranching communities of Alberta. Members of the cattle compact erected sumptuous ranch houses, which they decorated in the style of English country homes. They founded patrician clubs and artistic societies; they subscribed to the best London periodicals, entertained lavishly, and dressed for dinner. They imported the games and sports associated with the landed gentry. With the help of their well-bred wives and sisters, they instituted and nurtured a society that was as gracious and as "English" as the climate would allow.

The ranching patriarchs were able to establish and sustain their opulent style of life for several reasons. In the first instance, as pioneers in the area, they did not have to compete with a well-entrenched local elite; they had *carte blanche*, as it were, and so were able to set the tone for those who followed. Secondly, the nature of the ranching industry was conducive to the patrician lifestyle. Maintaining a large ranch required a great deal of capital for livestock, outbuildings, and equipment; cattlemen who had such capital at their disposal were not averse to demonstrating their wealth. Furthermore, large-scale operations like the Oxley ranches northwest of Fort Macleod depended on a substantial paid labour force, and this feature facilitated a social hierarchy. The socioeconomic structure of the ranching frontier in the 1880s was, accordingly, quite different from that of the Manitoba wheat lands where much of the land was held by small, independent and—as Captain Goodridge discovered—democratically minded farmers.

Of course the British-born ranchers in southern Alberta did not all live like the affluent cattle barons. Most of the cattlemen homesteaded, rather than leased; they settled in the southern foothills of the Rockies and counted their cattle in dozens, not in hundreds or thousands. Their homes were comparatively modest, and few of them had more than one or two hired hands. Nevertheless, the small ranch owners had much in common with the members of the ranching elite. Like the major leaseholders, they tended to be Conservative in their politics and Anglican in their religion. They also enjoyed the same pastimes as the prominent cattlemen and in many districts were responsible for introducing aristocratic sports and activities. At Pincher Creek, for example, it was the smaller stockmen who introduced polo to North America in 1884; homesteaders, not wealthy leaseholders, inaugurated the celebrated racing meets at Mosquito Creek the following year. Similarly, the smaller ranch owners brought the first hunt clubs to Alberta in 1886. These clubs proved to be phenomenally popular, despite the fact that the packs of imported hounds had to chase wild coyotes instead of English foxes.[5]

For Britons who had moderate means but aristocratic aspirations, the ranching districts of Alberta clearly offered many advantages. Apart from a healthy climate and a pleasing landscape, the foothills offered a kind of ease and leisure that few of the emigrants could have enjoyed in the Old Country. As Nesta Skrine, the wife of one of the sports-loving ranchers at High River, explained in the late 1890s:

> In England, on a narrow income there is no such thing as freedom. You cannot go where you please, or live where you please, or have what you please; you cannot join in amusements that are really amusing, because every form of sport is expensive; you cannot accept pleasant invitations because you cannot return them. . . . But with the same income in a country like this, you can live on equal terms with your neighbours, and all your surroundings will be entirely in your favour; you have only to make the most of them. Shooting, fishing, and hunting, just the things which would bring you to the verge of bankruptcy at home, you can enjoy here practically for nothing. You can have all the horses you want to ride or drive. . . . [6]

This gentlemen's paradise was enhanced further by the profits to be made raising livestock and by the satisfaction the ranchers found in their work. Indeed, the number of gentlemen who failed at ranching was appreciably lower than the number who failed in the wheat lands to the east and some commentators attributed this phenomenon to the British gentlemen's "inherent gift" for raising livestock.

Whether or not these gentlemen were especially gifted at handling cattle and horses is a moot point, for there were a great many successful Canadian, American, and European ranchers in the West. But there is no question that ranching had an almost hypnotic appeal for young gentlemen emigrants. From the mid-1880s on, public school boys and university men flocked to southwestern Alberta and literally overran many of the ranching districts. They were most evident in Calgary, which was universally acclaimed as one of the sportiest places on the continent. They were also highly visible in and about Millarville, High River, Lethbridge, and dozens of other ranching communities. James Francis Hogan, the Australian-born M.P. and colonial expert, was one of the many visitors who were struck by the number of well-bred youths in the territory. Hogan met the youths — whom he described as "a sort of high-class corps of amateur cowboys" — while on a round-the-world tour of the Empire in 1895. He was greatly impressed with the size and the spirit of the corps, and on returning to England declared that there were "more scions of nobility and young Britons of good family, leading a free, airy, open, healthy, and romantic life on the ranches of the North-West Territories... than in any other quarter of Greater Britain."[7]

Two young Britons whom Hogan might have encountered in the West were Herbert and Richard Church, whose Hadley Ranch was located on Sheep Creek, near Millarville, twenty-five miles south of Calgary. These two Englishmen were among the first homesteaders in the district. Herbert was twenty years old and "Dickie," his brother, was eighteen when they began ranching in 1888. By the mid-1890s the Hadley Ranch was paying its own way, and the owners were regarded in the district as knowledgeable cattlemen and experienced horsebreeders. They were also keen sportsmen and avid cricketers who, like Hogan's cowboys, rejoiced in the free lifestyle of the open range. But while theirs was obviously a satisfying life, it was also a challenging one, for like many of their neighbours, they had to learn the ranching business as they went along. They had to adjust to new conditions, discard romantic preconceptions, and endure a number of setbacks and hardships before they were established comfortably in the West.[8]

The Church brothers were not supernumerary gentlemen in the usual sense of the word. As grammar school boys, they were embryo adventurers who from an early age had been eager to see more of the world than London or East Retford, where their family had a summer home. Their father, Professor Alfred John Church, was aware of their interests and so was not surprised when, on a spring day in 1886, his sons asked him if they might emigrate to Canada; he was, however, reluctant to give his permission. He thought the boys were too young to be roughing it in the colonies. Besides, what did they know of frontier life, beyond the highly spiced tales they had absorbed from juvenile adventure novels and illustrated periodicals? What did they know about agriculture? They had kept bees in the back garden of their suburban London villa and had pruned a few fruit trees during their summers in Nottinghamshire, but they had no knowledge of cash crops or livestock. The two would-be ranchers could not even ride a horse. Professor Church, who was a classicist and historian at University College, London, also wondered whether the lads would be able to endure the harsh climate, the loneliness, and other hardships which, he understood, were an inseparable part of colonial life. Of course, the boys assured him that they could handle any difficulties they might face, and indeed as they stood eagerly in their father's study they seemed able to do so. Herbert was an inch shy of six feet and young Dickie was almost as tall. Both lads were healthy, well built, and physically strong. Eventually, after much discussion and soul-searching, the professor relented, but he insisted that before emigrating the boys take a course in first aid and acquire a few domestic skills, such as cooking and mending. He insisted, too, that they spend a year as pupils with an English farmer in Ontario before setting off on their own.

The boys left England in June 1886, carting a steamer trunk which London railway porters, used to handling heavy artillery pieces, dubbed the "Woolwich Infant." The huge trunk contained an outfit Professor Church said was appropriate for emigrants who had been raised in a gentleman's house. The outfit included over a dozen pairs of gloves, half a dozen suits, various jackets, jerseys, boots, vests, and linen. The "Woolwich Infant" also contained fishing rods and tackle, two twelve-gauge sporting rifles, tennis rackets, cricket bats, bandages, ointments, medical appliances, several dozen books, and a box of games. It was an impressive kit, to say the least, though the youths later found that they had neglected to pack two important items: a pneumatic India-rubber tub and a banjo. The tub was a great convenience when one performed one's morning ablutions on the open range, while the banjo offered solace and entertainment during the long prairie evenings.

The Church brothers undertook their apprenticeship with a gentleman farmer near Collingwood in southern Ontario. From him they received a pleasant, but not particularly profitable, introduction to colonial life. They spent most of the time doing menial chores or visiting neighbours rather than learning profitable methods of agriculture and stock raising, and like Frederick DelaFosse, they later regarded their apprenticeships as a waste of money. As soon as their articles expired, they accepted an invitation to join an uncle on the west coast and apart from occasional visits to Victoria for supplies, they spent the summer of 1887 on Texada Island in the Strait of Georgia. Their uncle hoped to find gold on Texada and land suitable for agriculture. He was disappointed on both counts and subsequently purchased a farm near Comox, on Vancouver Island. The Comox Valley contains some of the richest agricultural land in British Columbia and had the Church brothers accepted an offer to remain in the area, they would undoubtedly have prospered. However, Comox was a rather sleepy place and the damp air and incessant rain were not to Herbert's liking. The boys decided, therefore, to repack the "Woolwich Infant" and head for Calgary.

The Churches had had a glimpse of Calgary while travelling on the train to British Columbia. They had been struck by the crowds that came to the station to greet the train and, generally, by the bustling atmosphere of the town. They were more impressed on their return. There was a certain feeling in the clear, dry air—a kind of excitement and energy which they had not felt in southern Ontario or on Vancouver Island. Giving way to the atmosphere, Dickie immediately exchanged his Norfolk jacket and tweed trousers for a leather vest, chaps, and sombrero. Herbert was more reserved, though even he could not resist buying a fancy Western hunting knife at a cowboy outfitter's shop. Shortly afterwards, he gashed his leg while trying to master the art of knife throwing, and for the next few weeks he hobbled about painfully. But the pain did nothing to dampen his ardour and enthusiasm. He and his brother delighted in the characters and activity that surrounded them. They were intoxicated with the spirit of the rangelands. Both felt instinctively that they had found their métier.

Before leaving England, the Churches had imagined that ranching was a relatively easy occupation. A leisurely stroll around the paddock, a bracing ride across the prairie—what would be finer? They learned differently when they signed on, for a wage of $15 a month, as ranch hands with a Calgary cattleman. They were turned out at five o'clock each morning and it was often late in the evening before they were able to "hit the hay." On some days they were bruised and battered as they tried to corral unbroken horses; on other days they were saddle sore and exhausted after searching for maverick steers. Conditions were also more austere than they had imagined, and December found them huddled in a rickety shack which they shared with another young English rancher. Their diet consisted of salt pork and boiled beans, with an occasional treacle tart on Sundays. Nevertheless, the Churches remained cheerful. Indeed, as they sat down for their usual dinner on Christmas Eve in 1887, the two brothers were in exceedingly good spirits, for earlier that day they had received a telegram stating that their uncle was sending them a cheque for £200. The money would allow them to equip a small ranch of their own.

The Church brothers secured adjoining homesteads in the spring of the following year. They pre-empted an additional 160 acres each, and this gave them a 640-acre-block. Their location,

on the north side of Sheep Creek, was a good one: the land was
level and sheltered and spring water was abundant. Thanks to
their uncle's generosity they were able to purchase a wagon, a
team of horses, a mower and a rake. They were also able to purchase a stove and cooking utensils for the 36-foot by 20-foot log
cabin they built. The cabin, Herbert said later, was erected "by
main strength and awkwardness," for being inexperienced in
such matters, he and his brother had not thought to use skids
and rollers in constructing the high walls. Instead, they balanced
the stout logs on their shoulders; then, with a mighty effort, they
hefted each log into place.

The two-room cabin with its sod roof and rough lumber
floors was a great improvement over some of the bachelor
shacks in the area. Most of these shacks were one-room affairs
having tin roofs and dirt floors. The thin lumber walls—which,
if the shack was occupied by an Englishman, were invariably
papered with pages torn from the *Graphic* or the *Illustrated London News*—offered scant protection from the wind, the rain,
and the cold. The Churches' place, in contrast, was well insu-
lated; the log walls were chinked with wooden strips and made
tight with a straw-and-clay plaster. Even so, the first Hadley
ranch house was a far cry from the lavishly furnished residences
of some of the Alberta cattle barons. The boys' sleeping room
contained only a double bed and the ubiquitous steamer trunk.
The other room contained an iron stove, a bench made from a
couple of gun cases placed across two nail kegs, and a sturdy,
oilcloth-covered table. Sacks of oats for the horses along with
saddles, bridles, and harnesses were piled in the corners. Still, it
was a cozy little place, and over the next few months the
Churches transformed it into a comfortable, civilized home.
They added shelves lined with books and family photographs to
the living room/kitchen; hung cricket bats, hunting rifles,
fishing rods, and racquets on the walls, and placed a cougar-skin
rug on the floor. By the end of the year the Churches' residence
resembled the homes of many English-born ranchers in the
southern foothills. These small ranch houses, a visitor noted in
1884, had a distinctive, rather incongruous feeling about them.
They seemed to the traveller to be a cross between an "out-of-

the-way shooting lodge in the Highlands" and the "temporary abode of an Oxford reading party."[9]

Like most homesteaders who began ranching without much capital, the Church boys spent their first few years working for neighbours. One of their closest neighbours was John Ware, Alberta's celebrated Negro cowboy. From Ware they learned how to handle wild horses, how to use their mower and rake, and how to combat prairie fires, which on several occasions threatened to destroy their homestead. To make ends meet, the boys also hauled freight along the trail from High River to Calgary and worked as harvesters on nearby farms and ranches. With every season they grew more competent and more confident. They became more prosperous, too, and by 1892, when they were joined by a younger brother, G.E. ("Teddy") Church, they reckoned their property to be worth several hundred dollars.

Hadley Ranch was a diversified operation, for besides beef cattle the Churches kept milk cows, pigs, and poultry. In addition, they grew vegetables, which they marketed in Calgary, and experimented with growing several varieties of wheat. However, horses were their specialty. Whenever possible, they invested their savings in wild stallions which could be purchased at small cost from some of the large ranches in the area. Using the skills they had acquired from Ware, the boys would "break" the horses, work them for a season on the Hadley spread, then sell them to local farmers, to the NWMP, or to European cavalry agents who came to Fort Macleod for remounts. The market for these horses tended to fluctuate more than the market for beef cattle, and profits were small except during such periods as the Boer War, when demands for army remounts were high. Despite the tenuous nature, this type of ranching suited the Church brothers, and by the late 1890s they could break stallions that had defied other horsemen in the district.

Professor Church was not pleased when he learned that the boys were "going in for horses." He equated horse dealers with gypsies and feared that his sons would be drawn into "low company." Herbert hastened to reassure him. Writing to his father in 1889, he reported that many of their neighbours raised horses and that "the proportion of gentlemen among horse-raisers

[was] quite as great as among cattlemen and farmers." "Our experience of them," Herbert added, "is that they are very decent
fellows and quite straight, and [bear] excellent characters throughout the country. In fact, the horse-dealers [in southern Alberta]
are quite a different sort of people . . . than are to be found in
England. . . . "[10] Indeed, had the professor visited the area, he
would doubtless have been surprised and impressed by the distinguished men who traded in horses. For example, just south of
the Churches' homestead, on the other side of Sheep Creek, was
the mammoth Quorn ranch, which specialized in raising horses
for the famous Quorn hunt in Leicestershire. Farther south was
the High River Horse Ranche. Established in 1885 by an ex-India
army officer and a senior manager of the Bank of England, it specialized in raising remounts for the 21st Lancers, the 13th
Hussars and other crack cavalry regiments. Likewise Maj. Gen.
T.B. Strange's Military Colonization Company, which owned
several ranches in the Calgary area, dealt extensively in horses.

For the most part, the cowboys who worked these ranches
were also "decent fellows" who boasted public school and university educations. The young Rugbeian Henry McGusty noted
the fact when he came to Alberta from Oak Lake, Manitoba, in
the spring of 1890. Mounted on a one-eyed cayuse he called
Polyphemus, McGusty spent over a year moseying around Red
Deer, Calgary, and High River. In almost every bunkhouse he
met old school chums or alumni from one of the other Great
Schools.[11] The prevalence of these public school Old Boys was
remarked upon by many visitors, some of whom wondered if the
boys' expensive classical educations were not wasted in the wilds
of the Canadian West. Alexander Stavely Hill, the Conservative
M.P. and Old Oxonian who was one of the directors of the
Oxley Ranch, assured such visitors that this was not the case. It
was his opinion that the "better [a boy's] education, the more
knowledge he has in his head . . . [and] the better calculated he is
to enjoy and appreciate a life where the old world reading will
constantly suggest in his frequent hours of solitude, pleasant
trains of thought."[12] Certainly no one would argue that for
those who tended the vast herds on the open ranges, there was
plenty of solitude.

Although Old Boys from many distinguished schools and colleges helped to people the West, one school was particularly well represented. Relative to its size, Uppingham School accounted for more gentlemen ranchers than any other public school in Britain. At Uppingham, a small school in Rutland County, the great reformer and educator, the Reverend Edward Thring, was headmaster. Thring used classical studies and organized games—the key features of the public school curriculum—in such a way as to promote independence, inquisitiveness, and self-confidence in his boys. He also used the chapel, the classroom, and the playing field to inspire his students with the ideals of Christian manliness. These ideals were later demonstrated to good effect in the Canadian West. Thring's students also developed a particularly strong sense of fraternity, which is one reason why the Uppingham contingent in Alberta was continually being reinforced during the late nineteenth century.

Robert Newbolt was among the first of Thring's pupils to take up ranching. The son of an army officer, Newbolt had intended to follow his father's profession on leaving school in the early 1880s. A badly strained leg muscle and the onset of varicose veins, which developed after a particularly strenuous boat race, forced a change in plans. Fortunately, he was able to find another means of satisfying his adventurous spirit, for his father provided him with a $1,000-share in Major General Strange's Military Colonization Company (MCC).

Newbolt arrived in Canada in the summer of 1884. He was eighteen years old. After reporting to the general, he was sent to Idaho where he and several other MCC shareholders were to take delivery of 3,000 head of cattle. The cattle were then to be driven north to the MCC's home ranch on the Bow River. Newbolt, resplendent in his shooting jacket, riding boots, and bowler hat, managed to carry out the general's orders, although in doing so he received what can only be described as a baptism by fire. First he had to evade a gang of Idaho desperadoes who were determined to steal the MCC bankroll. Next, he was caught up in a saloon brawl in Montana, and only by hiding under a large billiard table did he avoid being hit by flying chairs, bottles, and bullets. Later he was forced to spend some of his savings on a

new outfit, after a party of high-spirited cowpokes used his beloved bowler hat for target practice! By the time he staggered
into Fort Macleod, the young Englishman had matured considerably. He was, however, undaunted by the experience and the
following year served with General Strange's Alberta Field Force
in the North West Rebellion. He then left the MCC and founded
a homestead which became the nucleus of the renowned Bowchase Ranch. When he settled down and married in the 1890s,
Newbolt was "a top notch rancher." "I could ride and rope with
any of them," he boasted, "[and] could hold my own in a poker
game." He was also an active member of the Anglican Church,
an enthusiastic polo player, and a charter member of Calgary's
prestigious Ranchmen's Club (1891).[13]

The year Newbolt came to Alberta, twenty-four-year-old
Walter Claremont Skrine was elected president of the North
West Stockman's Association. The youngest son of a landed
family in Somersetshire, Skrine was one of Thring's brightest
pupils. In fact, he and his brothers (one of whom was later an
assistant master at Uppingham) led the school in both academic
and athletic fields. A sense of adventure plus a desire to take
advantage of the "beef bonanza" had prompted Skrine to
establish the Bar S Ranch near High River in 1883. He later
married the Irish author, Agnes ("Nesta") Higginson, who,
under the pseudonym Moira O'Neill, wrote a number of poems
that described the beauty of the southern foothills. "The North
West, Canada" is one of the best known of these poems:

> Oh would ye hear, and would ye hear,
>   Of the windy, wide North-West?
> Faith! 'tis a land as green as the sea,
> That rolls as far and rolls as free,
> With drifts of flowers, so many there be,
>   Where the cattle roam and rest.
>
> Oh could ye see, and could ye see
>   The great gold skies so clear,
> The rivers that race through the pine-shade dark,
> The mountainous snows that take no mark,
> Sun-lit and high on the Rockies stark,
>   So far they seem as near.

Then could ye feel, and could ye feel
  How fresh is a Western night!
When the long land-breezes rise and pass
And sigh the rustling prairie grass,
When the dark-blue skies are clear as glass,
  And the same old stars are bright.[14]

As is evident from the poem, and from Moira O'Neill's other writings, the Skrines found life in the foothills comfortable yet challenging, and infinitely more satisfying than the life they had known in Britain. Their neighbour, Charles Linzee Douglass, held a similar view. After a brief stint in the navy, Douglass came to Alberta in 1885 to work as manager of the Quorn Ranch. The work was hard, the hours were long, and the pay was not particularly good. Still, he enjoyed the life, as his younger brother, J.L. Douglass, discovered during a summer holiday on the Quorn in the late 1880s. "Charlie," whom J.L. remembered being neatly attired in an Uppingham school tie and flannel blazer, had been transformed into the complete cowboy: he walked with a swagger and sported leather chaps, a faded denim jacket, and a large slouch hat. J.L. chided his brother for looking like a "ruffian" but admitted privately that Charlie cut a rather dashing figure. J.L. also noted in his diary that his brother seemed "bronzed," "broadened," and eminently "manly."[15] Charles Douglass later established his own ranch near Bassano, on the Red Deer river. There he received his cousins, Cecil and Leslie Douglass. Both Cecil and Leslie, who were the sons of a distinguished Guards officer, had been at Uppingham. Both took up ranching in the Alberta foothills.

As might be expected, the lifestyles of men like Robert Newbolt, Walter Skrine, Herbert Church, and Charles Douglass attracted a great deal of interest in the Old Country, and scarcely a week went by without some laudatory article being published on Canada's "high class corps of cowboys." The lives of the gentlemen ranchers were also extolled and romanticized in countless novels during the period. These novels were quite different from those inspired by the American West: they depicted a rugged, yet cultured, frontier. The genre included juvenile adventure tales such as Robert Leighton's *Sergeant Silk, the Prairie*

Scout (1913), about the exploits of "the Hon. Percy Rapson, late of Eton College, now of Rattlesnake Ranch"; didactic tales, such as Mrs. Humphrey Ward's *Canadian Born* (1910); the romantic adventure tales of Harold Bindloss, the English author who gave his name to a small town in Alberta, and such well-known works as *The Sky Pilot* (1899) by Ralph Connor (the Reverend Charles Gordon).

The Sky Pilot, set in Cochrane, Alberta, in the 1880s, was as popular in England as it was in Canada and the United States. It dealt with "men of adventurous spirit, who left homes of comfort, often of luxury, because of the stirring in them to be and to do some worthy thing." The characters in the novel are not all paragons of virtue, yet one cannot help but marvel at the young men who make up the "Company of the Noble Seven":

> Well-born and delicately bred in that atmosphere of culture mingled with a sturdy common sense and a certain high chivalry which surrounds the stately homes of Britain, these young lads, freed from the restraints of custom and surrounding, soon shed all that was superficial in their make-up and stood forth in the naked simplicity of their native manhood. . . .

The Company was led by "the Hon. Fred Ashley . . . sometime of Ashley Court, England." He was "a big, good-natured man with a magnificent physique, a good income from home, and a beautiful wife, the Lady Charlotte, daughter of a noble English Family." "At Ashley Ranch," Connor wrote,

> the traditions of Ashley Court were preserved as far as possible. The Hon. Fred appeared at the wolf-hunts in riding-breeches and top boots, with hunting crop and English saddle, while in all the appointments of the house the customs of the English home were observed.

Then there was the mysterious "Duke," a man whose background was shadowy but whose personality was compelling. "He was a perfect picture of a man and in all Western virtues was easily the first. He could rope a steer, bunch cattle, play poker, or drink whisky to the admiration of his friends and the confusion of his foes, of whom he had few. . . ." [16]

The Ontario-born Connor may have been guilty of exaggerating some of his characters, just as many British authors neglected to emphasize the risks and difficulties that were an integral part of the ranchers' lives. True or not, however, the ideas and images conveyed in such popular fiction pleased and flattered many of the English ranchers, some of whom made conscious efforts to live up to their stereotypes. More important, the literature excited the imaginations of many real-life Percy Rapsons who, as soon as they were able, packed up their own "Woolwich Infants" and headed for the Canadian West. The migration of these youths meant that the ranching districts of Alberta (and to a lesser extent Saskatchewan) were constantly receiving new blood and new money. The migration of new boys from the Old Country also meant that the coterie of Anglo-Canadian ranchers remained more or less intact, even during the early 1900s when non-British "sod busters" invaded the West and began subdividing the open range.

British gentlemen were also ranching on the western side of the Rockies, where former army officers like John Martley, Anglo-Irish gentry like Charles and Forbes Vernon, and gentlemen like the Cantabrigian Cornwall brothers had helped to establish the industry during the Cariboo gold rush. These men continued to play a leading role on the ranching frontier when the industry expanded during the last two decades of the century. They were among the first to realize the impact that the CPR would have on ranching and among the first to improve their herds in order to take advantage of new markets and high beef prices. At the same time, through their contacts in the financial capitals of Europe and America, the pioneer cattlemen were instrumental in attracting new investors and a new wave of gentlemen emigrants to British Columbia.

One of the wealthiest and most distinguished of the new investors was John Campbell Gordon, 7th Earl of Aberdeen. The earl, who served as Canada's governor general from 1893 to 1898, began his operations in the province in 1890 when he acquired almost 500 acres of property near Okanagan Mission in the Okanagan Valley. The Guisachan Ranch was managed by the earl's brother-in-law, the Honourable Coutts Marjoribanks.

Marjoribanks—who is still remembered in the valley as being "quite a gay blade"—had been farming, with little success, in the Dakota Territory and according to local tradition one of the earl's principal objects in establishing the Guisachan was to provide Marjoribanks with a new start. This may have been the case, although by all accounts "the Major," as Majoribanks was known, had little idea of, or interest in, successful property management. Festooned in embroidered flowery chaps, a beaded fringed-leather Indian jacket, a red bandana and a broad sombrero, he was much happier breaking horses, driving cattle, drinking with "the boys," and berating clergymen who objected to his salty language. "Hell, man!" Marjoribanks thundered on one occasion after being chastised by a Presbyterian minister for using lurid language in a stockyard, "I'm not teaching a Sunday school, I'm loading cattle... and I'll bet that Noah swore when he was loading his animals into the ark!" On another occasion, when asked how an aristocrat like himself had such coarse manners, the falstaffian Major replied: "You know, my sister [Lady Aberdeen, renowned for her propriety] has so much godliness that there wasn't enough left to go around the rest of the family!" [17] In any event, the earl regarded the Guisachan, which his wife had named after her home in Scotland, as a sideline. He was much more concerned with the nearby Coldstream Ranch which he purchased in 1891 from Forbes Vernon. This ranch was managed by W. Crawley Ricardo, a Cambridge graduate who had acquired an extensive knowledge of ranching in southern Alberta. During Ricardo's tenure the Coldstream was considered one of the leading cattle ranches in North America, although stock raising was but a part of the total operation. Thanks to an extensive irrigation system, the 13,000-acre ranch also exported fruit, wheat, barley, oats, and hops.

The British-born cattle ranchers who settled in the Okanagan maintained close ties with their counterparts in the Similkameen to the southwest and in the Nicola and Thompson valleys to the north. Marriage and a variety of sporting activities such as cricket, coyote hunting, and polo brought them together often. Yet British Columbia's cattle districts did not develop in quite the same manner as Alberta's. This was partly because the ranching industry in British Columbia was more diverse and cosmopolitan, with many of the large spreads being owned by Americans, Australians, and Europeans. Since the province did not favour the ranchers with generous leasing arrangements such as Ottawa offered in the North West Territory, mammoth organizations did not dominate ranching in British Columbia as the anglophile, conservative, cattle compact did in Alberta. In fact, with the exception of the Western Canada Ranching Company, which in 1888 acquired control of the gigantic Gang Ranch in the Chilcotin, large London-based consortiums did not begin operations in British Columbia until the turn of the century, when the province was relatively well settled. The diversity of the British Columbia economy and the fact that commerce was oriented towards the Pacific coast also helped to prevent a concentration of emigrants from developing in one part of the interior, as happened in the foothills of Alberta. Finally, although the gentlemen ranchers of British Columbia pursued many of the same social and sporting activities as their counterparts in Alberta, until the turn of the century at least, British Columbia's gentlefolk were inclined to look to the capital for the finer amenities of life.

CHAPTER VI

NATURE'S GENTLEMEN

By the 1880s Victoria had developed a style of society that made visiting Englishmen and gentlemen emigrants feel at home there. Coming to Victoria, they said, was like stepping from a busy, cacophonic thoroughfare into a quiet, secluded courtyard. The author and sportsman Clive Phillipps-Wolley, who paid his first visit to the city in 1884 after a transcontinental hunting expedition, declared, "I came across no place in America in which I would be so content to stay as in Victoria... [h]ere there is time to rest for a moment, and fancy... that there is something else in the world to live for besides the the accursed dollar."[1] The gentleman-tourist William Henry Barneby expressed similar feelings after his visit. In fact, he was so taken with Victoria that he purchased a "ranche" at Cordova Bay, a few miles from the city.[2] As it happened, Barneby inherited estates in England and so was unable to return to Victoria as planned. However, a great many gentlemen tourists and sportsmen did return in later years. Many brought their families with them, and though they were thousands of miles from home, most settled in easily within a matter of weeks. The fact that so many English gentlefolk established themselves there with such comparative ease was due partly to Victoria's Devonshire-like climate, its seaside location, and its people, many of whom spoke the English language with its native accent. Furthermore, Victoria's social life centred around three revered institutions dear to every English gentleman's heart. The Anglican church, represented by Christ Church cathedral, which Baroness Angela Burdett-Coutts had endowed in the 1860s, provided a spiritual focus for British Columbia's social elite. The cathedral stood on a hill overlooking the city, while on another hill stood the lieutenant governor's residence, Carey Castle. Although the castle itself was a rather ugly structure, it provided Victorians with a link to the monarchy and, ultimately, to the head of the royal family, the lady for whom their city was named. The Royal Navy's Pacific squadron, headquartered at nearby Esquimalt, represented the third institution, the British Empire. The presence of these three august institutions — church, monarchy, and empire — gave the city an air of security, tradition, and imperial importance.

Of course, Victoria had been considered an unusually civilized community since its founding in the 1840s. Remarkably, it managed to preserve its reputation even during the hectic days of the Fraser River and Cariboo gold rushes, when thousands of rough miners had passed through the city. However, Victoria's "English personality" did not fully blossom until the mid-1880s, when the city lost out to Vancouver as the western terminus of the CPR. Although some Victorians forever lamented the railway's decision not to extend to Vancouver Island, a number of residents realized at an early date that the loss could be turned into an advantage. They realized that if Victoria were not to become a great seat of industry and commerce, it might become an unsullied centre of culture and refinement. With this in mind, they began to emphasize the aesthetic, picturesque qualities of the city; they extolled its handsome setting, its mild climate, its civilized hotels and stately homes. They began to contrast Victoria's gentle atmosphere with the brassy, pushy, money-grubbing ways of its mainland rival. They accepted with pride visitors' pronouncements that Victoria was destined to be the Brighton or the Eastbourne of the Pacific coast of Canada.

Victoria's personality was perhaps most evident in its residents' love of floriculture, which found a splendid manifestation in Beacon Hill Park, a 150-acre tract of waterfront property which the city acquired in the late 1880s. The city employed John Blair, a British landscape gardener, to develop and enhance the parkland, which had been used earlier for cricket matches, picnics, and steeplechases. Blair added two artificial lakes, rock gardens, walkways and over 2,000 ornamental trees and shrubs, which the city's leading citizens donated. Captain Grant's yellow-flowering broom and hundreds of daffodils were also planted along the slopes of Beacon Hill. Had Wordsworth seen the park in springtime, he would have wept with joy. The grounds of the large estates located near the lieutenant governor's residence and the flower patches that surrounded many of the farmhouses gave further evidence of Victorians' devotion to gardening. A visitor in 1889 declared that he had rarely seen so many pleasing residences, such quaint cottages, such fragrant hedges, or so many pretty garden plots as he did "in this charming spot in the far Northwest."[3]

Victoria's reputation as a centre of culture and refinement also derived from the presence in the city of several clubs, lodges, and fraternal organizations. The most prestigious of these was the Union Club, founded in 1879 and patterned after the bastions of Pall Mall in London. Within the portals of the Union Club, members could enjoy a properly made gin and tonic while perusing a recent number of the *Field,* the *Standard,* or *The Times.* The club's large ex-India army fraternity could keep tabs on old acquaintances through the medium of the Allahabad *Pioneer Mail,* the Lahore *Civil and Military Gazette*, and kindred periodicals to which the club subscribed. For a long time the clubmen could also keep their hunting hounds in kennels adjacent to the premises, even though the clubhouse was located in the city core. That privilege, unfortunately, ended after repeated complaints from the incumbent of the Presbyterian church next door. Had the neighbouring clergyman been an Anglican, the sporting members of the Union Club might well have kept their hounds.

Admittedly, this city of gardens and gentility was not everyone's cup of tea. Certainly the Church brothers found Victoria much too quiet when they visited the city in 1887. Because of its narrow economic base, Victoria also offered limited employment opportunities, and as a result, many gentlemen emigrants were either without work or forced to toil in ungentlemanly occupations. One impecunious ex-Guardsman who had renounced the prairie winters for Victoria's balmy climate was discovered in 1890 working as an undertaker's assistant in the city's Chinatown. Several other gentlemen, including a number of clergymen's sons, were reported to have been working as waiters and dishwashers in some of the city's many saloons. The fact that so many young gentlemen experienced difficulties finding respectable or remunerative employment prompted several writers in the 1890s and early 1900s to advise impoverished emigrants *not* to come to Victoria—unless, of course, they had relatives or friends who would support them, or were prepared to take up some rather curious callings. On the other hand, most commentators agreed that if one had capital or a guaranteed income, a taste for a leisurely life, and a longing for familiar institutions, then Victoria was definitely the place to be.

Thirty miles north of Victoria, across a mountainous stretch known as the Malahat, is the Cowichan Valley, which James Douglas opened for settlement in 1862. The valley was blessed with sunshine and fresh water, a good supply of marketable timber, and substantial tracts of fertile bottomland; in 1882 William Henry Barneby called it "the pleasantest and most prosperous" area in British Columbia.⁴ When the Esquimalt and Nanaimo Railway (E & N) was pushed through four years later, the eastern part of the valley became even more prosperous as agriculture, lumbering and fishing expanded to take advantage of newly accessible markets in Victoria. The population of the valley increased in a corresponding manner, and Duncan— or Duncan's, as it was known prior to its incorporation in 1912—became the leading community in the district. Despite the extravagant promises of local promoters, Duncan never rivalled Victoria in size or in commercial importance, but it more than held its own in matters of gentility and refinement. Relative to its size, the small town adjacent to the Cowichan River probably claimed more gentlemen emigrants than any other community in Canada.

The emigrants who settled in Duncan and in neighbouring

hamlets such as Cowichan Station, Corfield, Maple Bay, and Cobble Hill engaged in a variety of occupations. Some were managers of local timber companies; others were engineers in nearby coal and copper mines. Several gentlemen settlers worked as general merchants, but those who did so were never in any danger of losing "caste." Emigration frequently involved a transposition of social values; thus running a store in the colonies was considered an acceptable occupation for a gentleman whereas selling groceries in a village in England was definitely not. In any event, most of the settlers were neither professionals nor merchants. The majority were farmers who kept dairy cattle and poultry and who, in the appropriate seasons grew vegetables, fruit, and flowers. By prairie standards, most of their operations were small, and profits were marginal. But the land was relatively inexpensive and the cost of living less than it was in most parts of the Dominion. Moreover, the climate was good, the neighbours congenial, and the scenery beautiful.

The British settlers in the Cowichan Valley were known as "longstockings," a generic expression derived from the ex-army officers' habit of wearing short puttees and knickerbockers. Over the years the term came to refer to retired naval officers from the base at Esquimalt who came to Duncan when they found Victoria too rich for their pensions, to Oxbridge men who had come to the valley after giving up teaching posts in the Old Country, and to the sometime homesteaders who had fled Manitoba and Assiniboia in search of a gentler way of life. The expression also applied to well-bred English girls, otherwise known as "lady helps," who were employed as lady's companions and general factotums by the well-to-do families of the area. Most of the longstockings lived in homes that bore names like "The Maples" or "The Bungalow." They tended to gravitate to the Tzouhalem Hotel (once renowned for its kippers-and-grilled-kidney breakfasts), to the Agricultural Society Hall, or to Mrs. Sutton's tea shop in the Duncan High Street. A relatively gregarious crowd, the longstockings were on good terms with the "shortstockings," the Canadian-born farmers, and with the "no stockings," the native Indians.

The Chemainus Valley, a few miles north, supported a very

similar society, although most of the early Chemainus residents were engaged in sheep raising rather than mixed farming. The village of Westholme (named after the home of the local post-master, a retired Royal Navy captain) was the principal gathering place. As was the case in the Duncan area, many of the settlers around Westholme took in "farm pupils." The pupils were mainly former public school boys and a number of them purchased property in the area after completing their one- or two-year apprenticeships.

Mr. and Mrs. Henry Burchell, who arrived from England in 1891, were responsible for bringing out a good many of these pupils. The Burchells lived on Thetis Island, three miles off Chemainus, in a large home known as Preedy Hall. This commodious structure incorporated a dozen guest rooms, a tennis court, and a private chapel. The well-manicured estate also included a sawmill, a model dairy, and an elaborate poultry run. Burchell, who favoured a striped college blazer and straw boater, was a skilled linguist and an enthusiastic sailor. He was also the magistrate for the area. He combined his talents and interests as he putted along in his naptha launch, *Sunbeam*, trading with the native Indians and administering justice in neighbouring communities. A popular man, Burchell gathered about him on Thetis Island a group of approximately thirty former farm pupils. By 1900 this informal colony had trebled in size as the young colonists sent for their aunts, mothers, sisters, and sweethearts.[5]

Geographically, Thetis Island is part of the archipelago known as the Gulf Islands. On some of these islands — notably Galiano, Saltspring, South Pender, and Saturna — British gentlefolk also resided. Because the Gulf Islands were relatively isolated, British settlers were free to create their own society. They could be very British and indulge in formal dinner parties, "at homes," and private tutors for the children; or they could opt for an unstructured, bohemian way of life. Either way, they did not have to conform to the manners or traditions of the host country. At the same time, they were within a few hours by steamer of Victoria and Vancouver. Of course, before they could settle into this utopia, they had to clear land for the farms and sheep runs that provided an income for most of the residents. Yet here, too, they were in a favoured position, for the Gulf Islands were not nearly as heavily timbered as most parts of the Pacific coast. Besides, for a small sum island residents could import Oriental labourers from Victoria to do the heavy work.

Among the British settlers on the Gulf Islands were a number of colourful, rather eccentric characters: Henry Wright Bullock, the "Squire of Saltspring," is one of the best known. Bullock was a clergyman's son and only twenty-four years old when he came to Saltspring Island in 1891; yet even then he looked much older than his years. Perhaps it was his portly frame and long bushy beard, or his habitual costume—a long black frock coat and black silk top hat—that made him seem prematurely old. Soon after he arrived on Saltspring, Bullock purchased a 300-acre estate near the lake that now bears his name. Behind a wall of lofty yews and neatly clipped laurel hedges, he erected a sumptuous home which he filled with oil paintings by the Old Masters, antique silver, and porcelain bric-a-brac. Japanese gardeners received fifty cents a day for tending the grounds of the estate; they were responsible for maintaining the nurseries, the creamery, the chicken runs, and the hundred-odd beehives. The electrified photographic developing laboratory located near the house was the squire's domain.

Bullock, who has been described as "the epitome of British formality and conservatism on the Gulf Islands,"[6] had definite ideas on a variety of subjects, including appearance and etiquette. He liked women to wear jewelry, veils, and long gloves, and he often presented these items to the ladies whom he invited to his seven-course dinner parties and formal balls. He also maintained that all women should have eighteen-inch waists and wear five-inch heels, and he could frequently be seen in the village of Ganges lecturing lady residents on the subject. Bullock also had pronounced views on raising children and on children's attire. Local boys, he believed, were much too lax in matters of dress, and he endeavoured to correct this fault by importing boxes of top hats and Eton suits to the island. The squire offered to pay the boys ten cents a day if they would wear these outfits. Youths who agreed to wear their suits to the Anglican church on Sundays received an additional nickel.

Squire Bullock never married, but this did not prevent him from having a family of sorts. With the help of his housekeeper, he secured young lads from the Protestant orphanage in Victoria whom he trained and employed as cooks, butlers, and chauffeurs. The lads were dressed in a distinctive brown and green livery which included a short jacket with rows of brass buttons, and one of the lads invariably stood at the squire's right hand during the formal dinner parties. The attendant's principal duty was to dispense a spoonful of sherry into the guests' soup—a ritual that the squire always insisted upon. The outlandishly outfitted orphans often had to endure the taunts of neighbourhood boys and the giggles of the schoolgirls who came to visit, but in the end, the boys were amply rewarded for their services, for when they reached manhood they were given a one-hundred-acre farm which their mentor equipped and stocked. Thus, despite his eccentricities, Bullock came to be regarded as "the beloved squire," and when he died in 1946 he was widely mourned.

Until the turn of the century, many Gulf Islanders, the squire included, derived a considerable portion of their incomes from horticulture. Many grew apples, cherries, and plums and marketed them as far afield as Winnipeg. With the advent of large-scale horticulture in the Okanagan Valley, the Gulf Island orchards declined, and many of the residents cut down their fruit trees and turned to sheep farming, which became the economic mainstay of the islands. The growth of the mainland fruit industry also led many emigrants who might otherwise have settled on the islands to settle instead in the new communities that sprang up in and around the Okanagan. Emigrants there were caught up in British Columbia's "fruit mania," a phenomenon that was every bit as hectic as the Manitoba "wheat boom" of the 1870s and the Alberta "beef bonanza" of the 1880s.

Settlers had been growing fruit in the Okanagan since the 1850s, but the commercial potential of fruit farming was not fully realized until the last decade of the century, when Lord Aberdeen began exporting produce from the orchards of his Coldstream Ranch. The whole valley then turned from cattle ranching to fruit growing, and by the early 1900s the countryside along Okanagan Lake, from Penticton to Vernon, was one vast orchard. Planting and marketing techniques improved during the Edwardian years and the number of fruit trees increased by over 525 per cent between 1901 and the outbreak of the Great War. Land values around communities with enticing names such as Naramata, Peachland, and Summerland rose in a similar fashion: property that sold for a dollar an acre in 1898 was fetching $1,000 an acre ten years later. As so often happened in land booms, most of the profits made in the Okanagan accrued to large development companies with headquarters in Vancouver, London, and several European capitals.[7]

Many of the companies, including the one Lord Aberdeen launched in 1906 to develop small holdings on the Coldstream, tried to lure upper-middle-class Britons with glossy advertising brochures and promotional booklets which extolled "fruit-ranching" as the most civilized form of agriculture. In their advertising, many promoters quoted Albert Henry George, the 4th Earl Grey and Canada's governor general from 1904 to 1911. Earl Grey, who owned a small fruit ranch in the Kootenay Valley, pronounced fruit growers to be "par excellence Nature's Gentlemen." Horticulture, the earl declared, was "a beautiful art as well as a most profitable industry" and as such was a natural calling for Englishmen of "refinement, culture, and distinction."[8] The appeals were a great success, and from about 1892, when the town of Vernon was connected by rail to the CPR mainline at Sicamous, gentlemen emigrants literally poured into the valley. The newcomers included, an early resident recalled, "retired officers of the army and navy, retired Indian civil servants, men who had gone broke growing oranges or tea and thought apples and peaches might put them on their feet again, . . . professional men, fed up with their professions, . . . shopkeepers looking for business openings, and ladies looking for husbands. . . ."[9] The latter could choose from hundreds of young British bachelors who had succumbed to the blandishments of real estate developers and purchased forty-acre "fruit ranches" of their own. These young Englishmen were known as cheechakos, a Chinook Indian term for greenhorn. In the words of one of the bachelors, the cheechakos "didn't know what the hell they were coming out to in the first place. They just sort of imagined a sort of beautiful halo around everything."[10] They were under the impression that they had only to plant their trees and wait for the fruit to ripen in order to reap enormous profits. While they waited for the bountiful harvests, they devoted themselves to croquet tourneys, paper chases, and gymkhanas, or to Kipling's poetry, which was then all the rage. Fortunately some of the young emigrants realized before they lost their savings that fruit farming, like any other type of agriculture, required a considerable amount of knowledge and dedication. Those who did not soon joined the ranks of the valley's large regiment of well-bred but impoverished gentlemen. Yet despite finding themselves in "Queer Street," a good number of the impecunious young men remained in the area and supported themselves by working as ranch hands, hunting guides, prospectors, or farm labourers. Aside from the money they left in lakeside hotels, these youths did little for the local economy. They did, however, add to the "tone" of the valley, and in company with their more successful compatriots, they accounted for the relaxed, sophisticated manners that were characteristic of some of British Columbia's fruit-growing communities.

Another important group of gentleman emigrants during the Victorian-Edwardian years were the big-game hunters, many of whom sported double-barrelled surnames as well as double-barrelled shotguns. These sportsmen left their mark on Victoria's Union Club, which for many years was decorated with mounted heads, animal skins, and spent cartridges, and also on the economic development of the province through mining companies, railroads, canals, and various other projects in which they became interested while stalking bears, bighorn sheep and other creatures in the mountains and forests of the Pacific slope. Clive (later Sir Clive) Phillipps-Wolley, who was active in the cultural, political and economic life of pre-World War I British Columbia, was among the most important of these gentlemen.

The man whom the Vancouver *World* once called a "curious blend of dreamer and soldier" was born Edward Clive Oldnall Long Phillipps, in Dorsetshire, in 1854. He did not add the name Wolley until 1876 when he inherited the Wolley estate in Hanwood, Shropshire. Educated at Rossall School, he was gazetted a captain in the Royal South Wales Borderers and seconded to the diplomatic corps as vice-consul in Kerch, a seaport in southern Russia. He returned to England when he inherited the Wolley estate and in 1879 married Jane, second daughter of Rear Admiral W.H. Fenwick. Having resigned his commission, he studied law and was called to the bar from the Middle Temple in 1884. Six years later, after two hunting trips to North America, he settled in Victoria with his wife and four children.

When asked why he wished to emigrate to British Columbia, the hero of Phillipps-Wolley's novel, *One of the Broken Brigade* (1897), replies that he is passionately fond of sport. "It is not the only thing worth living for, I grant you, but it is better than money-grubbing. If there is no sport in America, there would have been mighty few Englishmen developing it to-day. It is the love of sport, or something uncommonly like it, which makes Englishmen colonize at all." Certainly a love of sport was an important factor in Phillipps-Wolley's decision to emigrate to British Columbia. He had always delighted in what he called "the enjoyments of barbarism," an expression he used to refer to the pleasure he derived from hiking across rugged terrain in search of exotic and elusive quadrupeds. He had hunted in the Crimea and in the Caucasus, in the barren reaches of Spitzbergen, and in the forests of the Laurentians and the Adirondacks, but nowhere had he found such sport and adventure, and such an impressive landscape, as in British Columbia. The title of one of his most popular works, *A Sportsman's Eden* (1888), sums up his view of the province. Of course as a gentleman he also enjoyed the amenities of civilized life, and it was for this reason that he chose to settle in Oak Bay, the most anglophile of Victoria's municipalities. There, amid sixteen acres of oaks and formal gardens, he built a brick and half-timbered mansion which he named Woodhall, in memory of his estate in Shropshire. The mansion was magnificent with stained glass windows, beamed ceilings, and ornately carved fireplaces; it contained one of the finest private libraries in the Pacific Northwest and enough rooms to require the attention of three full-time servants. Over the main doorway of this residence was an inscription from Horace,

coelum non animum mutant qui trans mare currant, which may
be translated as "those who cross the seas change their heaven
but not their spirit." When applied to the owner of Woodhall the
inscription may be translated more simply to mean "Once an
English gentleman, always an English gentleman." [11]

When he was not hunting, Phillipps-Wolley devoted much of
his time to literature. He wrote poetry as well as prose, was a
consulting editor for the *Badminton Library,* and a frequent con-
tributor to the *Spectator.* He was active, too, in literary and
newspaper circles in British Columbia. He owned a newspaper
in the mining town of Nelson, served briefly as editor of the
Vancouver *Province,* and was a mainstay of local publications
such as the *Week* and *Westward Ho!* Phillipps-Wolley, whose
family motto was *ducit amor patriae*—let love of country
lead—was also devoted to the Empire; indeed, the Toronto
Globe (9 July 1918) described him as "the Imperialist of Imperialists." He worked tirelessly to promote the twin causes of imperial unity and military preparedness and was greatly disappointed when he failed to gain a seat as a Conservative imperialist in the federal election of 1904. He was rewarded eleven years
later, however, when he was knighted for organizing branches
of the Navy League in western Canada.

Although he decried "money-grubbing" and disliked "money-
grubbing real estate agents," Phillipps-Wolley actually made a
great deal of money from real estate. He owned a commercial
block in downtown Victoria, several of the smaller Gulf Islands,
and a number of lots near Duncan, where he and his family resettled in the early 1900s. He also owned property which he had
first seen during his various hunting expeditions in the interior.
He was, in fact, one of the province's leading capitalists. Among
Phillipps-Wolley's most ambitious investments were the companies he launched with his fellow sportsman, Warburton Pike.
One of these companies was engaged in mining copper in the
Cassiar Mountains; another ran a steam paddle-wheeler and
pack trains into the Klondike gold fields. Phillipps-Wolley
attracted the capital for these and other ventures with the help of
articles and business reports which he contributed to influential
financial organs such as the London *Mining News.*

Warburton Mayer Pike's career was similar to that of his friend and business partner; he was born in the same county as Phillipps-Wolley and by coincidence arrived in Victoria on the same day in 1884. Prior to coming to Victoria, Pike had attended Rugby and had spent several years at Oxford. He left without taking a degree and spent a number of months knocking about the East End of London. Although his was one of the most distinguished families in the West Country, he had, a friend recalled, "a penchant for slumming."[12] Since he had a private income, he was able to indulge in another penchant—hunting— and before he reached his majority he had hunted in Scandinavia, Iceland, and in several American states. For a time he also punched cattle in Texas and Oregon, so that when he reached Victoria, the twenty-three-year-old sportsman was very much a man of the world.

Soon after he arrived in British Columbia, Warburton Pike teamed up with another gentleman emigrant and hunting enthusiast, Charles Payne, and purchased a large farm on Saturna Island. This farm, which included a valuable sandstone quarry, plus property Pike owned on other Gulf Islands and in Victoria, made him one of the wealthiest men in the area. Few people who met Pike for the first time would have guessed as much. He rarely carried any money with him, preferred to go barefoot whenever possible, and because of his ragged clothes and tatty rucksack was often mistaken for a tramp. The fastidious squire of neighbouring Saltspring was no doubt appalled by his appearance, though Warburton Pike's fellow members at the Union Club were usually indulgent towards his eccentricities and mishaps. "Pikey," they chuckled, on hearing that he had been turned away from a theatre for not being properly attired or had been put off a streetcar for not having the fare, "was a rare old sport, game all the way through." Only when he received a native Indian woman in the clubhouse did they express disapproval of "Pikey's" behaviour.

In 1889 Warburton Pike undertook the first of his celebrated hunting expeditions to the far north. He had heard tales about the northern musk ox from Hudson's Bay Company trappers and was determined to test his skills in the inhospitable regions where the musk oxen lived. The expedition, which he detailed in his first book, *The Barren Ground of Northern Canada* (1892), involved a trek from Edmonton to Fort Resolution on Great Slave Lake. There he secured the services of two Indian guides who accompanied him on the twenty-month odyssey. Having shot several of the shaggy beasts, he returned through the uncharted territory of northern British Columbia. The journey involved crossing some of the most difficult terrain on the continent in the middle of winter: the mountains were sheer, the forests were almost impenetrable, and the wind, which blew constantly, was bitterly cold. When they eventually staggered into the settlement of Hudson's Hope, Pike and his native companions were exhausted, frostbitten, and on the verge of starvation.

"Pikey" thrived on this kind of adventure, and in 1892 he undertook another expedition which was more arduous than the first. This time he made his way across the Stikine Plateau in northwestern British Columbia; then, in a small canoe, he followed the Pelling and Yukon rivers across Alaska and down to the Bering Sea. The expedition, which formed the subject of his second book, *Through the Sub-Arctic Forest* (1896), made him a celebrity among the international sporting fraternity, and thereafter he was on intimate terms with such luminaries as Frederick Selous, a fellow Rugbeian, and Theodore Roosevelt. Following the expedition, he was also invited to represent the Dominion in many of the international shooting and field sports exhibitions which were held in Europe during the early 1900s.

Pike's second expedition took him through the remote Cassiar Mountains, on the British Columbia-Yukon border. The experience led to the founding of a mining company in partnership with Phillipps-Wolley, Lord Osborne Beauclerc, and other sportsmen. The trip also resulted in the creation of the Cassiar Central Railway Company which Pike and his colleagues chartered in 1897. The company had plans to build an eighty-mile narrow gauge railway line across the wilderness from Telegraph Creek to Dease Lake, and in consideration, the provincial government granted the company over 700,000 acres of land, along with mineral, timber, and water rights to the area.

As with other development schemes in B.C. during this period, the 2.5-million-dollar railway was never built, though Pike and company retained their land grant. Opposition politicians in Victoria were outraged and launched a campaign that rocked the already precarious administration of Premier J. H. Turner. The Turner government fell soon after, but Pike and his sporting associates weathered the storm with equanimity. In fact, they went on to charter other mining and transportation companies and to secure other lucrative land grants.

The Cassiar Railway scheme was one example of a venture that brought rugged big-game hunters into bed with effete politicians and financiers. An earlier, more controversial venture was the Kootenay Flats reclamation scheme which William Adolph Baillie-Grohman promoted from the mid-1880s to the early 1920s. The scheme involved draining the rich black floodlands south of Kootenay Lake near the British Columbia-United States border. This was to be accomplished by widening the outlet of the Kootenay River into Columbia Lake and by constructing a canal through the area now known as Canal Flats. Baillie-Grohman first concocted the scheme in 1882, while he and his friend Teddy Roosevelt were hunting mountain goats in the Kootenay Valley. Baillie-Grohman was impressed by the agricultural potential of the floodlands and felt certain that if the area could be drained he could established a thriving colony. The colony never materialized and though a small canal was constructed, it was years before Baillie-Grohman's drainage scheme was followed up. However, through various development companies which he registered in London, Baillie-Grohman managed to secure at least 78,000 acres in land grants plus several thousand dollars in cash subsidies.[13]

Every gentleman emigrant, tourist, and entrepreneur who came to Canada in the last decades of the nineteenth century seemed to know Baillie-Grohman. No doubt this was partly because Baillie-Grohman was constantly flitting back and forth across the Atlantic, raising money for his companies, promoting real estate transactions, and exhibiting his hunting trophies. He was also a memorable character, both suave and entertaining. He would settle into the lounge of a first-class railway carriage or steamship and regale his fellow passengers with tales concerning his exotic family background, how he shot his first bear before he was ten years old, how he redecorated Schloss Wolfgang, his castle in the Austrian Alps, and how he planned to develop the far, far West. People also remembered Baillie-Grohman for the articles he wrote in the *Geographical Journal*, the *Nineteenth Century,* the *Field*, and the *English Illustrated Magazine.*

The sportsman who often wrote under the pseudonym "Stalker" was born in London in 1851. He was related on his mother's side to the Duke of Wellington and on his father's to the Austrian aristocracy. He was educated privately and at Elizabeth College in Guernsey. He practised law in the metropolis for a few years but found the work tedious and so doffed his wig and dickie in favour of canvas trousers and hunting jacket. In 1878 he made his first trip to North America. The expedition, which he described in his book, *Camps in the Rockies* (1882), took him through the southern states, across the American midwest to the cattle ranches of Wyoming, and along the Pacific seaboard. As a result of his earlier publications, Baillie-Grohman was regarded as an alpinist and sportsman of the first rank, and on the 1878 tour he was accorded a warm welcome wherever he rambled.

Like his fellow barrister, Phillipps-Wolley, Baillie-Grohman found Victoria a pleasant change from the American West. "The men one met in the streets of Victoria were the English country-town type," he wrote twenty years later, "sturdy, well-nurtured, florid-complexioned men—beings that took life easily, that ate their dinners of wholesome roast beef in a tranquil frame of mind. . . . " He also admired the climate and the quaint cottages which he recalled were covered with clematis and festooned with "old-fashioned flowers so dear to those who have turned their backs on their native land."[14] The city, he realized, was an ideal base camp for his hunting expeditions and financial forays, and in the late eighties he and his wife established a home there. In the interval, Baillie-Grohman explored the interior of the province, practised law, and made a small fortune with shares he held in the celebrated Bluebell silver mine. Despite criticism from several British Columbia newspapers, and despite being involved in a number of complicated lawsuits, he also pressed on with his plans to reclaim and colonize the Kootenay Valley.

Baillie-Grohman, Phillipps-Wolley, and Warburton Pike were but some of the big-game hunters who left their mark on the Pacific slope during the last decades of the nineteenth century. As the Victoria *Daily News* reported on 21 April 1892, they were moneyed emigrants who had come initially "for the sake of a few hides and heads," but had remained in British Columbia to exploit and develop the province's natural resources. Their schemes were often quixotic, and they were certainly guilty of ignoring environmental and ecological concerns. However, people were barely aware of such concerns in the 1880s and 1890s, and for the most part local residents applauded the big-game hunters for attracting so much British capital into the province. Their prowess with a rifle was also admired, and for many years Warburton Pike's stuffed musk-ox was exhibited with pride in the museums of Victoria and Vancouver. Ironically, though, the very men who had done so much to develop the resources of the province came to lament the changes which followed economic development. And though they all contributed to a popular series of monographs entitled *Fishing and Shooting Along the Line of the Canadian Pacific Railway,* they later greatly resented the building of railway branch lines. The railways, they said, were bringing far too many tourists and settlers into the province — individuals who had little appreciation for the "enjoyments of barbarism." What was worse, the newcomers, the railways, the mining syndicates, and the timber companies were ruining their hunting grounds and driving away the best game. Progress, they blustered, as they counted their share certificates and polished their rifles, was ruining the sportsman's Eden.

CHAPTER VII

REMITTANCE MEN

By 1900, British gentlemen had been involved in the settlement of Canada for over three-quarters of a century. Gentlemen emigrants were largely responsible for clearing the backwoods of southern Ontario, for opening the Ottawa Valley, and for making the first assault on the muskegs of Muskoka. They were among the first to turn the sod in the wheat lands of Manitoba and Assiniboia; they played a crucial role in Alberta's ranching industry and in the orchards of British Columbia. They had opened new mines, chartered new railways, and provided capital for innumerable secondary industries. Socially and politically, gentlemen emigrants had also been a force. They had established literary and scientific institutes, theatrical guilds and athletic clubs from Halifax to Victoria; they had endowed churches, schools, universities, and philanthropic organizations. They had provided the Dominion with a corps of administrators, lawyers, doctors, and militia officers; they had rendered valuable service as justices of the peace, gold commissioners, postmasters, and customs officials. In short, they had made significant contributions in all walks of life and in all parts of the country.

Yet although the emigrants' contributions were considerable, their image and reputation had become considerably tarnished by the turn of the century. In the early 1900s, Montreal's English-language press was publishing editorials and cartoons that lampooned the English gentleman. In Toronto music halls, large crowds gathered to laugh at the antics of "stage Englishmen"—monocled, overdressed buffoons who peppered their monologues with "I say!" "deucedly clever," and "don'tcher know." In Vancouver, civic officials were grumbling about "knickerbockered toffs," while in Winnipeg, employment notices were appearing which stated, "No Englishmen Need Apply." The cartoons, the discouraging employment notices, and the muttered insults were but a few indicators of the Canadian public's attitude towards the gentlemen emigrants, especially the English emigrants. No longer were these gentlemen regarded as energetic, innovative pioneers; rather, they were viewed as disreputable, languid fops. In fact, attitudes had changed to such an extent that by 1900 the term "gentleman emigrant" had virtually disappeared and been replaced by a new, derogatory term—"remittance man."

Strictly speaking, a remittance man was any individual who received an allowance—a remittance—from family or friends at home. In its literal sense, the term applied to a great many of the young gentlemen who came to Canada before 1900: Clement Cornwall, Edward ffolkes, Frederick DelaFosse, Herbert Church all received remittances from their families during the early stages of their careers in Canada. In popular usage, however, the term "remittance man" meant bounder, scapegrace, and ne'er-do-well; it implied a social outcast, an emigrant who had been exiled to the colonies and who was paid to remain there because he was an embarrassment to his family in Britain.

The Australians coined the term "remittance man" in the 1880s, but the phrase soon became popular with Canadians as well. William Caine, a British traveller, encountered the expression for the first time when he visited Winnipeg in 1887. "The town is full of [young immigrants] sent out by friends in England," Caine reported. "They go by the name of 'Remittance Men,' because their chief occupation is borrowing dollars, 'till they get their remittance from home.'" Another British traveller, the Reverend Alexander Boddy, was also struck by the expression when he visited the Gateway City a few years later. "There is a class of men here who are called 'Remitters' or 'Remittance-men,'" he explained. "They are loafers who go round trying to negotiate loans. They are always expecting a remittance in a few posts from the Old Country."[1] By the turn of the century the expression was so familiar in both western and eastern Canada that contemporary writers no longer bothered to define it for their readers. They simply assumed that everyone had first-hand knowledge of the ubiquitous remitter.

The prominence of the remittance man and the Canadian public's negative attitude towards the gentleman emigrant were due partly to changes that took place in Canadian society after Confederation. Generally speaking, Canadians became more sophisticated, more independent-minded, more nationalistic—in a word, more Canadian. As they became prouder of their accomplishments and growing stature in the world, so they became more sensitive to criticism or, as was more often the case, to lack of recognition. They had little patience, for example, with poorly informed Britons who arrived in the Dominion expecting to find teepees and log huts, instead of modern cities and model farms. Similarly, they were quick to react to marble-mouthed English tourists and emigrants who affected what seemed to be patronizing manners. An early instance of this pride and sensitivity is to be found in a satirical pamphlet entitled *The Englishman in Canada* (1880), by an author who identified himself as "Mac." The subject of the tract is a languid and opinionated bachelor who decides to "explore" Canada on behalf of an organization called "The Society for the Promotion of Cosmopolitan Ideas." Mac's Englishman proposes to begin his journey in St. John's, Newfoundland, which he believes is within walking distance of Montreal. There, he feels certain, he will conquer savages, wild beasts, and "other unknown terrors." Having done that, he plans to take in Toronto, board a street-car, and tour the suburbs of Manitoba and British Columbia. His progress, needless to say, is quixotic and calamitous, and at every stage of the journey he makes some ludicrous statement regarding the nature of colonial society. Wherever Mac's picaroon goes, he is buffeted by bustling, progressive, confident men and women, none of whom are in the least impressed by his ideas concerning the innate superiority of Old World culture. He is convinced, nevertheless, that the "colonials" are in need of his services, and the pamphlet concludes with his stumbling up to Ottawa, where he expects to be offered the post of "Inspector General of Curling and Skating Rinks for the Dominion of Canada." The appointment, he imagines, will pay at least £1,000 per annum. Anything less would hardly be adequate for a gentleman like himself.

Mac's satire was mild and relatively good natured: it chided, rather than chastised. Much the same spirit pervaded Arthur G. Racey's cartoon series, "The Englishman in Canada," which appeared in the Montreal *Star* in the autumn of 1901. Racey, a third generation Canadian and one of Canada's most famous political cartoonists, did not object to gentlemen emigrants per se, but like many of his contemporaries, he was exasperated with some of the emigrants who arrived in the Dominion with ideas derived from spurious "settlers' manuals." Written by character's like Mac's Englishman, these paperback manuals depicted Canada as the "Great Lone Land," as a place where settlers constantly battled howling blizzards and hostile natives. These highly coloured manuals were often endorsed by colonial outfitters in London who stood to profit by selling emigrants superfluous equipment; they were accepted as gospel by gullible souls like Racey's character, Clarence de Brown-Jones, who arrives in Montreal brandishing snowshoes, bowie knives, and revolvers. Of course these innocents soon discarded their outlandish accoutrements, along with their erroneous notions and preconceptions of Canadian life. As Racey shows in his cartoons, however, the transition period was often painful, both for the emigrant and for members of the host society, who had to endure the novices' antics and *faux pas*.

Clarence de Brown-Jones, a character who provided a model for many of the stage Englishmen who strutted across the boards of Toronto music halls, did not, so far as we know, venture to the prairie West. It was just as well he did not, for emigrants of his type were objects of derision and even barbed invective. Moreover, they were not simply called "Brits," "Englishmen," or "remitters"; they were saddled with other epithets, such as tenderfoot, greenhorn, and broncho. The latter term, John Sandilands explained in his *Western Canadian Dictionary and Phrase-Book* (1912), referred to "an Englishman who still clings to Old-Country manners and speech; so called because he requires some 'breaking in.'" Sandilands added that once "broken in," erstwhile "bronchos" might be called "Improved Britishers," a title which signified that the bearer was almost, but not quite, acceptable to the no-nonsense Westerner.[2]

Certain emigrants in western Canada were also likely to find themselves referred to as "dudes," a term derived from the German "dudendop," or lazy fellow. The Alberta *Tribune* (2 July 1895) used the expression in this manner when it railed against the "dudes" who gravitated to Calgary. "Dudes" the paper defined as young Englishmen who, in trying to appear as seasoned ranchers, "dress themselves up in the garb of cowboys, [with] spurs the size of small cart wheels [and] hats cut with a scissor and covered with mud to look old and tough." "As a rule," the *Tribune* said, dudes "do little but ride round the country on a half-starved cayuse. Too lazy to plough, and too shiftless to own cattle, they eke out an existence on the remittance plan. Their only redeeming quality is that they do not marry and are not therefore likely to perpetuate the breed."

The unflattering remarks that appeared in the *Tribune,* and with disturbing frequency in other prairie newspapers during the late-Victorian and Edwardian years, point to the fact that western Canada, like eastern Canada, was changing. By the mid-1890s, the West was no longer an unstructured frontier but a developing settlement area, with conventions, traditions, and codes which newcomers were expected to honour. Readers of the western press, like subscribers to eastern papers, also expected newcomers to appreciate local realities and to conduct themselves in a manner that was compatible with those realities. Thus fancily dressed "dudes" who paraded through burgeoning centres like Calgary, Regina, or Winnipeg could expect to be met with hoots of derision; they could expect to be ostracized by residents who prided themselves on founding progressive, up-to-date communities; they could expect to be made the butt of innumerable jokes, insulting newspaper columns, and denigrating cartoons.

Indeed the dudes who ventured to the West, especially those who came to the prairie wheat lands, could expect to be regarded less favourably than they might have been regarded in the relatively cosmopolitan centres of the East. In some parts of Manitoba and Assiniboia, in fact, the dandified gentleman was met with overt hostility. This hostility is not surprising, given conditions on the prairies and the character of the prairie wheat farmers. Many of these farmers had come to the West from Ontario or the Maritimes in the late seventies and early eighties; by exerting an enormous effort they had, in the years that followed, succeeded in building prosperous farms. An efficient, utilitarian, dour breed of men, successful wheat farmers could not countenance newcomers who seemed to devote more time and energy to their appearance than to their work. These same farmers, moreover, had developed a certain pride and confidence which comes to those who have weathered setbacks and triumphed over obstacles. They were, accordingly, acutely conscious of English greenhorns who had the audacity to lecture them on how much better the squire's estate was managed in the Old Country. Farmers who suffered these lectures did so but once. Thereafter, when posting notices for chore boys or farm hands in the Farm Help Register in Winnipeg, they simply scribbled "No Englishmen Need Apply" at the bottom of their advertisements.

By the same token, the gentleman emigrant who wandered into the wheat lands of the West had to tread very warily in communities that had been established by labourers, mechanics, and others who had come originally from the lower ranks of British society. In many instances, these settlers had fled the Old Country because they felt restricted and/or abused by the upper classes. They were, consequently, not overly disposed towards the youngers sons of upper- or even middle-class families. Nor were Britons who had come to the West with little or no capital sympathetic towards the remittance man who could fall back on his allowance or, if need be, wire the guv'nor for extra funds. For these farmers, who had come to Canada to build a new life for their families, there was no bountiful guv'nor, no outside income, and no home to return to if the going got rough.

As a result of demographic changes on the ranching frontier and rivalries between cattlemen and "sod busters," the status of gentlemen emigrants in southern Alberta also altered. In the early 1880s, wealthy cattlemen from Britain and eastern Canada had established a society there that was gracious, cultured, and sporty. The successful members of this ranching fraternity constituted a charitable elite who had tolerated the failures and foibles of a younger generation of emigrants. The older ranchers had recognized, as one of them put it, "that the vicissitudes of life frequently occurring in those early days were often startling."[3] Since they held similar social and political beliefs, enjoyed the same sporting activities, and had attended the same schools, young gentlemen emigrants had in fact been welcomed by the established cattlemen. In the last decade of the century, however, the fabric of Alberta society changed and, in relative terms, the charitable ranching elite declined. When that happened, Tom Brown's halcyon days in the foothills began drawing to a close.

The society that British public school boys had so enjoyed on the ranching frontier began to change as early as 1891, when Ottawa introduced new leasing arrangements which were more favourable to farmers and small stockmen. The new legislation was not welcomed by the owners of large ranches, and the early nineties were marked by hostility between the cattlemen, who depended on vast, open ranges, and "sod busters," who ploughed up the bunch grass and marked off the grazing lands with barbed wire fences. The farmers, who ultimately won the struggle for control of the rangeland, fiercely resented the newly arrived gentlemen, who tended to ally themselves with the old guard. The resentment manifested itself in a variety of ways that included branding the Tom Browns who came to the territory as a pack of worthless remittance men.

Following the Liberal party's victory of 1896, the new Minister of the Interior, Clifford Sifton, launched a vigorous advertising campaign which brought approximately two million immigrants into the Dominion over a period of fifteen years. Most of these immigrants took up farming in the West, many in areas

that only a few years earlier had been a playground for the
British gentleman. This, too, affected Tom Brown's status in the
West. The new immigrants came primarily from humble backgrounds: they were working-class Britons, American-born farmers, and peasants from Russia, Austria, and the Ukraine. Altogether, they had little respect for the public schools' ethos and
little sympathy for the supernumerary gentleman who relied on
remittances from home.

A similar development occurred west of the Rockies, in British Columbia. As immigration to the province increased, gentlemen emigrants were apt to be jostled by railway navvies from
southern Europe and by miners and factory workers from the
United States and Britain. Happily for the young British gentlemen, many of B.C.'s new working-class immigrants settled in
the Kootenays or in Vancouver, where opportunities for
advancement were greatest. As a result, newly arrived gentlemen
could still count on a friendly reception in places like Victoria,
Vernon, or Duncan, where the anglophile elite was well entrenched. Even so, gentlemen emigrants who came to this most
British of provinces were likely to find themselves regarded as
exiles and ne'er-do-wells. During the last years of the nineteenth
century, they might even have heard themselves ridiculed in
popular songs and ballads such as "The Young British Rauncher
[sic]":

> When the half-baked remittance man comes to the West,
> Arrayed in short pants, which he thinks suit him best,
> He parades around town while he takes a short rest,
> Ere assuming the role of a rancher.
>
> Chorus:
> Role, role, role of a rancher,
> A Rauncher [sic] of B.C., etc.

This song, which included at least six additional stanzas, sati-
rized the remittance man's sporting enthusiasms and his overall
incompetence as a practical rancher. First sung on Vancouver
Island in 1897, the ballad soon echoed in barrooms and bunk-
houses from Vancouver to the Peace River.[4]

The Canadian attitude towards gentlemen emigrants had

changed by the end of the nineteenth century, but so, too, had the gentlemen emigrants themselves. Generally speaking, the supernumerary gentlemen were younger and less worldly than the half-pay officers who had come to British North America during the first half of the century. Furthermore, while the Tom Browns who came to the Dominion were fortunate in being able to turn to an earlier generation of emigrants for assistance, the assistance they received was necessarily limited. Once they left the established towns and cities where the first wave of emigrants had settled, the new emigrants had to rely upon their own devices. And it was at this point that the differences between early and late-Victorian emigrants were most pronounced. The first wave of emigrants, which included men like Samuel Strickland and Tiger Dunlop, came from a Britain that was still predominantly rural. The first generation of gentlemen emigrants had, accordingly, at least a cursory knowledge of country life: they had travelled on horseback, were familiar with livestock, had warmed themselves by open fires, and had read by candlelight even before they came to the colonies. The Tom Browns who came to Canada three-quarters of a century later came from a very different Britain. They had been raised in an age of steam, diesel power, and electricity. They had grown up, most of them, in the suburbs of large cities. They had become used to products and services which were luxuries in the Canadian northwest. The adjustments they had to make were, therefore, all the greater.

The attitudes of many of the young emigrants who came to post-Confederation Canada also made life difficult for them. They had been raised in an age of empire, an age characterized by intense nationalism. Their schoolmasters and clergymen, along with the authors and editors of the popular press, were constantly drawing attention to the greatness of the British Empire, to the accomplishments of British heroes, and, generally, to the glories of Britain. This nationalism was particularly acute in England and so it is not surprising that the Tom Browns who immigrated during the period remained intensely devoted to the Old Country. Obviously, though, it was advisable for them to temper their expressions of devotion once they settled in the increasingly nationalistic Dominion. Otherwise—as Mrs. Charles Inderwick's letters make clear—the emigrants were likely to exasperate and offend their Canadian hosts.

Mary Ella (née Lees) Inderwick, a native of Perth, Ontario, was the wife of an easy-going English gentleman who had originally come to Canada as aide-de-camp to the governor general, Lord Lansdowne. F.C. Inderwick subsequently moved to the Northwest where he and a friend began ranching. He met Mary, who was visiting her brother in Calgary, in 1884, and soon after, she became chatelaine of the Inderwick spread near Pincher Creek. The North Fork, as Inderwick's ranch was named, was a favourite stopping place for English gentlemen who were travelling through the Alberta foothills.

A well-educated woman who had been raised in a wealthy, cultured home, Mary had much in common with her husband's friends. But some of the gentlemen she found "trying." She noted in one of her letters, for instance, that she had spent the day with one of Charles's school chums, "a fresh Englishman" who insisted on comparing the charms of Oxford with what he termed the "uncouthness" of Winnipeg. To this Mrs. Inderwick remarked that it was absurd to compare "a young and lusty baby with a learned, polished, and very beautiful woman." In another letter she complained that Charles's friends exhibited a want of "tact" when speaking of Canada and Canadians: "The crowning insult to me is the way they say 'but we do not look on *you* as a Canadian,' and they mistake this for a compliment! It makes my Canadian blood boil! I answer that though I have married an Englishman, I have not lost my identity, and I am purely Canadian and proud of it." Yet her husband's friends were inclined to patronize her; they continued to regale her with talk of England's glories, England's prowess, England's beauties—"a never ending laudation of England" which she sometimes found unbearable. "Oh, don't England me any more!" she exclaimed one evening to a party of bumptious Old Boys. "I am *so* sick of it!"[5]

Difficulties also arose because some of the public school emigrants were inordinately devoted to games and other leisure activities. Their fondness for sport and their faith in games was, of course, part of the public school ethos. But the ethos, like other aspects of the gentlemen emigrants' background, had to be adapted to conditions in Canada—a fact that many of the young bloods failed to appreciate. Free from parental restraints and unfamiliar with the demands of agriculture, they neglected their farms and ranches in favour of fowling, fishing, cricket, football and billiards. "It makes one blush as an Englishman," a conscientious homesteader remarked, referring to the games-playing schoolboys and remittance men who cavorted around Brandon. "The most useless men I ever saw were young fellows who were said to have had 'the best education,' but were positive fools."[6] Certainly many Canadian farmers would have endorsed the homesteader's view, although most would have elaborated considerably upon his remarks. After long experience, they concluded that Old Boys from the Old Country were more than occasionally tactless, more than a little foolish. The emigrants were also, critics charged, supercilious and vain, mollycoddled and naive, incompetent and intemperate.

In 1907, W.H.P. Jarvis, a Prince Edward Islander who had spent many years in Manitoba, published a serio-comic tale entitled *The Letters of a Remittance Man to His Mother*. Reginald Brown, the "author" of the fictitious letters, represents in an exaggerated sort of way the kind of emigrant westerners came to decry. Attired in riding breeches and shooting jacket, Reggie begins his progress in Winnipeg, a city he regards as "a beastly, horrid place." He forms this opinion of the city after an altercation with an hotel clerk. The altercation arises when the clerk refuses to reschedule the hotel's luncheon so that Reggie can enjoy a refreshing bath. "Had anyone told me such a thing was possible I would not have believed it," he writes afterwards, recounting the incident. "I do not know what most gentlemen would consider the proper course under such conditions, but I exclaimed—*sotto voce*—'Extraordinary creature!' and marched out of the place with becoming dignity."

Recoiling from the "odious familiarity" of Winnipeggers, Reggie spends $3,000 on a 200-acre "improved farm" some distance from the city. The Oaks, as the farm is christened ("in honour . . . of the dear old place at home") turns out to be valueless, since most of the property is covered with a slough. But this does not upset the owner. On the contrary, he thinks the slough adds a picturesque quality to his estate. Besides, the slough attracts wild fowl and prairie chickens, which Reggie "pots" in order to relieve "the monotony of toil." As for his farmhouse, it is a tumbledown shack, blistering hot in the summer and freezing cold in the winter. It is, however, a well-stocked shack, for during his first months in Manitoba, Reggie lays in over $200 worth of marmalade, jam, and biscuits.

Reggie's other major investment is an emaciated horse, which he imagines is an English thoroughbred. "Possessing a hunter of one's own will make it possible to fancy oneself a squire at home and so utterly apart from these commonplace Canadians," he informs his "mater." The commonplace Canadians, however, are not impressed with the figure he cuts when he swaggers into town for supplies; nor do the storekeepers show him the deference he feels is his due as an English gentleman. He finds their attitudes perplexing, and says so in the letters he submits to the local newspapers. He is perplexed, too, by their sense of humour. "Ho! Sam," he hears a "colonial" shout to a neighbour, "did you ever hear a remittance man's description of farming in Manitoba? It is this: 'Tis nice upon the wintah's morning to get up and look out upon the open prairie, and see the little buttahflies making buttah and the grawshoppahs making graws!" Reggie suspects the remark was made for his benefit, but for the life of him, he cannot imagine why.[7]

Such jokes were legion in the West. Indeed, the jokes were so common that English gentlemen emigrants—who in the popular mind all answered either to Bertie, Monty, Reggie, or Teddy—became local celebrities. Every homesteader, it seemed, had a favourite anecdote about gentlemen emigrants, and in prairie communities people competed with each other in recounting fantastic tales of eccentric remittance men. Each of the jokes and anecdotes drew attention to a particular foible or failing of the "greenhorn Englishman." L.V. Kelly included a number of these tales in *The Range Men* (1913). Having homesteaded in southern Alberta at the turn of the century, Kelly concluded that the English remittance men were singularly incompetent and naive. To illustrate his point, he told the tale of the remittance man who visits a livery stable and spies two mules placidly munching oats from nosebags. "I say," the remittance man exclaims, turning to the stableman, "do you always have to keep these beasts muzzled?" A similar tale, which originated in Saskatchewan, concerned a remittance man who was instructed to fetch a team of horses and proceed with the ploughing. When after a considerable time the man did not reappear, the farmer went to the barn to investigate. There he discovered that the remittance man had hitched one horse between the two handles of the plough and was sitting on a bale of straw, scratching his head and wondering what to do with the other horse.[8]

British Columbians, not to be outdone, had their own repertoire of remittance man tales. One of these tales, told in the Kootenays, concerned a newly arrived Englishman who was charged with selling liquor to an Indian. The young English man's plea—that he thought the Indian was a Romany gypsy— was rejected by the magistrate, and the youth was subsequently sentenced to a few days in jail where, according to the custom then, he was kept busy cutting cordwood. A short while later the magistrate received a letter from the youth's father. "I don't know how to thank you for your kindness to my son...," the letter began. "He writes that he is cutting cordwood for the government. I don't know what cordwood is, but to get a government contract almost as soon as he arrived shows that he has some business ability. For young men able and willing to work, there are evidently openings in our colonies...." Another tale which circulated west of the Rockies concerned a well-bred Englishman who lost his way in the woods and was found half-dead of thirst beside a river. When his rescuers asked why he had not drunk the water at hand, the fastidious emigrant replied: "Why, I didn't have a bally drinking cup, don'tcher know!"[9]

There were also many stories about how the remittance man ensured a supply of funds from home. One story featured a young man who informed his guv'nor that he was running a herd of 700 full-blooded gophers on his ranch. The youth reported that although the animals were in good condition, he would need an extra $1,000 to keep them in shape for the spring market; naturally, the youth's father wired the money forthwith.[10] A variation on the same theme is the story about the remittance man whose father decides to pay a brief visit to his son's ranch. The son, in fact, had no ranch but lived in a squalid shack. However, in order to impress his benefactor, the remittance man persuades a neighbour to switch places with him for a few hours. Thus, when the pater arrives, he finds his boy comfortably installed in a large ranch house and apparently in command of several thousand head of cattle. The father—who in most versions of the story is cast as a doddering peer or a clergyman—is taken in by the charade. Indeed, he is so impressed that he rewards his son with a large sum of money; on returning to England he also increases the boy's quarterly remittances, so that the latter can make further improvements to the ranch. The same type of remittance man, devious but ingenious, was featured in another tale which circulated in all four western provinces. This tale concerned an impecunious remitter whose family had threatened to cut off his allowance on the grounds that he had nothing to show for the money they had previously lavished on him. Determined to prove that he deserved their continued support, the young Englishman borrowed a handsome stallion and a camera and hired a uniformed fireman to pose with the horse in front of a local hotel. The youth then sent the photo to his people in the Old Country. On the back of the photo he scribbled: "A recent snap of my ranch house showing one of my grooms with one of my hunters."[11]

Then there were the jokes and anecdotes that dealt with "gentleman topers" and "thirsty" Englishmen. Asked by visiting antiquarians if the area contained any notable ruins similar to those found in Britain or on the Continent, residents of most western towns were apt to reply in the affirmative. "Sure we got ruins—plenty of 'em," they would say, pointing to the local saloon. "We call 'em remittance men."

"Thirsty" gentlemen were scarcely a new phenomenon in the late Victorian-Edwardian years; nor were they confined to the Canadian West. In the 1840s, Mrs. Traill observed that intemperance was the prevailing vice among settlers in the backwoods of Upper Canada; she added, with "a blush," that the vice was most prevalent "among those that consider themselves among the better class of emigrants." Catharine's sister, Mrs. Moodie, also blushed when speaking of the "low debauchery" of the "broken-down gentlemen loafers" she had observed in the 1850s. As we have seen, John Gwynn Swain's companion, Hugh Gibson, came to a sorry end through drink, while Frederick Dela-Fosse confessed that drunkenness was the great failing of his remitter friends in Muskoka. Young Edward ffolkes also commented on the problem during his early days in Guelph. "Whiskey is the curse of the country . . . ," he informed his mother, "I have never tasted it. Once taste it and they say it is like opium — it is nearly impossible to give it up. It is a curse to a Canadian, but a double curse to an Englishman."[12] In Canadian folklore, however, the drunken Englishman, or, more accurately, the drunken remittance man, was most often associated with the West.

Winnipeg was famous, or as the case may be, infamous, for its gentlemen topers. Their haven at the turn of the century was the Garry Club, where one of their favourite drinks was a "Rajah's Peg" — a powerful concoction made of equal parts of brandy and champagne. The Grotto, in the basement of the Mariaggi Hotel, and the Giffo Club, near the stately Royal Alexandra Hotel, were also popular watering holes. Most of the habitués of these resorts wore "Ascot ties, caps, vivid waistcoats, and shaggy tweeds," one of their number recalled fondly. "They played better than average billiards and backed their chances of filling an inside straight as if the Count of Monte Cristo were their uncle." The Methodist reformer, J. S. Woodsworth, however, was not impressed by their connections or their skills at billiards. Younger sons and remittance men, he complained, were a blight on the Gateway City. "Useless at home, they are worse than useless here. The saloon gains most largely by their presence."[13]

Farther west, near Portage la Prairie, the remittance men's "whiskey sprees" were said to be "an institution," while at Brandon, one aristocratic settler was known to bathe in champagne. Up north, in Edmonton, a bartender told a *Times* reporter in the mid-nineties that young sparks from the Old Country were "positive devils for drink." "Rum-punch all the morning, then brandy and soda till 3 or 4, when they are paralyzed and have to sleep some hours, then whisky toddy till bed-time," the bartender said, pointing to two of his best customers. Similar reports came from Calgary and from several of the smaller ranching communities in the North West Territory.[14]

The Territories, it should be noted, were nominally "dry" from 1872 to 1895. The law, which was designed to keep liquor from native Indians, prohibited the manufacture, import or sale of alcohol, save for that required for medicinal or sacramental purposes, and even then those who wished to use intoxicants had to acquire a special permit which was available only from the lieutenant governor, a member of the territorial council, or a magistrate. The law, however, was not strictly enforced, for while the NWMP came down heavily on anyone who dealt in large amounts of contraband, or who provided liquor to the Indians, as often as not they turned a blind eye to white settlers who kept liquor for their own use. As one ex-trooper wrote in 1889, "Whiskey hunting is not popular with the corps; and a man who persistently prosecutes for this offence is looked upon with contempt."[15] Furthermore, as Ralph Connor lamented in The Sky Pilot (1899), permits were not hard to come by, if one knew the right people, as most gentlemen emigrants did. In any case, the remittance man was, if nothing else, an ingenious character, and if he had a mind to drink he invariably managed to do so.

Most of the toper stories were amusing, like the tales of high-spirited young ranchers who rode their horses into hotel bars. Shouting "Drinks for the house!" the remittance ranchers would knock back a quart of whiskey while mounted on their steeds. In High River, a character known as "Sir John, the Astronomer," reputedly earned that sobriquet because he had discovered the fourth star on Hennessey's "Three Star Brandy." Stories also circulated concerning "Lord Dutton," an aristocratic spendthrift whose sister refused to send him any more money on account of his drinking. When pleading and wheedling failed to soften the matron's heart, the erstwhile remittance man sent a cable under an assumed name to his sister's home. The cable announced

"Lord Dutton's" death and requested that money be sent for funeral expenses. It was a desperate ploy, but a successful one, for the money he received kept "Lord Dutton" in hootch for quite some time. [16]

Bob Edwards, the celebrated editor of the Calgary *Eye-Opener,* drew upon many of the bibulous High River remittance men in creating one of the most memorable of his characters, "Albert Buzzard-Cholomondeley, late of Skookingham Hall, Skookingham, Leics., England." Edwards recounted Bertie's adventures in a series of articles entitled "Letters from a Badly Made Son to His Father in England." The letters, which have been reprinted many times since, were first published in the *Eye-Opener* between October 1903 and April 1904.

Young Buzzard-Cholomondeley spent his early days in the West shooting craps, "a different species of game from grouse or partridge," as he informed his father in one of the letters. He then tried his hand at farming, but soon lost £1,000 with the help of his "dear friends," Messrs. Walker, Seagram, Dewar, and Gordon. Bertie's other letters recounted how he failed as a newspaper proprietor, a bartender, and a politician, and how he narrowly avoided the gallows and the territorial lunatic asylum. Bertie invariably added a request for more money and a veiled threat that if funds were not forthcoming he might be inclined to return to "dear old Skookingham." The guv'nor, anxious to keep his scapegrace son safely exiled in the colonies, usually acceded to Bertie's request.

Amusing as these stories were, there was another side to the humorous picture which Edwards and other raconteurs created. The other side featured unhappy alcoholics who had lost their patrimony through gambling, youths who had become crippled after falling drunkenly from their horses, and former public school boys who were found writhing and ranting from the effects of delerium tremens. Leroy Kelly drew attention to this side of the picture when he recalled the scions of good families who had become drink-beggars and hotel hangers-on: "They rolled in the gutters, they rode through the streets, they drank with everyone, and they made pitiful exhibitions of themselves."[17]

Why did the well-bred schoolboys and youthful remittance men drink excessively? Some drank in order to compensate for the years they had spent with reproving parents and schoolmasters; once they felt clear of those authorities they became libertines. Some drank in imitation of the hard-living cowboys who were stock characters in the penny dreadfuls and dime novels of the day. Others drank simply to let off steam or, as one pioneer put it, "because everyone else was doing it." [18] They drank, too, to relieve tedium, to compensate for a diet that so often consisted of black tea, salt pork and beans, to escape dismal surroundings, and to inure themselves against isolation and loneliness. References to feeling isolated and lonely are among the most striking features in the emigrants' diaries and journals and in the letters they sent home to England. The same feelings also underlay the songs that English bachelors in the West sang to amuse themselves. One of the most popular songs was entitled "Life in a Prairie Shack." Sung to the tune of "Life on an Ocean Wave," the chorus and first two stanzas were as follows:

> Oh, its life in a prairie shack,
> When the rain begins to fall;
> It drips through the mud on the roof,
> And the wind comes through the wall.

> Chorus: And the tenderfoot curses his luck
> And feebly murmurs "Ah!
> The blooming country's a fraud,
> And I want to go home to my ma."

> Then they set him chopping wood,
> When it's forty-five below,
> He aims a blow at a log,
> And amputates a toe. [19]

Henry McGusty frequently heard this song when he visited bachelor shacks in southern Alberta in the early 1890s, although a saltier version had been sung in the Moose Mountains of southern Saskatchewan at least a generation earlier. Both versions of the song, in any case, point to the deplorable conditions that many emigrants endured, as well as to their disillusionment and despair. Both versions call to mind a situation where one might easily seek refuge in the bottom of a glass.

Contemporaries also attributed the emigrants' intemperance to a dearth of women. They believed that the young sparks would have been more responsible, more industrious and more moderate in their drinking had they been exposed to the refining influences of women. Certainly women were scarce in the newly opened areas of the Dominion, and many young emigrants had little or no contact with the opposite sex. One Oxonian cattleman, for example, reported in 1905 that he had not even seen a woman in nearly three years.[20] Of course, most emigrants were not quite so unfortunate, and some—such as John Gwynn Swain—suffered from an embarrassment of riches. "It is a strange thing," Swain noted in one of his letters, "wherever I go, I can't get rid of the girls."[21] Bachelors who lived in Vernon, British Columbia, in the 1890s were not so lucky, but on one occasion, they were befriended by Richard Marpole, the superintendant of the CPR Pacific division. Sympathizing with the young fellows who were unable to hold a dance because of a shortage of partners, Marpole imported a carload of pretty girls from Vancouver. The young horticulturalists could scarcely believe their good fortune.[22]

Still, for most bachelors, especially those who resided in tiny hovels in isolated districts on the prairies, the chances of finding a suitable spouse or companion were definitely limited. Ladies like Mary Inderwick and Nesta Skrine understandably found the established gentlemen more attractive, and prairie-bred Canadian girls were not inclined to take up with fellows whom their fathers denounced as "no-good remittance men." As for the emigrants who took up with native Indian girls, unhappily they ran the risk of being vilified and ostracized as "squaw men"; they were regarded with even more contempt than the proverbial remittance man.[23] All in all, the young gentleman emigrant was in a predicament where female companionship was concerned. Some probably endeavoured to ease their trials with the help of a bottle.

Despite their various shortcomings, there were very few

"bounders" among the members of what Clive Phillipps-Wolley called "the broken-brigade." Although Canadians poked fun at the remittance men's incompetence and intemperance, they readily conceded that gentlemen emigrants were generally honest, cheerful, and well-mannered. "Remittance men," a pioneer at Pincher Creek recalled, "were a happy-go-lucky lot, always satisfied with what was done for them, uncomplaining." The wife of another early settler in Alberta recalled that the remittance men of her acquaintance were "very courteous, very appreciative, very considerate.... If one said 'd——' a finger would go up to another's lips in warning, and an apology was quickly forthcoming."[24] Furthermore, as Henry Bashford noted in his novel, *The Manitoban* (1904), the basic qualities of the public school man still shone through in even the most incorrigible remitters. In this respect Bashford's portrait of Henry Laville might be taken as representative of thousands of remittance men:

> Henry Laville, a big invertebrate younger son of good English stock, was a remittance man of the worst type, receiving every quarter a cheque sufficiently large to obviate the absolute necessity of farming his land well, and thus, since it was largely expended on drinks of varying sizes and quality, perfectly successful in keeping him perpetually and, to the majority of his neighbours, contemptibly poor.
>
> Yet he had certain qualities that commanded some amount of respect. He was kindly and honourable.... No man had heard him lie, or known him to make a shady bargain, and these in a Manitoban town were attributes beyond praise. And he was recognized as being the best fighter in [town], bringing an English training to the assistance of the magnificent physique with which nature, ever prodigal to younger sons, had endowed him.[25]

But as Bashford, who had homesteaded in Manitoba, knew, being manly and athletic, honest and good-natured, was not enough — at least as far as most Canadians were concerned. As another character in his novel observes, "To be English stood for debt and drink, gentlemanly manners and general inefficiency. To be Canadian stood probably for a balance at the bank, a seat in the Bible class, and a reputation for hard work and the best side of bargains."[26]

The poor reputation of young gentlemen emigrants did not go unnoticed in Britain. Travellers and missionaries often returned from Canada with disturbing reports of public school failures and gentlemanly derelicts, while the emigrants' follies were the subject of a number of short stories and novels. The press, too, devoted considerable attention to the declining status of the emigrants, particularly to those who had settled on the Canadian prairies. "To speak broadly, it must be said that the young Englishman of the better classes sent out to the North-West to be a farmer is not a success," a correspondent for *The Times* noted (31 January 1894):

> The consensus of opinion which I discovered among practical men upon this point was very striking, and the general statement is not disproved by the many exceptions. The labouring man coming from the Eastern Provinces or the Old Country to the West with scarce a dollar, will in a few years be a fairly prosperous and contented settler, with a good farm and an increasing stock. The young Englishman, coming with apparent advantage of some capital, and a quarterly or half-yearly remittance from home, at the end of the same time has not got nearly so far....

Although the youths had health and physical strength, the correspondent said, they seemed to be unable to apply themselves diligently to tasks at hand. The correspondent likened the young Englishmen to thoroughbred racehorses, full of dash and high spirits. But what they needed in Canada, he said, was "the patient force of the steady draught horse."

The reports, understandably, disturbed Britain's leading educators, who feared that unsuccessful Old Boys would bring the public school system into disrepute. The reports also worried emigration authorities who feared, with good reason, that remittance men would blacken the reputations of industrious Englishmen who wanted to establish themselves in the Dominion. Many Britons including some who were not directly connected with the elite schools, the middle class, or the aristocracy, felt that steps had to be taken to ensure the success of the young gentlemen abroad. But how was that to be accomplished? How were remittance men to be discouraged? How were the thoroughbred racers to be turned into steady and industrious draught horses? According to those who grappled with these questions, the first step was to ensure that prospective emigrants possessed a suitable character. Inveterate fools, the authorities said, would never amount to anything in a country whose citizenry prided themselves on their industry and intelligence. Authorities like Harvey Philpot also warned English parents not to think that there was something in the bracing Canadian air that would magically transform youths who had previously been unmanageable. "Let me warn the disappointed parent against sending to Canada the son who, through his dissipation and extravagant habits, has brought discredit upon his family in England, hoping thereby to give him a chance of 'sowing his wild oats' and eventually becoming respectable. Never was a more cruel mistake made, nor one attended in most cases with more disastrous consequences," Philpot wrote in his Canadian guidebook:

> The poor youth feels himself cut adrift from all endearing ties and influences, which if kindly and wisely exercised might in time have subdued and brought him to a sense of his folly. His hands, more accustomed to dealing cards and handling champagne glasses, are totally unfit to handle a plough or cradle a field of wheat; his ideas do not harmonize in the least with the ruder ones of his practical neighbours; he soon becomes discouraged and, finally, disgusted with the life he is compelled to enter upon; his natural pride forsakes him; he sinks lower and lower in the human scale. We find him at last an outcast from society, living with a few more of his stamp in some remote settlement, long ago lamented as dead by his friends in the Old Country and where known at all, known as a "loafer" among his more fortunate neighbours.

Philpot then turned to the emigrants themselves and warned them against appearing conceited, prejudiced, and critical in the eyes of Canadians. He also urged them to cultivate a little bonhomie and, if possible, to shake themselves free of the "fog of reserve" which, regrettably, so often characterized the Englishman abroad.[27]

William Stamer offered similar advice when he stated unequivocally that well-born immigrants would have to climb off their "high horses" if they expected to "secure the good will and kind offices of [their] neighbours" in Canada. For example, Stamer said that married gentlemen should not recoil when greeted by a bluff backwoodsman who asks "How's the woman?" Instead of responding frigidly, "Mrs. Greene is tolerably well, I thank you," the answer, according to Stamer, should be "Spry, thankee; how's yourn?"[28] John Rowan, addressing "bachelors of good family," made much the same point when he warned readers against "squirearchical stiffbackedness" and "social exclusiveness." The only traits young gentlemen would require in the Dominion, he said, were "pluck," "energy," and "honourable ambition."[29]

Repeatedly, young emigrants were reminded that Canada was essentially a democratic country — a country where a man's worth was not judged by the length of his genealogical tree. "Good pure blood and spotless pedigrees are valuable recommendations in this country to horses, pigs, cattle, and even dogs," a Manitoba periodical declared in 1886, "but they are valueless to men." Another authority warned gentlemen emigrants who intended to take up ranching or farming in the West not to expect to find eager tenants in a country where every adult male, irrespective of his social class, was entitled to 160 acres of free land. This writer invited British youths to adjust to the idea that during their first few years in the West they might even find themselves working for their father's ex-coachman.[30]

While enjoining young gentlemen to democratize their thinking and prepare for hard work, the authors of emigrant guidebooks also advised readers to temper their athletic enthusiasms. The Dominion of Canada, the counsellors said, was one portion of the British Empire that had not been won on the playing fields of Eton. At the same time, youths were urged to revise their ideas concerning the Empire. "If an [emigrant] will persist in feeling, and making it known, that he is a kind of pocket edition of all that the great British Empire stands for, while the Dominion is 'one of our colonies,' and the Canadians are 'just colonials," warned an Edwardian counsellor, "he will probably get into trouble in a week with the men whom he undertakes to work for or amongst." Elaborating upon this point, another counsellor, a public school headmaster, informed his readers that although Canada was assuredly a part of the Empire, Canadians were not to be confused with the "submissive races" who inhabited imperial possessions in Africa or Asia. Young Britons who settled in Canada, he said, would find themselves among a people who were "not accustomed to obey..., a people entirely free from subservience to rank or wealth, a people intolerant therefore of dictation of condescension."[31]

THE ENGLISHMAN IN CANADA

(From A.G. Racey's 18-part cartoon series, Montreal *Star*, autumn 1901)

(*McCord Museum, McGill University, Montreal*)

Clarence, the younger son and dead game sport of the de Brown family, decides to go to Canada. His parents sorrowfully give their consent.

He bids farewell to his club and is presented with a couple of "vewy
hawndy awticles, don't cher know" by the members.

During the voyage over he is talkative.

He lands at Montreal.

(*Glenbow-Alberta Institute*)

He suddenly comes across the only species of Indian and Bear that is well known in Canada today.

He is overcome by the heat in Canada.

Disgusted at being a victim to the dense ignorance displayed in the Old Country with regard to Canada he disposes of his arsenal, furs, guide books and other impedimentia.

He is delighted with the beautiful Canadian winter season, which is very different from what he was led to expect at home, and he finds Canadians very much like any other people, only smarter, more practical, independent and prosperous and too busy chasing the almighty $ to pay any attention to the wild fairy tales told about Canada. He finds Canadian girls prettier and nicer than the girls of any other country—one girl especially.

CHAPTER VIII

CLOISTERED COLONISTS

A conscientious attitude, an accommodating disposition, and a realistic appreciation of local conditions would certainly have eased the gentleman emigrant's progress in Canada. But in the opinion of most counsellors, a knowledge of agriculture and stock raising was of primary importance, especially for those who were intending to make their way in the Canadian West. Many of these counsellors felt, though, that it was extremely difficult for young gentlemen to acquire such knowledge. Laura Johnstone, an English lady who served as a matron in a boys' school near Qu'Appelle in the 1890s, stated that she could think of but one instance where a young aristocrat, completely inexperienced in the ways of agriculture, was hired by a prairie farmer; in that particular case the youth was hired simply so that the farmer could have "the pleasure of telling everybody that he had Lord —— in his pay." As for the middle-class boys who came west seeking wages and experience, most of them had to endure spartan living quarters, wretched working conditions, and inedible food. Small wonder, she suggested, the youths went to the bad.[1]

Miss Johnstone's view was unduly pessimistic. Indeed, it was fallacious, considering the many gentlemen who received a start working on farms and ranches in Manitoba and the Northwest.

However, many Britons shared the same view, and these Britons were usually among the first to endorse the idea of special colonies for gentlefolk. Self-contained communities, operating on the principles of co-operation and collective security would, proponents believed, alleviate a great number of the problems faced by emigrant gentlemen in the West. First of all, emigrants would not lose confidence, for by living among other gentlefolk, they would be shielded from the barbs and insults that Canadians so often hurled at greenhorns. Secondly, since gentlewomen would play an active role in these communities, young bachelors would be compelled to conduct themselves with propriety and decorum. Thirdly, emigrants would be introduced gently and safely into the new country: established members of the community would advise newcomers on how to invest their capital and remittances, as well as on the arts of agriculture and stock raising. Fourthly, emigrants could take advantage of the economic opportunities in the new land while still enjoying the traditions, the manners, the pastimes, and the people they had known in the Old Country. Regarded in this way, colonies of gentlefolk seemed to offer emigrants the best of both worlds.

The Canadian West appeared to be an ideal location for such colonies. Land was plentiful and inexpensive, the soil was rich, the waters were clear, game abounded. There, if anywhere, could arcadian dreams be realized. Yet while visions of utopia undoubtedly played a part in the founding of gentlemen's colonies in the West, spiritual considerations were not usually mentioned when the subject was raised, as it frequently was in books and articles about emigrant gentlemen. The authors of this literature were more concerned with practical matters. Would such colonies be economically viable? How should the communities be organized? These were among the questions Maj. Gen. the Honourable William Feilding addressed in one of the articles he wrote for the *Nineteenth Century* in 1883.

Feilding argued that "special settlements" of expatriate British gentlefolk offered a number of advantages: permanent residents of the settlements could share their knowledge, labour, and if necessary, capital and so develop a community that would be the envy of the country at large. The community Feilding envisaged would also serve as a halfway house and training centre for prospective homesteaders of "the better class." The experienced colonists in the settlement, he explained, could introduce new chums to local agricultural techniques; they could instruct their countrymen in animal husbandry and show novices how to erect inexpensive but comfortable dwellings. Feilding suggested that after spending a year or two in the settlement, young emigrants should secure a homestead or improved farm in the neighbourhood and offer their services and expertise to the next wave of emigrants. "In this manner," the general said, "young men would be able to live with their equals, to accustom themselves gradually to the hard life of a settler and to develop their property under the supervision of an experienced gentleman of their own class in society."[2]

Feilding, along with John Rowan and several other writers of the period, believed that these communities would obviate many of "the evils, the discomforts, and the difficulties attendant on the first stages of colonial life."[3] Although the idea had merit, there were serious drawbacks to the special settlements they proposed. William Stamer, who had lived with British immigrants in the United States and Australia as well as in Canada, very much doubted whether cohesive, aristocratic communities could function harmoniously for an extended period of time. Residents' interests would not always coincide, their resources would be unequal, and jealousies among colonists were bound to arise, he said. Furthermore, he suspected that "black sheep" would be attracted to the colonies and that their presence would lower the moral tone of the communities. But the greatest disadvantage of special aristocratic communities, Stamer said, would be the poor relationships that would develop between the colonists and their neighbours. "In a new country," he warned, "any attempt at exclusiveness would be sure to raise the ire of the 'sovereign people.' The 'gentleman's settlement' would be held up to derision in the district . . . and any and every obstacle that human ingenuity could devise would be thrown in the way of the aristocrats."[4]

As it happened, Canadians did not actively attempt to thwart aristocratic settlements, though misunderstandings and tensions certainly did arise between Canadian and British-born settlers in districts that contained tightly knit British communities. As Stamer predicted, the gentlemen's settlements were occasionally rent by internal squabbles, while in at least one of the colonies "black sheep" did creep in to graze. Yet there were a number of other factors that Stamer did not foresee. One was leadership, for a strong leader was necessary to muster and direct the colony's resources and to maintain its distinctive spirit. The attitudes, experience, and resources of the colonists were equally important: members had to be prepared to subordinate their interests to the good of the community; they had to have, or quickly acquire, agricultural experience; and they had to have sufficient funds and the manpower to carry out their plans. Finally, though the colonies might remain socially, culturally, and intellectually removed from neighbouring communities, for economic survival they had to have access to outside markets.

The importance of these factors was demonstrated in the histories of aristocratic colonies in the United States after the Civil War. The Victoria colony, for example, was established near Fort Hays, Kansas, in 1874 and collapsed five years later following the death of its founder. Runnymede, an English community in Harper County, Kansas, folded in 1892, six years after its founding, when it was by-passed by the railway. The aristocratic community at Le Mars, Iowa, was established in 1877 by the Close brothers of Cambridge University; it collapsed within a decade as a result of acrimony that developed between high-spirited colonists and neighbouring farmers. At Rugby, Tennessee, a colony went bankrupt three years after it opened in 1879; inefficient managers, the colonists' preoccupation with sport, poor soil conditions, and hostile neighbours were the principal reasons for the failure.[5]

Each of these colonies had been launched with great fanfare in Britain, and when they failed, the press discussed and analyzed their demise. The Rugby failure received particular attention since the respected author of *Tom Brown's Schooldays* had founded the colony himself as a refuge for supernumerary gentlemen. The press commended Thomas Hughes's efforts, although when the postmortem was over and when the histories of

Victoria, Runnymede, and half a dozen others had been considered, several erstwhile proponents of aristocratic communities concluded that perhaps such settlements were untenable after all. Capt. Edward Pierce, a volunteer artillery officer from Somersetshire, was not among this group. In 1882, the year Hughes's settlement collapsed, the captain launched a similar colony called Cannington Manor in the Canadian Northwest.

Edward Mitchell Pierce was born in the village of Merriott in 1832. At the age of twenty he married Lydia Bishop Bowdage, a Devon woman seven years his senior. She bore him nine children — five boys and four girls. A vintner by trade, Pierce owned and rented several large homes in the West Country; he entertained grandly and generally lived the life of a country squire. With a reported income of £4,000 per year, he could well afford to do so. In 1880, however, he lost heavily in a bank failure; most of his savings and investments disappeared, and he was left with a total capital of only £2,000. It was this financial misfortune, plus failing health, that prompted him to consider the possibility of building a new life for himself and his family in the Canadian West. But though he planned to take up free homestead land, he had no intention of becoming a common farmer: "grubbing about the land," as he once wrote, was not his style.[6] The captain was a dreamer, a promoter, an organizer, and he determined even before he left England to found a colony where gentlemen like himself could be free of high rents, excessive taxes, and (presumably) insolvent banks.

The Pierces emigrated in the summer of 1882. After settling Mrs. Pierce and the youngest children with friends in Toronto, the captain and his two eldest sons headed west to Assiniboia. They scouted carefully and after several weeks found what they were seeking near the Moose Mountains, approximately forty miles south of present-day Moosomin. The soil was fertile, the countryside was dotted with small lakes and copses of birch and poplar; elk, deer, and wild fowl were to be seen everywhere. Viewed in the summer sunshine, the undulating parkland seemed ideal for the proposed community, and so Pierce was especially disappointed when he learned that the area was temporarily closed for settlement. But Pierce, whose family crest bore the motto *Nils Desperandum*, was not to be denied. He travelled to Ottawa where he secured an interview with Senator David (later Sir David) Macpherson—financier, railway promoter, and soon-to-be Minister of the Interior, responsible for prairie settlement. Pierce's visit was timely, for only a few months earlier the Conservative government had passed legislation that encouraged group settlements. Although the captain's resources were not equal to those of some of the colonization companies, which were then vying for blocks of land, his proposal for a colony of English gentlefolk impressed Macpherson, who introduced Pierce to the prime minister. On Sir John A. Macdonald's own instructions, the Moose Mountain district was reopened so that Pierce and his three eldest sons could file for homesteads and pre-emptions. The government and the CPR, which owned land in the area, also agreed to reserve sections adjacent to the Pierce property for English families.[7]

Pierce returned to the property immediately after his interview in Ottawa, and with the help of a North West Mounted Police trooper, he and his sons erected a log farmhouse. The dwelling was comfortable but small, as Mrs. Pierce discovered when she and the children moved out from Toronto early in 1883. Still, the building was nobly christened Gitchee Wa Teepee, which the captain said meant Great White House, and indeed it was not long before the house grew into its name. Pierce enlarged and improved it every year and by 1887 Gitchee Wa Teepee boasted a dozen bedrooms, several drawing rooms, a ballroom, and a handsome belfry.

Captain Pierce was not the first colonist in the area; the Baptist church had opened a mission station at Moose Mountain, and a dozen squatters were farming in the vicinity when the captain arrived. But Pierce was the district's most prominent and most energetic settler. He provided the community with the name Cannington, chosen in honour of his mother's village in north Somerset, and he added the lofty and aristocratic suffix, Manor, so as to avoid confusion with the town of Cannington, Ontario; he also endowed All Saints, the Anglican church which was consecrated in 1884 and named in remembrance of its patron's parish in Merriott. Although he failed to realize an ambition to win a parliamentary seat, Pierce was, as he himself put it, "doctor, lawyer, law-giver, and general referee" in the area.[8]

As justice of the peace and land commissioner, he was in a position to vet homesteaders who wished to settle in the community; being the largest landowner, next to the CPR, he was able to determine the selling price of land in the district. Pierce was also one of the founding partners of the Moose Mountain Trading Company, which controlled the general store, the grist-mill, the dairy, and the hotel in Cannington Manor. In addition, Pierce, more than any other individual, was responsible for promoting the community, for extolling its charms among British expatriates in eastern Canada, and for advertising its advantages among gentlefolk in England. In notices sent to English newspapers, he depicted Cannington Manor as a veritable paradise. "With cheap living, no rents, rates, taxes, nor coal merchant's bills, fine sporting, fishing, and boating, and good society, this settlement must prove a paradise to the heavily handicapped *paterfamilias* at home," Pierce wrote enthusiastically. "With a few hundreds a year, he can lead and enjoy an English squire's existence of a century ago!" Young men who possessed a little capital but were without prospects in England were told of the handsome profits to be made in agriculture; professional men toiling in grimy cities were told of the salubrious climate and the beauties of the countryside around Cannington Manor. "You will still fancy yourself in England, only without England's worries and anxieties," Pierce wrote to a prospective colonist in 1887. "Get two or three good families to come out with you—the more the merrier!"[9]

The people who responded to Pierce's appeals were a diverse lot, though most could lay claim to the title of gentlefolk. One of the captain's partners in the Moose Mountain Trading Company was an ex-India civil servant. Pierce's other partners were Old Cliftonians: one had been a master brewer in Cornwall, the other a mining engineer in Mexico and Algeria. The gentleman who operated Cannington Manor's pork packing and cheese processing plant had been a marine architect in Barrow-on-Furness; the local land agent, an ex-army officer, was the son of an equerry in the Court of St. James. Other early members of the colony had been bankers, diplomats, and solicitors.

In order to supplement their incomes, Captain Pierce and the heads of other large families in the colony began advertising for farm pupils. Their notices, offering "expert tuition to young men of good birth and education," were well received, and as a result young bachelors—most fresh out of the public schools—became an important element within the community. "Eton, Harrow, Fettes, Loretto, Cheltenham, Clifton, Marlborough, Shrewsbury were all represented," an early resident recalled.[10] Indeed, the response to the notices was so great that Captain Pierce and several other tutors had to build wings onto their residences in order to accommodate the youths. Many of these young men were transient, and after spending a year or two at the Manor they continued their adventures farther west. But a fair number of the pupils remained, either as hired hands or as landowners in their own right. Two who remained were Ernest and William ("Billy") Beckton, graduates of King William's College, Isle of Man. The Beckton brothers, having spent some time in Le Mars, Iowa, came to the Manor in 1885 to undertake an agricultural apprenticeship with the captain. Two years later they were joined by their younger brother Herbert ("Bertie"), also an Old Boy of the Manx college.[11]

The Beckton boys were members of two of northern England's wealthiest families. Their maternal grandfather, Matthew Curtis, was the archetypical "Manchester Man." Starting life as an apprentice in a textile mill, he made his first fortune when he developed a device that revolutionized the manufacture of wire-cards used in cotton-carding machinery. After marrying the daughter of a venerated Yorkshire family, Curtis went on to found one of England's largest textile mills and to serve an unprecedented three terms as lord mayor of Manchester. The Beckton's paternal grandfather, a Salford man, had also made a fortune in textiles. Their father, Joseph, was director of one of Manchester's largest machine works.

When Matthew Curtis died in 1887, his grandsons, twenty-year-old Ernest, nineteen-year-old Billy, and eighteen-year-old Bertie, inherited a large fortune. They used part of their legacy to purchase 2,600 acres of land near Cannington Manor. Part of the legacy was also spent on erecting a sumptuous ranch house which the boys named Didsbury. The house was named in honour of their birthplace, a quiet, leafy, gracious suburb a few miles south of Manchester.

The twenty-six-room mansion was not built to an architectural plan. Instead, it was designed "off-the-cuff," with young Ernest, Billy, and Bertie suggesting an alteration here, or an addition there, as the building progressed. Despite its erratic design and construction, Didsbury was remarkably handsome. A two-storey building, with a high, gabled roof, bay windows, a broad verandah, and a crenellated entranceway, it was constructed of limestone and faced with blue rolling stone which had been quarried from a site nearby. It was easily the most striking house in southern Saskatchewan and, as a reporter for the Moosomin *Courier* (18 October 1891) noted, "one is rather staggered at seeing such a place on the prairie." Staggering, too, were the hand-carved fireplace mantles, the polished mirrors, the gilt-framed oil paintings, the Hepplewhite furniture, and the Turkey carpets which graced Didsbury's interior.

The Becktons also used prairie stone to construct a residence for their foreman, for the bunkhouse, which housed eighteen labourers, and for the kennels, located behind the main residence. But perhaps the most impressive part of the estate, aside from the ranch house, were the stables, which were built of stone and panelled with mahogany. These stables, which the MacLeod *Gazette* (3 September 1891) conceded were "the best appointed ... west of Winnipeg," provided shelter for some of the finest thoroughbreds in North America. Each horse had a commodious stall, and each stall was marked with a brass plaque engraved with the name and pedigree of the stall's occupant. At the entrance to the stables was a trophy room, its cases crowded with gleaming cups, shields, and ribbons bearing the Becktons' orange-and-black racing colours. The trophies were testimony to the talents of Reginald Purser, the "gentleman jockey" whom Billy brought with him from Le Mars, and to the dedicated work of the head groom, whom Ernest had lured from Lord Yarborough's celebrated stables in Lincolnshire. And of course the trophies were testimony to the money that the Mancunian brothers spent in vast amounts on horse breeding and racing.

Ernest was the titular head of the estate and when he married

Captain Pierce's daughter, Frances, in 1889, his brothers built their own homes in the neighbourhood. Yet though the squire married, he did not abandon a bachelor's way of life. In fact, in the early nineties he added a bachelor's wing to Didsbury. Known locally as the "Ram's Pasture," the new wing provided accommodation for Cannington Manor's "sporting faction," or "dudes," a high-spirited group of young men who were easily recognized in their grey flannels, striped blazers, and "wide-awake" hats. The dudes were attended by Ernest's valets, two old soldiers who served drinks in the billiard room, maintained the guests' sporting rifles, and ironed the weekly newspapers. With its rooms ringing with laughter and the clinking of glasses, Didsbury took on the appearance of a hunting lodge-cum-fraternity house. "What good times!" one of the dudes recalled. "What good fellows!" [12]

In 1888, six years after its founding, Cannington Manor had a permanent population of almost 150. In May of that year, John Donkin, a NWMP trooper, passed through the community with a police patrol. Donkin, who had spent a number of years in the West, was struck by the beauty and orderliness of the village and by the refined manners and prosperous appearance of the residents. He commented on the flocks of Cotswold and Leicester sheep, the herds of dairy cows, the flocks of well-fed poultry. He was impressed by the trim, whitewashed houses and the neatly kept barns and byres. He was charmed by the chubby-faced children who gazed in awe as the redcoats went jingling past, and by the surpliced choir he heard singing outside the church. It was like a dream world, the English trooper wrote, a dream world that was "so painfully suggestive of the dear land across the sea." [13]

Harold Bindloss, the Liverpool-born writer who spent some time at the Manor a few years later, was also fascinated by the community; his view, however, was different from that of visitors like Donkin, who had but a fleeting glimpse of the community. Bindloss recorded his impressions in three novels: *A Sower of Wheat* (1901), *Winston of the Prairie* (1907), and *Harding of Allenwood* (1915). In the first of the novels, the community is called Carrington Manor; in *Winston* it is called Silverdale, and in *Harding* it appears as Allenwood Grange. The communities are all located in Assiniboia and all were founded by retired British army colonels. A number of the Canningtonians who afterwards read these novels complained that Bindloss had exaggerated, indeed maligned, their community. Others stated that his description of life at the Manor was disconcertingly faithful.[14]

Bindloss's colonels were big, bluff, burly men—imperious autocrats who ruled over their colonies with an iron hand. Colonists were expected to obey the colonels at all times, or run the risk of being "frozen out" of the community. Although Bindloss came to Cannington Manor after Pierce's death, his description fits the captain in many respects. The "Skipper," as Pierce was known in the colony, appeared to at least some of the residents as a feudal baron, and those who opposed his wishes or contravened some rule of etiquette in the colony were indeed "frozen out." One resident was ostracized for some unrecorded offence for over a year. He continued to live in the area, but was "cut" by most of his fellows, rather like a non-conforming schoolboy is "cut" by his classmates in a public school. "I was taboo to all the English in the settlement," the resident recalled, "[and] it was then [that] I found out what kind-hearted people our Canadian neighbours were."[15] Yet while the captain sometimes appeared to be unbending and uncharitable, he was, like the Bindloss colonels, a deeply religious man. Of this his followers were well aware. However, they were also aware that as far as the Skipper was concerned there was but one church and that, of course, was the Church of England. Dissenters, another resident recalled, were threatened with frozen crops in this life, and "a visit to a hotter place" in the next![16]

The communities in the Bindloss novels were as similar to Cannington Manor as their leaders were to Captain Pierce. Like Cannington, the Grange in *Harding of Allenwood* was designed

> to enable a certain stamp of Englishman to enjoy a life that was becoming more difficult without large means at home. A man with simple tastes could find healthy occupation out of doors, and get as much shooting as he wanted. So long as his farming covered, or nearly covered, his expenses, that was all that was required.

In *Winston of the Prairie*, the founder of Silverdale, Colonel Barrington, brings to the community farm pupils very like those Captain Pierce attracted to Cannington Manor. They were predominantly "the younger sons of English gentlemen who had no inclination for commerce" and who, for a variety of reasons, were debarred from prestigious careers in Britain. Like many of the older residents, these youths "played" at agriculture, rather than worked at it. "They were growers of wheat who combined a good deal of amusement with a little, not very profitable, farming. . . . "[17]

Bindloss described the community amusements very well: hunting, card parties, picnics, and musical evenings were all popular at Cannington Manor, as they were at Silverdale, Allenwood Grange, and Carrington Manor. Amateur theatricals were popular, too, and in the Cannington Manor schoolhouse operettas, melodramas, pantomines and even Shakespearean plays were performed. Curiously, Bindloss did not emphasize the colonists' love of tennis or the steeplechases and flat races which were held at the Cannington Manor race track. Nor did he mention the colonists' passion for cricket and the happy matches which took place between the gentlemen's XI and the ladies' XI. (In these matches the women played with regulation cricket bats while the men used broom sticks.) Bindloss did, however, note that many of the colonists made annual or semi-annual visits to the Old Country, and that in the winter months, when the wheat fields, the tennis courts, and the race tracks were covered with snow, several of the residents migrated to the balmier parts of the United States or British Columbia.

While Bindloss succeeded in capturing much of the flavour and spirit of the Manor, he did overdraw the colony's aristocratic character. Cannington Manor was never exclusively upper class; in fact, the community included a relatively large number of Canadian-born residents and unpedigreed Britons. These residents were known as the "drones," and were generally acknowledged to have been the most industrious, the most progressive, and the most gregarious members of the community. They owned or managed the most profitable farms in the district and they provided such essential services as smithing, carting, and building construction. By including such settlers, Cannington Manor managed to stave off some of the problems that had beset Runnymede and other colonies in America which were comprised exclusively of Englishmen who lacked practical experience in the ways of the West. Still, although the two groups worked together, relations between the drones and the gentlefolk were not particularly warm. They rarely fraternized and there was no intermarriage among Canadian and upper-class English families. The colony's founder, moreover, took a dim view of Manorites who identified themselves with anything Canadian. This facet of Pierce's character was illustrated during an exchange he had with one of his employees' daughters. The captain asked the girl, who had been born in Manitoba, her nationality. She answered that she was a Canadian. "Canadian?!" the captain boomed. "You can't be a Canadian! Where were your parents born?" "Scotland, sir," the girl replied. "Well, then, you are Scotch," Pierce declared. "If a man was born in a stable, would he be a horse?" [18]

Captain Pierce and some of his followers could be unreasonably ethnocentric, and some of the dudes were inordinately devoted to sport. Even so, the prospects for Cannington Manor seemed good: the residents had considerable capital, the community was well organized, and thanks to the drone element, the colonists possessed a skilled labour force. The project failed, nevertheless. It failed for several reasons, one of which was the untimely death of its founder. Pierce died in June 1888. His death did not immediately affect the colony's rhythm, for on the afternoon of his death the Manorites continued gaily with their annual Sports Day. But it was soon apparent that the colony had lost some of its discipline, cohesion, and moral tone. Pierce had been very particular about keeping up standards, and though some of the colonists had balked at his rigid ideas, his fastidious manners, and his iron hand, standards proved to be very important to the colony. As long as the Skipper was at the helm, there was no danger of unbridled frivolity, licentiousness, or intemperance. But after his death, discipline in the "ultra-English" colony slackened, as farm pupils began spending less time at their lessons and proportionately more time in the saloon bar of the

Mitre Hotel. Inevitably, perhaps, "black sheep" also crept into the happy meadow. The newcomers drank excessively, and some even endeavoured to have affairs with the married women of the Manor. The attitudes and antics of these young men imposed strains upon the community, and their behaviour led to the departure of a number of the old English families.[19]

As the community lost some of its tone, it lost some of its character, drive and purpose as well. Basil Hamilton, a Canadian government surveyor, noticed this when he was working in the district in 1896. The colony, which Hamilton described as "a mild bohemia in the wilderness," had a worn, rather seedy appearance. The houses were not so brightly painted, the barns and byres were not so neatly kept, the choir at All Saints was not so melodious. The model community was beginning to fray around the edges. Hamilton remarked further that while a few of the "gallants" still "kept up the old forms and ceremonies" like the annual hunt club suppers and racing weeks, they did so in a comparatively "tame" manner. All in all, he said, the colony was not as large and not nearly so gay as it once had been.[20]

By 1896 it was clear that Cannington Manor had failed to establish a solid economic base: the pork factory, the cheese processing plant, the rolling mill—none of these had ever managed to show a profit. Pierce had deliberately discouraged manufacturing industries on the grounds that such industries were vulgar, while the growth of Moosomin and Regina prevented the colony from developing into a market town or centre of government. Since many of the colonists were indifferent farmers and stock growers, Cannington Manor could not even claim to be an agricultural community. The crowning blow, however, came in 1900, when the eagerly anticipated CPR branch line by-passed the community in favour of a route six miles to the south. Without a railway, without a sound economy, and without a leader, the flamboyant but naive colony stood little chance of survival.

When the CPR by-passed Cannington Manor, a handful of the colonists removed to a new location on the railway branch line. They took with them the Moose Mountain company store and the "Manor" half of the colony's name. The elite English families and the high-spirited dudes, however, did not follow on to Manor, Saskatchewan. The former sold or abandoned their large homes and either returned to England or relocated in British Columbia. The dudes either went to the Yukon to try their hands in the Klondike gold fields, or volunteered for service in the Boer War, or continued their adventures elsewhere in the Empire. By 1902, when the town of Manor was formally established, the ultra-English colony, the "mild Bohemia," had all but disappeared. The cricket pitch was choked with weeds, the tennis courts were overgrown, the paddocks at the race track were empty. The colony which Captain Pierce had hoped would provide a perpetual haven for English gentlefolk had survived for only twenty years.

Few prairie communities rivalled Cannington Manor in wealth and extravagance, though several communities—some utopian, some socialistic, others simply ethnic—easily matched the Manor in naivety. Each of the communities was intended as a western Eden and, like the biblical Eden, they were all short lived.[21] The notable exception was the Barr, or Britannia Colony, established in 1902 on the Saskatchewan-Alberta border and renamed Lloydminster in 1903. Although this "all-British" community had to struggle for survival during its first year because of irresponsible leadership, it quickly developed into a prosperous, progressive town. It succeeded principally because it avoided the mistakes of the gentlemen's colonies in North America. The Barr colony was, for example, comprised of settlers drawn from a number of occupations and social classes: in addition to city clerks and tradesmen, the colony included artisans, professionals, mechanics, and agricultural labourers. The latter were especially important in the colony's early days, since they possessed skills that could be adapted to the northern prairie. In addition, the colony included a large number of married men who were accompanied by their wives and children. These men, who are invariably described in contemporary accounts as "solid, hard-working" individuals, acted as a check on some of the footloose bachelors in the community. The Barr colonists also mixed readily and easily with surrounding homesteaders, and as a result the community was able to rely upon experienced neighbours for encouragement and assistance. Finally, the members of the community at Lloydminster had little time or inclination for the leisure activities that had played so large a part in communities like Cannington Manor. At Lloydminster, athletic and cultural organizations were established only after the community had taken secure root, and even then these activities took second place to events sponsored by the local farmers' and stock growers' associations.

Upper-class Britons were not easily persuaded to abandon or alter their traditional attitudes and interests, however; nor were they ready to give up the idea of gaining a gentlemen's Eden in the New World. Undaunted by the collapse of Cannington Manor, and by the failure of the Manor's counterparts in nineteenth-century America, Edwardian gentlefolk moved farther west to British Columbia. There, in the Thompson River Valley, they established the village of Walhachin, the last of the aristocratic colonies in Canada.

Founded in 1910, this community thirty-five miles west of Kamloops was intended as a haven for well-bred families who wished to escape the economic uncertainties, industrial unrest, and political tensions that marked Edwardian Britain. The colonists at Walhachin engaged in fruit farming, one of the most gentlemanly forms of agriculture. Within a short period of time, they had built an extensive irrigation system. The valley blossomed, the colonists prospered. Then came August 1914, and the men of Walhachin marched off to war. Few survived the fighting, and their families, who had remained behind in the valley, were unable to maintain the orchards. Like some of the delicate fruits the colony had grown, Walhachin simply withered on the vine. By 1919 it was a ghost town.

The very moving story of Walhachin has appeared in a number of romantic versions, including verse.[22] But the true story of Walhachin, though tragic, is less romantic. The Great War alone did not kill the colony: the venture was undermined by a variety of social, political and economic factors. These factors, identified in recent studies of the community,[23] may have been apparent to the Walhachin men who did return, albeit briefly, to the valley after the war. The tragedy is that the colonists did not anticipate the problems nine years earlier.

Walhachin had much in common with the aristocratic communities that preceded it. Like the Victoria colony in Kansas, for instance, Walhachin was established in an area that was undergoing an economic boom. The province of British Columbia was prosperous: immigration was increasing, property prices were skyrocketing, new resource industries, frontiers, and markets were opening daily. The semi-arid Thompson River Valley, which had hitherto been given over to cattle ranching, shared in the boom. Two transcontinental railways (the CPR and the newly chartered Canadian Northern Pacific) served the district, and most people believed that the waters of the Thompson could be used to irrigate the lands adjacent to the railways. Once irrigated, enthusiasts believed, the valley would bloom, just as the Okanagan Valley was blooming a few miles to the southeast. The area seemed ideal for a large horticultural settlement. Moreover, like the Close brothers' colony in Iowa and Thomas Hughes's settlement in Tennessee, Walhachin had the backing of a joint-stock company. To be sure, elaborate planning had not prevented the demise of either Le Mars or Rugby, but the backers of Walhachin hoped that they could avoid the problems that dogged the American settlements; they also hoped that by conducting Walhachin on business principles, they would be spared some of the financial difficulties that had beset Cannington Manor, where Captain Pierce had largely controlled investment. Walhachin's parent, the British Columbia Development Association (BCDA), seemed strong enough to avoid economic problems. The association had been registered in London in 1895, and by the early 1900s it was one of the financial giants in British Columbia, with investments in ranching, mining, lumbering, and shipping. In addition to its impressive and profitable portfolio, the BCDA could claim several peers, knights, and wealthy commoners among its shareholders and directors. All of the directors played a part in founding and promoting Walhachin, but Sir William Bass, the brewery baronet, took a leading role.

Sir William saw the Thompson Valley in 1907 when a land surveyor and property developer in Ashcroft invited him to come and investigate the agricultural potential of the area. During his tour, Sir William received reports which indicated that decid-

uous fruits, then being grown in the Okanagan, could be grown
with greater success in the Thompson region; the reports stated,
in fact, that the Thompson River Valley, with its dry winters and
hot summers, was "the best adapted district in the whole of British Columbia for the growing of fruit." As for irrigating the
semi-arid valley, this could be carried out at "a minimum of
cost." [24] Sir William was excited by the reports, and he returned
to England convinced that the valley could support not only
choice varieties of fruit but also a champion colony of gentlemen
horticulturists. The BCDA took the first steps towards establishing such a colony by launching two subsidiary companies,
one to plan and promote a townsite in the valley and another to
market the valley's produce.

The proposed colony was to have been called Sunnymede, a
name suggested by Sir Talbot Chetwynd, manager of the BCDA's
111 Mile Ranch in the Cariboo. Sunnymede had a rather warm
ring to it and was reminiscent of Merrie England. But it was also
reminiscent of the unfortunate Runnymede colony in Kansas,
and no doubt some of the BCDA directors knew of that community's ill-starred history. In any case, the association rejected Sir
Talbot's suggestion and settled on the name Walhachin. A Shu-
swap Indian word, Walhachin (or Walhassen, as the district was
first called) meant "land of round rocks." Directly translated, the
name was not particularly inspiring, so the BCDA, employing
what might best be called poetic licence, concocted its own
translation. "Walhachin," the BCDA brochures stated, meant
"bountiful valley" or "an abundance of food products of the
earth." [25]

Just as the BCDA showed flair and originality in translating
the name of its proposed settlement, so, too, it showed skill in
recruiting individuals who would help promote the venture. A
key member of the advertising team was the journalist John Fitzgerald Studdert Redmayne, whose book, *Fruit Farming on the
"Dry Belt" of British Columbia* (1909), enjoyed large sales in England. Redmayne, who had valuable contacts in Fleet Street,
was on the BCDA's payroll, and his book — which pointedly recommended fruit farming for "men of better class" and "people of
education and refinement" — was available through one of the

BCDA offices in London. The office was located in Waterloo Place, next to British Columbia House, where the BCDA also had good friends and contacts. The agent general and former premier of British Columbia, John Turner, was a member of the BCDA's board of directors, and the then premier of the province, Sir Richard McBride, and the provincial deputy minister of agriculture, W.E. Scott, openly supported the association's plans. Altogether, Redmayne's glossy and lavishly illustrated book, the kind words from provincial government officials, and the encouraging remarks made by Governors General Lord Aberdeen and Earl Grey concerning "fruit ranching" in the Far West greatly aroused the public's interest in the embryo colony, and when Walhachin opened officially in 1910, it had no difficulty in attracting residents and investors.

As William Close had done at Le Mars, the BCDA provided ready-built cottages for its settlers at Walhachin. The cottages, consisting of four bedrooms, a parlour, and a kitchen, sold for $1,100. Residents who desired larger premises could order these beforehand from the builder at an additional cost of $125 per room. Ten-acre parcels of land in the colony sold for $3,000 undeveloped, while ten-acre "ready-made estates," planted with young apple, peach and cherry trees, could be purchased for $3,500. For those who wished to invest in the colony but were not immediately able to take up residence, the BCDA provided a further service: the association would plant and tend estates for a fee of $25 to $50 per acre. The association recommended this service particularly to "Anglo-Indian Officers and Civilians about to retire on pension" and to English public school boys who had not yet completed their education.[26] The BCDA and its subsidiaries also laid out the townsite of Walhachin and began construction of the 130-mile network of wooden flumes which would provide water for the colonists' orchards.

The well-planned, tailor-made community grew quickly; by 1912 it had a church, a school, and a community hall as well as a livery stable, a bakery, two tea rooms, and several dry-goods stores. The estimated permanent population of Walhachin at that time was just under 200. As the BCDA had hoped, the residents were people of education and refinement: among the first

settlers were several large families who had left England because
of the high cost of living, a few city bankers, several ex-civil
servants, and a corps of ex-army officers. Walhachin was also
home to a large number of well-bred young bachelors who, following the BCDA's advice, had settled on adjoining holdings
"for the sake of social companionship." These young men, one
author has alleged, were "rejects," in that they had one of three
backgrounds:

> one of repeated failure and/or behavioural problems in
> schools such as Eton and Marlborough, one of personal scan-
> dal or legal "difficulties," or one of military or civil service ex-
> pulsion. Generally, their families were at a loss as to what to
> do with them, so the boys were encouraged to go overseas to
> manage the family's newly acquired property at Walhachin.[27]

The allegation is unflattering and unfounded. In the first place,
only a handful of the young men of Walhachin had been sent to
manage their families' estates; most of the cheechakos came to
learn fruit farming or some other type of agriculture. Secondly,
few if any of the youths had been expelled from their schools or
the services, though some of the youths may have failed to pass
the civil service or army entrance examinations. By and large,
the young men at Walhachin were either adventurers or supernumerary gentlemen. They may have been rumbustious, but
they could scarcely be called "rejects."

Since many of the colonists at Walhachin were relatively
affluent, they were able to employ a large number of domestic
servants and field hands. Fifty Chinese servants worked there on
a permanent basis, and in the summer months over a hundred
labourers were hired to assist with the harvest. The large
numbers of domestic servants and field hands, plus the seasonal
nature of the colony's economy, meant that residents of Walhachin had plenty of time for leisure activities. Indoor recrea-
tions included whist parties, amateur theatricals, and fancy dress
balls. The balls were held in the Walhachin community hall,
which boasted the finest sprung dance floor north of Vancouver.
Outdoor activities included tennis, shooting, cricket, golf, and
polo. The venues at Walhachin attracted sportsmen from as far

away as Calgary, and so popular were the events that a special committee was formed to co-ordinate the colony's social and sporting calendar. This committee usually met in the Walhachin Hotel, a commodious two-storey building opened with great ceremony in 1910 by the prime minister, Sir Wilfred Laurier. Advertised as being "equal to or better than any hotel in the Upper Country of British Columbia," the Walhachin was under the management of Miss Flowerdew, an English gentlewoman. Unlike the Mitre Hotel after Captain Pierce's time, the Walhachin was never an unruly place, and by all accounts even the young sparks who frequented the hotel's two saloon bars were always well behaved. But Miss Flowerdew's was more than a drinking place, for the hotel included a number of comfortably furnished reading rooms, a billiard parlour, a smoking lounge, and a dining hall. In the winter, the Walhachin's large fireplaces provided warmth and cheer for incoming colonists who were awaiting the completion of their cottages in the village; in the summer, when the temperature hovered in the high nineties, the hotel verandah provided a shady refuge for sunburnt sportsmen and fruit ranchers.

The Walhachin was a well-conducted establishment, but the social and sporting activities which centred around the hotel added nothing to the colony's revenues. In fact, although a number of new orchards were planted between 1912 and 1914, the increase in the colony's agricultural output was negligible. Social activities also contributed to the chilly relations that unfortunately developed between the colonists and the ranchers and railway employees who resided in the area. The railwaymen and stock growers referred derisively to Walhachin as "Little England," and looked upon the colony's hunts, dances, and parties as frivolous and indeed decadent.[28] The colonists, in turn, became increasingly defensive and isolated. It was a classic situation, with inevitable tragic consequences. The English colonists lacked experience in dry-land agriculture, but they neither requested nor were offered assistance from their knowledgeable neighbours. Instead, they blundered along, resolutely but unproductively. As they did so, their investments and the community itself suffered.

The colonists' inexperience in agriculture, the emphasis they placed on leisure activities, and their insularity were among the principal causes of Walhachin's collapse; but there were other factors. Notwithstanding the reports that had so excited Sir William Bass and his BCDA colleagues, the Walhachin area was not suitable for growing fruit. The Thompson River Valley, while situated close to the Okanagan Valley, did not have the soil or the annual rainfall to permit fruit farming on a large and profitable scale. Furthermore, Walhachin's irrigation network of flumes and ditches proved to be unreliable and almost impossible to maintain. The system was constantly in need of repair, and repairs were expensive, both in time and money. As if these were not liabilities enough, the sun-kissed colony was afflicted with administrative problems. These surfaced in 1913, after the 6th Marquis of Anglesey acquired the BCDA's holdings at Walhachin. Anglesey moved to the colony and built a large home, complete with swimming pool and a special room for his concert piano. But although the home was impressive, the owner was unable to provide the shaky community with firm leadership. The twenty-eight-year-old peer was also unable to inspire much confidence among Walhachin's absentee investors, since it was well known that he had made several bad investments previously and was plagued with the astronomical debts that he had inherited from his cousin, the 5th marquis.

Walhachin was already in a precarious position prior to August 1914, and in all likelihood it would have collapsed anyway had its men not gone off to war; but the war certainly exacerbated the colony's situation and hastened its collapse. The elderly men and the women who remained in the community did not have the skills or the stamina to maintain the orchards, the ditches, and the irrigation flumes. Nor, as the war dragged on, were they able to muster the necessary capital or the manpower they had once employed. Faced with these difficulties, the residents of Walhachin began leaving the valley. Most went to Vancouver or Victoria to await their loved ones' return from overseas. During their absence, Walhachin fell into disrepair, and by 1919 it was beyond reclamation. That, in any case, was the feeling of most of the veterans who returned to the valley after the war. After a brief tour of the almost empty townsite, the broken flumes, the clogged ditches and the parched orchards, they concluded that the colony could not be restored to its former self. Besides, many of the veterans were physically disabled and had lost their enthusiasm for exotic colonial ventures after four years in the trenches. Accordingly, they disposed of their holdings as best they could and either rejoined their families in Victoria or Vancouver or returned to England.

The Marquis of Anglesey, burdened with more debts following an unsuccessful foray into the Alberta oil fields, was also anxious to cut his losses at Walhachin, though he had great difficulty in doing so. Sir Richard McBride, a confirmed anglophile and lover of the aristocracy, had died in 1915 and British Columbia's post-war premier, John Oliver, was a very different character. An ex-pit boy who had been raised in the Derbyshire coalfields, the doughty Oliver felt no compunction about denying tax concessions or any other assistance to the marquis. Even Anglesey's offer of Walhachin as a site for one of the province's post-war soldier settlements was refused. Rebuffed by the provincial government, the marquis leased the townsite to a local cattleman and returned to Britain. Not until after the Second World War did the Anglesey family manage to dispose of the property, by which time there were few traces of the Edwardian emigrants' Arcadia.

William Stamer predicted Walhachin's demise in 1874, just as he predicted the collapse of Cannington Manor and the failure of the aristocratic colonies in the United States. Although planned as model communities, the colonies developed into bastions, socially, culturally, and economically removed from their environments. They provided only one of the advantages promised by Major General Feilding and other proponents of "special settlements": they offered gentlefolk a refuge where they could mix with people of their own class. The colonies did not, however, obviate the "evils, discomforts, and difficulties attendant on the first stages of colonial life." If anything, they actually increased and aggravated the difficulties. Because they were elitist and oriented to leisure, the settlements encouraged the very attitudes and behaviour that counsellors had warned against: specifically, the colonies encouraged members to retain their social prejudices and passion for sport while discouraging them from joining the mainstream of Canadian society. Further-more, despite assurances given by Feilding, Laura Johnstone, John Rowan and others, the colonies did not inure young gentle-men to the hard life of a Canadian settler. Indeed, it is difficult to imagine anything further removed from the harsh realities of the frontier than the "Ram's Pasture" at Didsbury or the centrally heated dance hall at Walhachin. Most important and most re-grettable, though pensioners may have derived some economic benefit from living in such cloistered gentility, the young men who came to these settlements did not acquire the knowledge and the skills which would allow them to compete with the men of the soil in the Dominion.

CHAPTER IX

MUDPUPS & PREMIUM HUNTERS

Because aristocratic colonies failed to provide sufficient practical benefits to their members, gentlemen emigrants felt compelled to look for other ways to learn the arts of agriculture and stock raising. Of the many methods they considered, one of the most favoured was the premium farm-pupil system, a controversial and in some cases ruinously expensive form of agricultural apprenticeship. The system was built around naive young gentlemen who came to the Dominion in the thousands because they believed the claims made by those who stood to profit from the scheme.

The idea on which young gentlemen and their parents pinned such hopes seemed straightforward enough. A farmer or rancher in Canada would place an advertisement in the British press offering to teach intending settlers local agricultural techniques. The advertisements promised students expert tuition, a comfortable home, and congenial society. In exchange for these services, the advertisers charged a fee, or "premium," for each pupil. In the 1880s these premiums ranged from about £30 ($150) to £200 ($1,000) per year.

The advertisements were placed in quality periodicals so as to attract the more affluent emigrants. The following notice, which appeared in the *Field* on 4 February 1882, is representative:

> An English Gentleman (married), two years resident in Manitoba, is willing to RECEIVE a few GENTLEMEN'S SONS who desire to obtain a KNOWLEDGE OF COLONIAL LIFE. Good references. . . .

The quality periodicals also carried notices placed by families who were seeking colonial instructors for their sons. Again the *Field* (1 April 1882) provides a good example:

> A GENTLEMAN is desirous of placing his SON, between 17 and 18 years of age, where he would have the opportunity of acquiring a knowledge of REARING STOCK and GROWING CORN. It is essential that he be required to work himself, as he would be sent with a view to his becoming in some measure acquainted with the work and life he would have to lead as a settler in the colonies. . . .

Once contact between the two parties had been made, necessary arrangements were carried out with the assistance of an agency or middleman in England. The agent would provide a schedule for the payment of the premiums, arrange for the pupil's passage, and prepare a document or contract outlining the terms of the agreement. The contracts varied, although usually they stipulated advance payment of annual premiums and a two- to three-year course of instruction. The premiums covered the cost of tuition, the pupil's room and board, and a small allowance which the farm instructor would convey to his charge at regular intervals. (The allowance was often termed a wage, but since it derived from the pupil's father, the payment was more in the nature of a remittance.) Occasionally, the documents would include other clauses dealing with holidays, accommodation (i.e., private or shared quarters), or food and clothing.

The system appeared to offer many advantages. The inexperienced young emigrant would be received by a solicitous gentleman farmer, in whose home he would enjoy many of the amenities of civilized life. The experience would broaden the youth's horizons and provide him with valuable friends and contacts. More important, the youth would be introduced to the mysteries of agriculture, and the knowledge he gained would prove invaluable when he began farming or ranching on his own. The experience would also stand him in good stead should he desire to seek employment, and in this respect many farm instructors provided their pupils with graduating diplomas. The diplomas declared the bearers to be qualified agriculturalists, who possessed any number of skills pertaining to horticulture, cereal farming, and animal husbandry.

On the surface all this seemed highly commendable, but in fact the system was a sham and a swindle. The reasons were numerous. In the first place, professional farmers or ranchers who depended on delicate crops, expensive livestock, and complicated machinery were not usually prepared to entrust these to inexperienced schoolboys. As a result, many farm pupils found that they had paid for a course in digging holes for fence posts, cutting cordwood, or shovelling manure. In addition, many of the so-called farm instructors were themselves inexperienced and so had little practical knowledge to offer; in fact it was not at all uncommon for a new emigrant to advertise for pupils— whom he styled "agricultural apprentices" or "agricultural cadets"—in order to supplement his income and do some of the onerous chores. The system was iniquitous, too, because it did not provide pupils with the discipline and incentive normally associated with paid employment. So long as the father paid the premium, the pupil could consider himself a paying guest, and if he did not get too much underfoot he could lead an aimless existence. Most Canadian-born farmers and ranchers were aware of this, and as a result they regarded the pupils' diplomas or "certificates of skill" with amusement and contempt.

Unfortunately, many Canadians also looked with contempt upon the farm pupils. In their minds, it was almost inconceivable, in a country where labour was scarce, that someone would actually pay for the privilege of doing another's work. No one with any self-respect would be party to such an arrangement; no one save the most incompetent or untrustworthy of characters would have to resort to such a practice. Because of this thinking, the ill-advised but well-intentioned farm pupil was invariably branded as a failure or a misfit. In western Canada the pupils were known derisively as "mudpups," and mudpups in most frontier communities were relegated to the bottom rungs of the social ladder.

The stigma of being a mudpup was perhaps the most iniquitous aspect of the premium farm-pupil system; this was tragic and ironic, for the system was originally conceived to help young men take a respected and useful place in the rural society. Instead, the system had the opposite effect: it segregated the fee-paying pupil from his wage-earning neighbours, put him in an artificial position, and saddled him with an unenviable reputation.

The inherent disadvantages of the system should have been apparent, after careful reflection, to the harried paterfamilias who scrutinized the notices in the *Field* and similar publications. The fallacies of the system should have been apparent, too, from the many reports that came back to England from disillusioned and disgruntled farm pupils. Then there were the warnings that appeared in travellers' accounts, settlers' manuals, and government immigration literature, and the sensational scandals and criminal cases in which the system was implicated. Yet despite the criticisms it provoked, the system persisted. It did so partly because it seemed to meet a need and partly because its advocates were so skillful in refuting or discrediting their critics.

Proponents of the premium farm-pupil system played on parents' fears and insecurities. They said that public school boys who attempted to earn wages and experience as common labourers would lose "caste." They argued that young gentlemen who came to the Dominion "on spec" were likely to be abused, cheated, or in some way exploited by a host of blackguards and scoundrels. They painted an alarming picture of sensitive youths being jostled and jeered at by uncouth colonials; they told poignant stories of downcast youths wandering friendless and penniless across the empty prairie.

Of course, the case for the farm-pupil system was argued in subtler, more rational ways in some of the articles and essays that appeared in respected British periodicals. One such article, entitled "Farm Pupils in the Colonies," appeared in *Macmillan's Magazine* in 1890. The article was unsigned, and on first reading it seemed to be an objective, balanced consideration of employment opportunities for emigrants. The article was written, however, by A.G. Bradley, an English gentlemen later well-known as a travel writer and historian. When Bradley wrote the article, he was operating a farm-pupil agency in London.

Bradley, who had farmed in Ontario, conceded that the work-for-wages system had its advantages: it offered youths some financial rewards and provided them with an opportunity to observe the habits and customs of colonial farmers. He pointed out, though, that youths who came to the Dominion with the intention of beginning their careers as labourers would first have to compete with Canadians, a race of men who, apparently, were almost impossible to best: "The regular Canadian hired man . . . does more work in a day than any farm-labourer in the world; half as much again as an Englishman, twice as much as an Irishman at home. It is with this man that the young gentleman, fresh from a public school, has to be compared." Bradley went on to explain that Johnny Canuck had been born to a life of toil and from his infancy had become inured to the hardest of labour. "His powers of endurance have been developed to the highest pitch that the human frame is capable of." What chance, then, had the tender novice of competing with these almost superhuman men? Little chance, according to Bradley. He claimed that scarcely half of the young emigrants would be able to endure the demanding regimen and the spartan living conditions that Canadians accepted as commonplace. The other half—"the less robust, the very young, the half-hearted"— would find the life more than they could bear. Such youths would likely become discouraged and depressed, and to relieve their depression, they might well turn to drink. In the end, they would become pitiful derelicts.

Clearly, what was needed was a gentler means of initiating the youths to the life of a settler. The farm-pupil system was that means. Bradley argued that contrary to popular belief, the farmers who participated in the system were not "swindlers" who demanded exorbitant premiums; rather, they were by and large highly trained, respectable men who simply expected a reasonable fee for service. The apprenticeships would make men

and farmers out of boys and do it in a manner that was compatible with and sympathetic to the characters of young gentlemen.
In Bradley's words, the English farm pupil would "board in the
family of people of his own social grade and education and have
much the same comforts and refinements he would have at
home, say in a farm-house of the better class, or in a quiet country vicarage, with the social advantages pertaining to that style
of life."[1] It was an attractive picture, and one that certainly
appealed to many parents whose sons were destined for the colonies. But as many a public school boy discovered, life as a colonial mudpup often bore very little resemblance to life in a quiet
country vicarage.

The colonial farm-pupil system was based on training prac-
tices that had existed for centuries in the crafts and professions.
In Britain individual craftsmen and guilds had traditionally
demanded fees from apprentices and trainees, and many professions, particularly law, required premiums as a matter of course
from articling students. The premium system was not common
in agriculture, however, until the middle years of the nineteenth
century, when a number of gentlemen farmers in the West Country began offering instruction to urban-bred gentlemen who intended to take up land overseas. The system persisted in England for many years, but it became much more prevalent in the
colonies because people assumed that pupils would receive
better training if they pursued an apprenticeship under the same
conditions they could expect to meet as settlers in a new land.

Samuel Strickland was among the first to promote the premium system in the colonies. Strickland was a student of character, and having observed the characters and the fortunes of
young gentlemen emigrants in Canada for over a quarter of a
century, he concluded that such youths needed a special regimen
if they were to make their way in the backwoods. He outlined
his views in his memoirs, *Twenty-Seven Years in Canada West*
(1853):

> The best plan . . . in regard to emigration, is for gentlemen to
> provide for their younger sons in this way. A premium for
> three years, paid to some respectable settler, to engage him to

instruct the young emigrant... would set a young gentleman
forward in life at a small expense to his friends.[2]

Strickland admitted that young gentlemen who were so provided
for might have to endure a few inconveniences; but "youth," he
said, "with its buoyant spirits, readily overcomes hardships and
difficulties." Besides, "the amusements of shooting and fishing,
riding and exploring excursions [would] quickly make newcomers much attached to the country."

Strickland publicized his views on the emigration of young
gentlemen when he returned to England for an extended visit in
1851: he discussed his ideas with friends at his family home at
Reydon Hall and in the informal lectures he gave in a number of
parishes in Norfolk. The lectures, plus the publication of his
memoirs, aroused considerable interest in the scheme, and
Strickland was inundated with queries. The encouraging response prompted him to put some of his ideas into practice, and
in 1853 he founded the "Agricultural Academy" at Lakefield.

The grandiously styled "academy" was in fact a rather humble establishment. It consisted of Strickland's own farm house
and a few log cabins which accommodated about a dozen farm
pupils. Strickland's Yankee neighbours were inclined to take a
dim view of the academy, which they thought was unnecessary,
but most tourists were favourably impressed. Charles Weld, an
Anglo-Irish barrister who visited the school a year after it
opened, thought it would provide valuable service to the community by bringing in young men with capital. Weld was also
impressed by the students who, though armed to the teeth with
rifles, knives, and other formidable weapons, turned out to be
jovial, well-behaved fellows. "Social conviviality," Weld reported, after describing an evening he had spent with the lads,
"never degenerated to coarseness; and though the red hunting-
shirts, looming through the tobacco-smoke gave the company a
brigandish appearance, gentlemanly conduct was as strongly
maintained as if the scene of our merriment had been in a
London drawing-room."[3]

Colonel Strickland's pups had good reason to be well behaved and jovial, for he provided them with plenty of food and
every opportunity for hunting, fishing, and fowling. Moreover,

pallid youths who were consigned to the colonel's care knew that
if they followed Strickland's regimen they would be transformed
into burly young men. Horton Rhys, an ex-army officer turned
actor, remarked upon this after meeting an old school chum at
the Lakefield academy in 1860. When Rhys had last seen his
friend at Eton he was a timid, weak, retiring soul and a favourite
target for the school bullies. When Rhys called upon the friend
at Lakefield, he was met by a "big, brawny, bellowing backwoodsman," who sported an enormous beard and a huge
mustache. "Heaven save the mark!" Rhys gasped, as he gazed up
at the Etonian Paul Bunyan.[4] But whether Rhys's friend had
been transformed into a competent agriculturalist is another
question. One of Strickland's other pups, a clergyman's son,
afterwards reported that while "many young Englishmen of
good family" did learn "the rudiments of farming as understood
by the genial colonel," those rudiments "consisted chiefly in a
thorough training in manly sports and a fine discrimination in
the selection of liquors."[5]

When Colonel Strickland died in 1867, the farm-pupil system
had become common in many parts of Ontario; indeed, in some
communities it was a veritable cottage industry. Some of the
farmers who operated training farms did provide their pupils
with useful knowledge as regards agriculture and stock raising,
but unfortunately such farmers were relatively rare. More often,
cadets were kept at heavy manual labour or allowed to pursue a
frivolous routine. Young Edward ffolkes discovered this when
he came to Toronto in 1880. While staying in his King Street
boarding house, ffolkes met Thomas Charles Patteson, an Old
Etonian and graduate of Merton College, Oxford. Patteson,
who was then the postmaster of Toronto, informed ffolkes that
only those who wished to lead a dissipated life, or who fancied
living on dry bread and water should begin their careers as colonial farm pupils. He then launched into a lurid description of
the vices and slovenly habits pupils acquired; these habits, Patteson said, were derived principally from "low, mean, selfish,
drunken" Canadians. Yet ffolkes's counsellor, one of the wealthiest and most influential men in Toronto, kept a large farm some
miles from the city for the very purpose of "training" mudpups

himself. This sagacious but paradoxical official even invited ffolkes to visit the farm, "just to see your brother Englishmen, whom I make work like slaves."[6] ffolkes was understandably stunned by Patteson's revelations, particularly since he was then contemplating an apprenticeship with another farmer. But after meeting Patteson he decided to make enquiries at the Ontario Agricultural College at Guelph, where he could be sure of receiving a decent education and decent treatment from his instructors.

The young Haileyburian was fortunate in being dissuaded from enlisting in Ontario's corps of agricultural cadets. Frederick DelaFosse, his contemporary from Wellington College, was not as lucky. Frederick's uncle made arrangements for his nephew to be apprenticed to a gentleman farmer in the Muskoka district. The farmer, a retired British army captain named Martin, was to train Frederick for a period of three years. Frederick had seen some of the letters Martin had sent to his guardian, and initially Frederick was pleased with the proposed arrangement: the prospect of a comfortable berth on a colonial estate, along with unlimited fishing and wild sport, seemed well worth £100 ($500) per year. As he neared his destination, though, the nineteen-year-old pupil began to have some qualms. His doubts were first aroused aboard the *Scandinavian,* where he met two Canadian magistrates who were returning to their homes in Manitoba. The magistrates denounced the arrangement that Frederick's uncle had entered into as "bare-faced robbery." The young mudpup's doubts were again aroused in Gravenhurst while he waited for the steamer that would convey him across Lake Muskoka to the town of Bracebridge. "My God!" one of the locals exclaimed, upon hearing of Frederick's premiums. "Of all the goldarned swindles I ever heard, this takes the cake." Even more discouraging were comments made by a group of backwoodsmen whom DelaFosse encountered "jaw ing" in the hotel at Bracebridge. The woodsmen were highly amused with DelaFosse's contract and much taken with the ingenuity of the ex-army captain who had secured the youth's services for three years. "Boys," drawled one of the cutters, turning to his grinning companions, "this here beats anything as ever I seed. Most Englishmen as I've knowed I've took to be kind of soft, but blamed if that there geezer as has got this here young cuss to pay him for clearing his own farm ain't got us all beat. He's a smart one, he is. Blowed if he ain't smart enough to be Primeer of Canady!"[7] This last remark elicited gales of laughter from the hotel patrons.

When DelaFosse eventually reached the Martin farm at Buck Lake, thirty miles from Bracebridge, he found that the captain already had three other pupils: two were public school boys; the other had just come down from Cambridge. The three proved to be agreeable companions, though their presence did little to mitigate the dismal surroundings. The captain's "estate" consisted of three acres of burned-out logs and unpulled stumps. Amid the wreckage were two log shanties: both were haphazardly built and both were covered with mud and manure plaster. The larger of the two accommodated the captain, Mrs. Martin, and the Cambridge man, who slept in a small cubicle partitioned off by a blanket from the main room. A rough wooden table, three decrepit chairs, and a couple of crudely constructed beds comprised the furnishings. The other shanty was even more austere, although in the summer months Frederick and his two colleagues rarely slept in it. Summer nights the boys spent outside, huddled over a smudge fire in a vain attempt to escape the mosquitoes.

During his first year, DelaFosse's curriculum included washing dishes, chopping wood, fetching water, burning brushwood, pulling stumps, and hauling out the occasional tree with the aid of the captain's emaciated oxen. The following year the programme expanded as Martin, flush with his pupil's premiums, was able to afford a barn and a new farm house. The house was an improvement on the mud-and-manure shack and was large enough to hold the grand piano which the captain purchased for his wife. But Martin's agricultural holdings developed slowly and painfully. A crop of alfalfa failed to mature in the rocky soil; a field of turnips was lost to a neighbour's cow. Only the oats ripened, and when they did, the captain endeavoured to introduce his apprentices to the "poetic charms" of harvesting. "You feel when you start in and lay aside swath after swath that here indeed is joy," the captain would bubble. "The glorious sunshine overhead, the rhythmical swing of the cradle as the back bows to the stroke.... Ah, yes! What more could one wish for."[8] Glorious sunshine notwithstanding, DelaFosse was not inspired by the work or impressed with his instructor, and shortly after his articles had expired, he shook the muskeg from his boots and headed west for Manitoba.

Looking back on the experience fifty years later, DelaFosse wrote that when he and his fellow pupils left Muskoka "we were about as well-equipped for practising husbandry as when we first came to the country." He acknowledged that the captain was kindly and well-meaning, but said that Martin had nonetheless hoodwinked them into coming to Muskoka with his highly coloured letters. Through the letters they had been misled as to the captain's agricultural qualifications and the agricultural potential of the district. DelaFosse added, "That the experience spoilt the careers of most of us goes without saying."[9]

Sixty miles, as the crow flies, southwest of Lake Muskoka is the town of Collingwood. Not far from the town, on a farm near the shores of Georgian Bay, Herbert and Dickie Church had their first introduction to colonial life. The soil around Collingwood is relatively good, so the Churches' apprenticeships were not nearly as difficult as DelaFosse's had been. Nevertheless, like DelaFosse, eighteen-year-old Herbert and his sixteen-year-old brother derived little practical benefit from their experience as agricultural cadets.

The Church brothers were apprenticed through the agency of A.G. Bradley to an English farmer at Collingwood. Premiums for the two boys were £80 ($400). Their first-class steamer tickets, which Bradley secured, plus the agency fee, came to an additional £80. The lads' extensive outfit, which Bradley advised them to take, added another £40 ($200) to the account. The arrangement thus cost the boys' father £1,000 ($5,000), no mean sum in 1886.

Professor Church conceded that he might have avoided the premiums: "It would have been easy to find farmers who would have taken the young fellows into their houses, and given them board and lodging in return for their labour. But in view both of the present and the future I wished to keep the two together. They would be happier and they would learn to work in concert." Like so many English parents, Professor Church also hoped that his sons might be introduced gradually and gently to colonial ways. "Life at a small farm, with its rough accommodation and coarse, monotonous fare might have disgusted them with their new life, and possibly have weakened their health," he wrote in an article directed to other fathers. "By this arrangement, then, they began their life in the midst of comforts quite as great as they were accustomed to enjoy at home."[10]

The Reverend Mr. Church sought to provide his sons with the country-vicarage-like environment that Bradley had referred to, and in this respect he succeeded, for Herbert and Dickie did enjoy congenial society at the Collingwood farm. They shared their quarters with a bishop's son, and the three were often entertained in the homes of other English families in the district. They played a great deal of lawn tennis and whist, and took part in picnics, dances, and boating excursions. This is not to say that their days were solely devoted to leisure. They rose most mornings at six o'clock to milk the cows, feed the horses, and clean the stables. They were responsible for the chicken coops and the pigsty. In the afternoons they stooked wheat and baled hay at a frantic pace. After feeding the livestock and bedding down the teams, it was often eight or nine o'clock before their chores were finished.[11]

As a result of this regimen, Herbert and his brother were soon bronzed and physically hardened, and by the end of their apprenticeships they had developed a proficiency in many basic skills. For example, when they first came to Collingwood, it had taken them an hour to milk a single cow; before they left, they could do it in three minutes flat. They could also stack hay at a rate of thirty forkfuls a minute and slaughter a hog without feeling too squeamish. But were these skills worth the premiums it had cost to acquire them? Herbert later said in his autobiography that the arrangement with Bradley and the Collingwood farmer was a mistake: "We would have learned just as much or more by working for board and lodging as some other young Englishmen were doing in the same district." He added that though he and his brother had enjoyed their leisure, they had also been eager to learn sophisticated farming techniques. But "the farmer's sole idea when we arrived was to get as much unskilled labour out of us as possible. We spent day after day loading manure on the waggons driven by regular teamsters, our request to be taught how to drive the teams being treated with scorn."[12] Since the two brothers were repeatedly assigned the most menial tasks, they quickly became frustrated, and it was their frustration as much as anything else that prompted them to abandon Collingwood and join their uncle out west.

The premium farm-pupil system followed the frontiers of settlement and by the 1880s it was as prevalent in Manitoba and the North West Territory as it was in Ontario. Soon, western newspapers were awash with editorials and articles decrying the system. Typical was the editorial which appeared in the *Emigrant*, a Winnipeg periodical, in 1886.

> Quite a number of young Englishmen are now scattered over the Northwest, supposed to be learning farm practices under the proper methods suitable to this country, and for which privilege they pay from one hundred to two hundred pounds, besides their labour. In some cases seen and others heard of, the supposed teacher himself didn't know how to farm, and in others the pupils were kept at the simplest, hardest work, and no pains taken to advance them. There are a few exceptions, but as a rule it is perfect nonsense to pay a premium and throw your labour in to learn farming here.

The *Emigrant*'s editorial brought forth a flood of letters from Manitoba homesteaders and farm pupils, all of whom denounced the system in unequivocal terms. Among the longest and most vitriolic of the letters was one from the Honourable Walter Clifford, younger son of the 8th Baron Clifford of Chudleigh. Clifford, who had a flourishing dairy farm near Virden, agreed that the premium system was "perfect nonsense" and charged that those who advertised for pupils were generally the least successful of farmers. But the twenty-four-year-old aristocrat also criticized English families who seemed to want their sons supervised and coddled in the West. The Old Country paterfamilias, Clifford said, should have more confidence in his sons and less fear of the new land. If youths were allowed to make their own way—as Clifford had done—the ubiquitous farm-pupil system would wither in short order.[13]

The system did not wither, and an army of agricultural cadets soon invaded the prairie province and the North West Territory. John Donkin, the NWMP trooper, met some of the cadets aboard the *Sarnia* when he came to Canada in 1884. He thought them extremely gullible, for all the bravado they exhibited; he also suspected that the "extraordinary agreements" they brandished, outlining the terms of their apprenticeships, were not worth the paper they were printed on. As it turned out, Donkin's suspicions were fully justified. One of the pupils went to a "bucolic professor" near Brandon; the lad was treated harshly and forced to sleep in a root cellar. He endured this abuse for only a few months before returning to Britain, dejected and generally disgusted with the Dominion. Another youth, the son of a Northumbrian vicar, spent his apprenticeship hoeing potatoes; he also fled the country in short order. A third pupil, whose father was a colonel in the army, enlisted as a bugler in the NWMP in order to escape his "bondage," while two other youths—whom Donkin described as having "money and brains in an inverse ratio"—later turned up in Prince Albert, driving commissariat wagons. Like the colonel's son, they had been badly treated during their apprenticeships and had turned to freighting as a relief from their rural taskmaster.[14]

Unfortunately, Donkin's account of his farm-pupil acquaintances reinforced the view, held in many quarters in England, that western Canadian farmers were mean, hard-hearted men who took a perverse delight in mistreating gentle newcomers. His account also added to the belief that the prairies swarmed with low-class "buckboard farmers," so called because they spent most of their days riding around in a buckboard wagon visiting their friends, while their hapless farm pupils toiled relentlessly on the homestead. This impression was reinforced further by some of the novels of the period, especially those which sought to warn readers against the farm-pupil system. In Harold Bindloss's *A Sower of Wheat* (1901), for example, we meet a buckboard farmer who is stout, smug, flabby, and illiterate; the pupil whom the man abuses is, in contrast, an endearing, well-educated fellow: "a curly-haired, brown-eyed stripling, with the look of good breeding about him." Clive Phillipps-Wolley's novel, *Snap* (1890), conveys much the same picture of "teacher" and pupil. As Edward ffolkes found, however, those who took in farm pupils were not always lowly cads. In fact, since the farm-pupil system was so lucrative, many well-bred young Englishmen participated in the scheme as instructors. Arthur Sherwood, a twenty-two-year-old university man who homesteaded near Portage la Prairie, is a case in point.

Not long after Sherwood arrived in Canada in 1882, he and his partner, who was also a young bachelor, started looking for English farm pupils. They succeeded in procuring two youths, a few years their junior, at £30 ($60) per annum. Although Sherwood and his partner appreciated the additional income, Sherwood emphasized in his letters home that he had no intention of exploiting his students. "I think we can teach them something, and make it comfortable for them," he wrote. Still, Sherwood's altruism was tinged with a bit of avarice, for in 1884 he reported that he was looking for two additional pupils. He planned to charge the new cadets £50 a year, "and as much more as you can screw out of them."[15]

Even Herbert and Dickie Church, who expressed such low opinions of the premium system after their experiences at Collingwood, took a pupil once they had secured a homestead in Alberta. They acquired their pup at Calgary in the summer of 1888. The youth was a public school boy and was, Herbert recalled, "as green as we were."[16] Unhappily for the Church brothers, their pupil was rather more careless.

When the Churches took on their apprentice, they were doing contract work for the Quorn Ranch; specifically, they had contracted to supply the Quorn with 200 tons of hay. Under the terms of their agreement, the boys were required to stack the hay, fence the stacks, and plough adequate firebreaks around them. The firebreaks were especially important since the parched prairie had been ravaged by a number of fires that summer. Herbert and Dickie carried out the work as prescribed. They raised and enclosed two great haystacks and around the first they ploughed two wide furroughs. They were just about to plough furroughs around the second when disaster struck. Their farm pupil, who was charged with watching over the first hay-stack, decided to relieve the tedium by smoking a cheroot. He lit up and within seconds the first stack was ablaze. Minutes later the second stack was in flames, too. Never again did the Church brothers take in farm pupils.

Although the Churches renounced the system, several ranches in southern Alberta—including large outfits like the Quorn, the Walrond, and the Oxley—took in a number of pu-pils each year. Pupils on these ranches were usually relatives or friends of the shareholders and undertook their course during the school holidays. For some of the lads the experience was a lark, an exciting relief from declining Latin nouns. For others— for quite a few others, in fact—the experience was valuable, and on leaving school many subsequently returned to the foothills as ranchers or as ranch managers. Those who derived real benefits from their ranching holidays did so because they were required to work alongside Canadian and American cowboys, hard-riding men who did not stand for much nonsense during the course of a working day.

The Oxley, the Quorn, and the other large spreads were clearly business ventures, not hobbies, and the men who directed, managed, and worked them were expected to be pro-ductive. But of course there were many smaller, less successful outfits in Alberta where a boy might also receive ranching in-struction. Messrs. Sturrock and Buckler ran one of them. Char-lie Sturrock was a Scots gentleman who came to the Millarville area at the age of eighteen in 1903. He took up with another young bachelor named Eric Buckler, from England. The two pooled their resources and proceeded to establish Buck Ranche, on Sheep Creek. Neither Charlie nor Eric, who are still remem-bered in the area as "classic remittance men," had any ranching experience; nevertheless, they had a small amount of capital, a great deal of enthusiasm, and some large ideas. One of their best ideas was to advertise for farm pupils in the *Field*.

By all accounts, the youths who were lured to the Buck Ranche were a colourful crew. They arrived with "brand new saddles of the best English make and rifles in beautiful leather cases. They wore tailored riding breeches, with high polished boots into which it was a work of art to wiggle their legs. They even brought with them hounds for coyote hunting and, to go after cougars, Irish wolfhounds, Scottish deer-hounds, a bull mastiff, and an assortment of fox-hounds." Needless to say, the canine-loving dudes learned little about ranching or farming. They were, however, supported by remittances, and for several years pupils and tutors had a "wizard time." They were soul-mates and sportsmen, who valued each other's company more than they did the practical aspects of agriculture.[17]

Farm pupils were also important in the social life of gentle-men's colonies such as Cannington Manor. In fact, the first pups arrived at the Manor in 1883, only a few months after the settle-ment was founded. They were apprenticed to Captain Pierce, who was a great believer in the system. The captain once claimed to have spent $300 in postage in the course of recruiting pupils in the Old Country. But any costs the Skipper and his colleagues incurred were amply repaid, for the farm pupils at Cannington Manor played a vital role, socially and economically. The youths spent their money freely, they reinforced the aristocratic tone of the colony and, of no little importance, they married their tutors' daughters.

The farm pupils who came to Cannington Manor were charged a fee of £100 ($500) per year—a hefty sum since the students were expected to pay their own way to the colony. They were, however, comfortably housed in the "collegiate" wing of Gitchee Wa Teepee, in the "Ram's Pasture" at Didsbury, or in the large homes of other Cannington residents; the youths were guaranteed congenial companions, and there was certainly no shortage of recreational activities. Surprisingly, considering the colony's preoccupation with sport, expert tuition was also available from some of the practical instructors whom Pierce re-tained. The best remembered of these was William "Scotty" Bryce, resident tutor at the Manor from 1886 to 1888. Bryce, who was later president of the Saskatchewan Livestock and Stockbreeders Association, was well qualified for the job, having farmed in Scotland and Northern Ireland prior to emigrating to

Canada. Imparting his knowledge to the cadets at Cannington Manor, however, was no easy task. Bryce complained that the youths were irresponsible and impetuous; they had no sense of urgency at seedtime or harvest and would down tools on the slightest pretext. A strict teetotaler, Bryce also lamented the boys' thirst. He afterwards declared that he was glad when the youths took up tennis, for he was then free to get on with his own work.[18]

The farm-pupil system was never as entrenched at Walhachin as it was at Cannington Manor, and indeed one of the promoters of the Thompson River Valley colony, J.F.S. Redmayne, denounced the system heatedly. "Respectable individuals," Redmayne said, "do not engage in the practice": that being so, it had no place in Walhachin.[19] Despite Redmayne's sanctimonious claims, the farm-pupil system was practised there, albeit on a limited scale. It could scarcely have been otherwise, for the premium system was rampant in Kelowna, in Vernon, and in the other fruit-growing communities of the Okanagan. It was prevalent, too, in some parts of the Kootenays, in the dairylands of the Fraser Valley, and even along the heavily wooded Howe Sound area, near Vancouver.[20] The majority of British Columbia's farm pupils, though, were to be found on the southern part of Vancouver Island. In the 1890s and early 1900s, the Cowichan and Chemainus valleys formed the heart of mud-pup land, for on almost every dairy farm and chicken ranch an agricultural cadet resided. The youths who served on these farms and ranches appear to have been happier than those who trained in the prairie West and Ontario. Whether their training was any better is a moot point.

Perhaps a few lost years and a few hundred pounds was a small price to pay for an introduction to the backwoods and the prairies. After all, the Church brothers, Frederick DelaFosse, and countless others who paid the price survived the system and ultimately prospered in the Dominion. And perhaps the youths who took part in the system deserve little sympathy: they entered into their agreements more or less voluntarily and actually suffered little during the course of their apprenticeships. Even the disgruntled young men whom John Donkin met did not endure nearly the same hardships as did some of the Barnardo boys and other pauper children who were sent to Canada. The premium farm-pupils and their parents were exploited, nonetheless, and the fact that they were exploited resulted in adverse publicity for the Dominion at a time when Canada was doing its utmost to recruit moneyed British immigrants.

Immigration officials in Ottawa were particularly upset by three well-publicized farm-pupil scandals: the "Shearman Swindle," the "Anglo-Canadian Affair," and the "Birchall Case." The Shearman Swindle took place in the United States, but Canadian authorities feared—rightly, as it turned out—that the public would assume that similar operations existed north of the border. The case involved a libel action which Henry Shearman, a British immigrant who operated a "farm school" in Minnesota, brought against the proprietors of the *Scotsman*. In 1884 the Edinburgh newspaper charged that Shearman's school was fraudulent and that his pupils (who paid from 60 to 75 guineas a year) did little more than "the meanest and most menial of labour."[21] Fearing a loss of business, Shearman launched a suit against the paper for £10,000 in damages. Yet though he resorted to a number of legal ploys and manoeuvres, Shearman was unable to refute the *Scotsman*'s charges and in 1885 his case was dismissed. In the process, as both plaintiff and defendant mustered their evidence, the British public was provided a picture of the farm-pupil system in the United States and in Canada. The public's reaction was not favourable.

The second case dragged on from the mid-1880s to the mid-1890s. It centred on an outfit called the Anglo-Canadian Farm Pupil Association (ACFPA), which operated principally around London, Ontario. The ACFPA was organized and conducted by a retired clergyman and a former justice of the peace. They did a brisk business placing aristocratic young emigrants with local farmers, until some of the pupils complained of the treatment they had received from their instructors. But the aggrieved pupils did not complain only to their parents; they also complained to the Colonial Office, to the Minister of the Interior, and to Canada's governor general, Lord Stanley. When immigration authorities began investigating the complaints they found that the ACFPA had been representing itself as a semi-official arm of the Canadian government. With the help of the Dominion Police and the Ontario Provincial Police, the ACFPA's activities were eventually curtailed, though not before the British press had made the issue a *cause célèbre*.

The Birchall case was even more embarrassing; in fact, it was one of the most notorious scandals of its day. The case involved Reginald Birchall, the Oxford-educated son of an English clergyman, who came to Woodstock, Ontario, in 1889. Posing as Lord and Lady Somerset, Birchall and his wife lured two young farm pupils to the district on the pretext of settling the youths on the Somerset estate. The estate was nonexistent, the youths were robbed, and one of them—Frederick Benwell—was murdered. Birchall was eventually caught by the indefatigable John Wilson Murray, Canada's "great detective," and was hung for murder at Woodstock in November 1890. The case created a sensation —partly because Murray, when seeking to identify the victim, had sent Benwell's photograph to newspapers throughout Canada, the United States, and Britain, and partly because during the trial Birchall was so forthright in admitting the dastardly plans he had for Benwell and other farm pupils. In England, where the trial was reported in the daily papers, it was said that Birchall was part of an organized conspiracy, dedicated to the wholesale slaughter of wealthy young Englishmen. Although the notion was absurd, the Dominion received a great deal of unfavourable publicity because of the Birchall case.[22]

To counter the adverse publicity, and to prevent other young emigrants from being abused, exploited, and even murdered, the Canadian government launched a campaign aimed at discrediting farm-pupil operators. The campaign was organized by Sir Charles Tupper, former premier of Nova Scotia and Canada's high commissioner in London from 1883 to 1896. Tupper began the campaign by inserting a notice warning of the system in the Dominion's *Official Handbook for Emigrants*. Next, he gave a series of well-publicized speeches in London and the provinces denouncing the system. He then printed special notices which were displayed in British post offices and railway stations. The notices read as follows:

CAUTION TO EMIGRANTS: The system of paying premiums
in this country to gain instruction in farming in Canada is considered by the Canadian Government to be unnecessary. Young
men who are going to Canada to obtain a knowledge of farming are advised to pay no fees of the kind to any private agency,
but to apply to the High Commissioner for Canada, 17 Victoria St., London, S.W., from whom full information on such
subjects may be obtained.

In addition, Tupper ordered Dominion immigration agents in
Liverpool, Southampton, and other embarkation points not to
deal with steamship companies who co-operated in any way with
premium farm-pupil agencies.[23]

Unfortunately, the high commissioner's campaigns did not
mark the end of disreputable agencies like the ACFPA. However, the campaigns, along with the Birchall case and related
scandals, did serve to discredit the farm-pupil system. As a
result, British parents and their sons became more cautious
when they perused advertisements that offered expert tuition to
"agricultural cadets." Because of the controversy that surrounded the system, late-Victorian and Edwardian gentlemen
also began to look for alternative ways of acquiring a knowledge
of farming and ranching. One alternative was to enroll in a
recognized agricultural college.

CHAPTER X

OLD BOYS & OLD COLONIALS

Until the last quarter of the nineteenth century few people gave much thought to the training of prospective emigrants. Apart from Samuel Strickland, who thought there should be special academies for settlers, most people expected emigrants to fend for themselves. The British government shared this laissez-faire attitude, and though the Canadian government was actively re-cruiting immigrants, it too lacked any interest in providing new-comers with colonial training. When people eventually began to consider the need for such training, they conceived the idea of agricultural colleges. Soon that subject became a topic of public discussion—a topic that was debated as intently as gentlemen's colonies and almost as intently as the premium farm-pupil system.

The debate over agricultural colleges revolved principally around three questions: would the schools provide useful train-ing to emigrants; should the schools be located in Britain or in the colonies; and at what age should students begin their train-ing? With regard to the first question, there were those who maintained that training colleges would serve no useful purpose. James Aspdin, one of the founders of the controversial Anglo-Canadian Farm Pupil Association, was among this group. Agri-cultural colleges, he said in his booklet, *Our Boys: What Shall We Do With Them?* (1889), would mislead and ultimately hamper intending colonists. He argued that conditions in the controlled environment of a college, irrespective of the college's location, would bear no similarity to conditions on a Canadian farm. Students confined to such colleges, he said, would never become physically strong and self-reliant, as they would if they undertook a course with a premium farmer. A.G. Bradley, who also had a personal and financial interest in the farm-pupil system, argued a similar view. "The very fact of being merely one of fifty or one hundred students at an institution cuts . . . a pupil off from all those inner and domestic matters that are really such an important feature in [a] farmer's life." If young gentlemen felt the need of some sort of training prior to emigrating, better they spend their time with the village blacksmith or carpenter, Bradley said.[1]

Bradley was being flippant, but the regimen he spoke of was by no means uncommon. In the early 1850s *Chambers' Edinburgh Journal* recommended that prospective emigrants prepare for their new life by renting a yeoman farmer's cottage in Britain for a few months. The farmer, who was to remain in attendance, would instruct his tenant in rustic arts, while the spartan conditions of the rural cottage would replicate, in a limited way, conditions in a backwoods cabin.[2] Prior to beginning their apprenticeships as farm pupils thirty years later, the Church brothers had received a few pointers from their local smithy. Although the knowledge they acquired was minimal, Professor Church believed that it would later prove useful to the boys once they settled in the Far West. And so it did. A similar regimen was recommended in several boys' weeklies which were devoted to promoting the idea of emigration within the Empire. *Boys of Our Empire*, for example, advised its urban subscribers to spend a month or two with local tradesmen, so as to familiarize themselves with the rudiments of carpentry and metal work. This periodical also suggested that youths cultivate a green thumb in their back gardens or in civic vegetable plots. It was good advice, as far as it went, although it is difficult to imagine young aristocrats grubbing about in a council allotment.[3]

Certainly Major General the Honourable William Feilding's young friends and relatives would not have been permitted to grub about in an allotment: had they done so they would have lost caste. Nor could the general stomach the thought of young gentlemen being exploited as farm pupils. Feilding, therefore, took the opposite view to Aspdin and Bradley and was among those who argued strongly in favour of colonists' academies. In his article, "Whither Shall I Send My Son?" the general called for special academies that would train young Englishmen in all aspects of colonial life. The schools he envisaged would provide a broad curriculum and would be conducted along the lines of a military academy. Among the subjects to be studied were ploughing, the breeding of livestock, surveying, "cooking with and without those culinary articles deemed necessary for civilized life," the curing of game, the preparation of hides, harness making, bookkeeping, geology, and "the construction of rafts and other contrivances for crossing lakes and streams." This programme, Feilding said, would prepare young gentlemen for almost every exigency in the colonies.[4]

William Stamer, whose views on immigration were usually sound, took a middle road in the debate. Emigrants' colleges similar to those proposed by Feilding would be a sham, he said. Such colleges, he suspected, would be conducted by theoreticians who would in all likelihood offer spurious "testamurs of efficiency" to their graduates. For a young man in the colonies to "represent himself as a graduate of the Gentlemen Emigrants' College would be to have the door shut in his face." Still, Stamer did not rule out the idea of preparatory schools entirely. He believed that they might prove useful if they were conducted on thoroughly practical lines, if instructors were artisans, not academics, and if students concentrated on developing manual skills. Assuming the colleges were located in England, Stamer said their curricula would have to be geared to colonial conditions. That is, students would have to learn to build wood-frame houses, not brick bungalows; they would have to learn to sit a Western saddle, and they would have to acquire a knowledge of such methods of agriculture as were practised overseas. Most important, if emigrants' colleges were to be viable, they would have to prepare students *mentally* for the life that lay ahead. The graduate of a successful college, Stamer said, "would have acquired habits of thrift and regularity; have discovered that riches are not absolutely essential to human happiness; that enough was as good as a feast; and last, but not least, that manual labour, if not exactly dignified, is very far from being derogatory."[5]

John Rowan echoed some of these sentiments two years later, in 1876. Speaking from personal experience, Rowan said that there was a great need for a college where prospective colonists could acquire a knowledge of "carpentry, saddlery, turning... [and] a hundred other things which the squatter or backwoods farmer may any day have to turn his hand to." Without such a college, boys might have to endure an expensive and "irksome" farm-pupil apprenticeship. Like Stamer, Rowan stressed that while the colleges would have to teach practical trades and handicrafts, they would also have to imbue their students with the philosophy of hard work. "This," he rightly said, "was a great point."[6]

Stamer suggested that those who intended to take courses in colonial life begin as early as possible, before they acquired too many luxurious tastes and refined habits. Twelve, he thought, might be a good age to begin. But since most young gentlemen did not contemplate emigrating before they left school, Stamer's suggestion was thought to be unrealistic. Most observers felt that eighteen or nineteen was the best age for students to enrol in a colonists' school. As regards the location of these schools, there was no consensus. Some argued that the schools should be located in England, so that students who found they were unsuited to agricultural life would not have to suffer the expense of emigrating. Others insisted that would-be colonial farmers should train in the area they intended to settle. Opinion remained divided, and in the end educational facilities were established on both sides of the Atlantic.

In Canada, the most respected of the training centres was the Ontario School of Agriculture and Experimental Farm in Guelph. The school was founded in 1874 to provide advanced courses in stock breeding and soil management to provincial farmers. When enrolment declined because of the economic depression in the late seventies, the government-operated school launched a vigorous campaign to attract young Britons. The campaign was an immediate success, and by 1880, when the school was renamed the Ontario Agricultural College (OAC), British students accounted for a third of the total enrolment.

The OAC offered courses in liberal arts as well as in agricultural science and engineering. Instruction was of a high calibre and fees were reasonable. Boarders who had previously spent a year with a local farmer were charged $50 (£10) per annum; those without practical experience paid $100. The full programme entailed three years of study, although students were permitted to take courses on a semester basis.

The philosophy of the college was *mens sana in corpore sano*, for students were encouraged to participate in a wide range of sporting and intellectual activities. The training of agriculturalists, however, was the primary aim, and to this end the OAC offered a comprehensive syllabus which included surveying, natural history, soil chemistry, and veterinary anatomy. Even the OAC's liberal arts courses, such as English literature and composition, were tailored to agricultural purposes, for students were often required to write critiques on pastoral poems. Practical instruction, which critics like Aspdin and Bradley said would suffer in an agricultural college, was not neglected, since students were required to spend at least four hours each day in the college fields, stables, or workshops. The students were even paid a wage for their labours. The wage was nominal—5 cents an hour for freshmen, 10 cents for sophomores—but it went some way to defraying the costs of meals, laundry, and other incidental expenses which were not covered by students' fees. The payment of wages was also intended to encourage habits of thrift—habits that the college superintendent, a Scotsman, regarded as cardinal virtues.

Edward ffolkes was a student at Guelph in 1880–81, and his diary provides an illuminating account of OAC life. On weekdays, ffolkes rose at 5:30 A.M. After attending morning prayers and having breakfast, he was usually at work by seven. His working days were divided between lectures and fieldwork. The former involved intensive courses in agricultural science and related subjects; the latter included haying, carpentry, attending to livestock, and repairing farm machinery. The working day concluded at six o'clock, though after supper ffolkes was required to keep up with his reading. His textbooks were the standard ones: *The Horse* by "Stonehenge" [J.H. Walsh], *Inorganic Chemistry* by R.L. Wilson, and William Youett's *The Complete Grazier... and Cattle-Breeders' Assistant.* ffolkes found the reading onerous, the lectures demanding, and the examinations "horrible." He much preferred working with hybrid plants and livestock at the OAC experimental farm or being out in the fields ploughing with a steam tractor. Even spreading manure and carrying sacks of potatoes—"nice work for strengthening the back and rounding the shoulders"—he found preferable to the "decidedly hard work" of the classroom. [7] Since young Edward had not been a distinguished scholar at Haileybury, his comments concerning the theoretical side of the programme at OAC are not surprising. But he did have a feeling for the soil, and although he failed inorganic chemistry and bookkeeping, he left Guelph with honours standing in agriculture. [8]

During his semester at Guelph, ffolkes managed to find time to play rugby for the college XV, to serve as vice-president of the literary society, and to join the debating club. He was joined in these activities by a number of his old school chums, one of whom was A.E. Cross. Although born and raised in Montreal, Cross had been sent by his father (a Quebec Court judge) to Haileybury to acquire an education befitting an English-Canadian gentlemen. On leaving the OAC in 1881, Cross attended the Montreal Veterinary College, then headed west as assistant manager of the British-American Horse Ranche. He later became a charter member of the prestigious Ranchmen's Club at Calgary, founded a brewing empire, and helped launch the Calgary Stampede. Another of ffolkes's school chums from Haileybury who was attending the OAC at the time was John Basil Feilding, the general's nephew. He subsequently became technical advisor to the Canadian Wildlife and Conservation Commission and was a member of both the Ontario and Nova Scotia fisheries departments. Young Edward was in good company.

ffolkes was also friendly with the OAC faculty members, though he was somewhat surprised at their intense nationalism.

When he arrived at Guelph he had been required to "kiss the Bible, swear an oath, and sign a document," promising that he would remain in the Dominion for at least four years after leaving the OAC. The college staff, he found, were very anxious to discourage emigration to the United States. One student, who inadvertently admitted that he was contemplating farming in Minnesota on graduation, was expelled within hours. Accordingly, Edward warned his brother, Robert, who was planning to enrol at the OAC and then settle in Iowa, to keep his plans secret: "Remember, that if the authorities get so much as an inkling that Bob is thinking of farming in Iowa they will fire him out before he has been here a day...."[9]

Edward's object in going to the OAC was to "learn the outline of farming and get hardy, and all that sort of thing."[10] He succeeded, and when he resettled in Manitoba he was physically fit, self-confident, and comfortable with livestock and farm implements. Yet while he obviously benefited from his semester at the Ontario college, he afterwards complained that he was unprepared for Manitoba soil conditions and farming methods. It would have been better had he actually trained in the prairie West. ffolkes' complaint was understandable, but at the time there was nowhere in the West where gentlemen emigrants could undertake comprehensive courses in agriculture. In fact, a programme similar to that which ffolkes desired was not available until the Right Reverend the Honourable A.J.R. Anson, bishop of Qu'Appelle, opened an agricultural school at St. John's College, Assiniboia, in 1885.

Bishop Anson understood gentlemen emigrants. He was the third son of the Earl of Lichfield and had been educated at Eton and Oxford. He had come to the prairies in 1884 as the first bishop of the new Diocese of Qu'Appelle. It was a time of growth in Assiniboia: the CPR was well underway, new lands were being opened for settlement, and an army of immigrants was pouring into the district. To provide for this ever-growing flock the bishop established St. John's (Anglican) Divinity College at Qu'Appelle Station in 1885. By establishing a seminary in the diocese, Bishop Anson hoped to train clergymen who would be attuned to the needs and conditions of the widely scattered homesteaders. He soon realized, though, that British emigrants, especially those of his own class, needed more than spiritual guidance, and for this reason he added a small agricultural academy to the divinity school.

St. John's Collegiate Farm, as the academy was officially known, comprised 640 acres. It was managed by a competent instructor who emphasized the practical, but did not exclude the theoretical, aspects of western farming. A variety of grains and vegetables were grown on the property, and sheep, as well as horses, pigs, cattle, and poultry, were raised. The Collegiate Farm accepted a new class of twelve students each year and offered a two-year programme. Freshmen fees were £60 ($300) per annum (inclusive of room and board); sophomores, who had gained some experience and who could help train the novices, were charged £50.[11]

Henry Greig, whose son was enrolled at the Collegiate Farm, visited Anson's academy in 1888. Greig, a North Country businessman, was impressed not only with the "thorough" training his son had received but also by the comfort, the decorum, and the discipline of the school. He published his impressions, along with his views on the needs of young gentlemen emigrants, on his return to Britain. His report was encouraging, and his opinions were typical of those held by many middle-class Victorian parents. "The transition from a comfortable home in these islands to the rough life of a North-West Canadian is often found trying by young men," Greig wrote:

> The change is too sudden, but [at St. John's College] the transition is gradual, and this is an important point. There is some home life at the College; the students have for comrades young gentlemen; there are daily services and the personal influence of the Bishop which is always a prominent feature in the life led there....[12]

With Greig's help the Collegiate Farm was promoted widely in England. Notices concerning the school were sent to local parishes, and advertisements were placed in the *Church Messenger*, the *Guardian*, the *Church Times,* and kindred periodicals. The campaign was a success, and by 1892 the school was on a firm and apparently permanent footing. Unfortunately, the seminary and the boys' preparatory school which Bishop Anson had also founded were less successful. The two were plagued with financial difficulties and in 1894, following Bishop Anson's retirement, they closed. The closures affected the Collegiate Farm, which had shared some of the seminary and school facilities, and in spite of the fact that the farm was self-supporting, synod officials decided to rent the estate to two local farmers. The farmers announced that they would continue to operate the property as a reception and training centre for young immigrants; however, student fees were raised and the quality of instruction declined. In private hands, the school was too much like a premium farm, and in 1895, in the wake of the Anglo-Canadian Affair, the school closed for good.

Although the Collegiate Farm had catered to relatively few students it had, under diocesan auspices, performed a valuable service, and its demise meant that public school boys who were planning to emigrate had to look for alternative facilities. Fortunately, such facilities were close at hand, for in 1887 Robert Johnson had opened the Colonial College at Hollesley Bay, near Woodbridge in Suffolk.

Robert Johnson was a remarkable man in an age of remarkable men. He is principally remembered as a prison reformer, as an advocate of leniency for first offenders, and as the founder of the Discharged Prisoners' Aid Society. A devout churchman, whose long white beard gave him a distinctly patriarchal appearance, Johnson was also instrumental in establishing savings banks for agricultural labourers, rural sick benefit societies, medical clubs, and many other benevolent associations. Urban planning, civic architecture, and the graphic arts were among his other interests. In each of his interests Johnson invested a great deal of time, energy, and money. The training school for gentlemen emigrants he conducted with the same magnanimity and zeal.[13]

As far as we know, Johnson never visited any of the settlement colonies; however, he had many colonial friends, and from them he learned of the problems faced by inexperienced British public school emigrants. A Canadian friend told him that "*most*... of the young men who are sent out from the Mother Country are miserably unfitted to grapple with the difficulties of a settler's life"; a South African correspondent told him of naive young emigrants who, lacking friends and experience in colonial matters, became "idle and reckless." From another friend, a long-time resident of Australia, Johnson learned of "the disastrous and cruel consequences of the too common practice of wrenching a young man suddenly from the comforts of home, and throwing him into a new country to make his way without preparation and training." Johnson found the reports upsetting, though they did not shake his belief in the efficacy of emigration. Rather, they convinced him that British public school boys, whom he regarded highly, needed special training, guidance and encouragement before they ventured to the Empire overseas. To provide for these youths Johnson established the Colonial College which, in its day, was the largest and best-equipped agricultural academy in Britain.[14]

In many ways, the college resembled a first-class public school and it was often referred to as the Public Schools' Colonial Training College. The main buildings were of imposing design, and students were provided with most of the extra-curricular activities normally found at the larger public schools. The college was not, in fact, formally affiliated with any of the schools, though public school headmasters fully endorsed its programmes and most of the young men who attended the College were former public school boys.[15]

Fees at Hollesley Bay were expensive: £108 ($540) for the first year and £126 ($630) for the second. But the Hollesley Bay curriculum was exceptional, for it included courses on veterinary science, soil chemistry, minor surgery and medicine, geology, silviculture, and surveying. Facilities were also exceptional since Johnson's 1,800-acre estate supported an orchard, a fully-equipped dairy, a market garden, and an experimental farm which was given over to various types of colonial-grown cereals.[16]

Major General Feilding approved of the college, especially as it offered courses in riding and shooting. William Stamer would have approved, too, since the resident staff included not only academics but also blacksmiths, wheelwrights, harness makers and carpenters. The British press was certainly enthusiastic, and the college was the subject of feature articles in journals from the *Daily Graphic* and the *Educator*, to the *Boy's Own Paper* and the *Captain*. Each of the journals referred to the college's "unique character," and indeed it was a unique institution. But it was the institute's ambience, as much as the instruction it offered, that made it so. Johnson intended the college to become "a depository of colonial lore"; its very atmosphere, he hoped, would make it "redolent of colonial life."[17] He succeeded admirably in creating and maintaining that atmosphere. Colonial flags, provincial coats-of-arms, wheat-sheaves, sheepskins, and cowhides from Canada and the other dominions graced the college halls. Colonial politicians and immigration officials spoke regularly at college functions, and a long line of successful ranchers, farmers, and backwoodsmen came to the college as guest lecturers. A colonial atmosphere was even evident in the Hollesley Bay stables. The college was renowned for breeding Suffolk Punches—heavy, strong, docile work horses. It was rather appropriate that such horses were raised at an institute devoted to transforming public school boys (whom *The Times* had likened to high-spirited, thoroughbred racers) into conscientious, hard-working homesteaders. In any event, the mares that were foaled at Johnson's stables were named so as to underscore the college's devotion to the colonies. Hence such prize winners as Tasmania 3205, Winnipeg 3494, Alberta 4195, Rhodesia 4196, and Calgary 4533.[18]

The institute's character was also reflected in the college song, a rousing, light-hearted number which reflected the interests, the confidence, and the good-natured humour of Johnson's students:

> I.   There's a wonderful College at Hollesley Bay,
>   Where Colonists blossom and bloom into day;
>   There's a dairy and farm, there are acres galore,
>   With harrows and rollers in bountiful store,
>   While of oxen and sheep there's numberless stock;
>   But the students themselves are the 'flower of the flock!'

Chorus:
    They can all of them dig, they can all of them plough,
    They can all of them wheedle the milk from a cow;
    They can all of them sow, they can all of them reap,
    They can all of them borrow the fleece from a sheep.

II. Australia and Canada thrill with our fame,
    And the kangaroo leaps at the sound of our name;
    Cecil Rhodes has a plan which he thinks will take shape
    To ship us by waggon-loads out to the Cape;
    While in distant New Zealand the Maories say,
    "Please send us more students from Hollesley Bay!"

III. Then here's to our founder and here's to the Queen,
    And here's to the Empire we never have seen;
    But though we've not seen it we do not forget
    That on its broad acres the sun cannot set,
    And we'll show when we get there we're chips of the block
    That was raised in Old England, the 'flower of the flock.'[19]

Between 1887 and 1900, over 700 young men passed through the Colonial College and, as the song promised, they made their way to all parts of the Empire. But while Old Colonials (as ex-collegians were termed) were drawn to the lands of the springbok, kiwi, and kangaroo, the majority settled in western Canada. They grew wheat in Manitoba and Assiniboia; they became dairy farmers and fruit growers in British Columbia. One Old Colonial acquired the whole of Sidney Island, near Victoria, for a sheep run. It was cattle ranching, though, that most appealed to the Hollesley Bay alumni, for the directories published in *Colonia*, the school magazine, indicate that a large number of Old Colonials were settled in the ranching districts of southern Alberta. Some, like the Honourable F.C. Lascelles, a son of the Earl of Harewood, had their own ranches; some, like G.E. ("Teddy") Church, Herbert's youngest brother, had teamed up with relatives; others, like H.B. Jameson, whose family was later well known in Alberta ranching circles, were employed by large outfits like the Quorn.

Henry McGusty was an Old Colonial, and when he and Polyphemus, his one-eyed horse, ambled through the foothills, they camped with several Hollesley Bay graduates. These young men were "going on famously" and had obviously benefited from their two years in Suffolk. McGusty, in contrast, only toyed with ranching, and on returning to England was mildly critical of the Hollesley Bay College.[20] He conceded that it had given him a general knowledge of agriculture and stock raising but complained that it had not given him a detailed understanding of western ranching. McGusty's view may have been shared by others, though as Robert Johnson noted after reading McGusty's book, the ex-Rugbeian had not been the most conscientious of students at Hollesley Bay.[21] Besides, the college offered a broad programme and sought to prepare those destined for the high veldt and the outback as well as those destined for the prairie West; thus, whatever the college lacked in depth it more than made up for in breadth. The success rate at Hollesley Bay was, in any case, very high, and few Old Colonials failed to "make good" in the Canadian West. Only one succumbed to the temptations of Cannington Manor, and only one, the Honourable Mountstuart Elphinstone, failed to appreciate and adapt to local conditions.

Elphinstone, younger son of the 15th Earl of Elphinstone, a director of the Canada North West Land Company, was a student at the Colonial College from 1888 to 1890. On graduating, he acquired 9,000 acres of land near Virden, Manitoba. There he erected a large stone residence ("a sort of palace," a visitor called it) and endeavoured to establish two tenant farms. It was not a successful venture — few tenanted farms in western Canada were — and the young Scottish aristocrat was forced to abandon it in the late nineties. He then tried his hand in the Klondike gold fields, was unsuccessful, and returned to Britain.[22] Yet even the Honourable Monty, remembered in the Virden area as a "classic remittance man," was not an out-and-out failure. In the early 1900s, he embarked on a new career as one of the directors of British Columbia Fruit Lands Ltd., a development company which owned and managed several successful ranches in British Columbia.

The programme at Hollesley Bay was described by the *Army and Navy Gazette* as being "pre-eminently good." The *Field* declared that "it is difficult to put too high a value on the training boys receive at the Colonial College."[23] The commendations were well deserved, and at the turn of the century there was every indication that the Colonial College would enjoy many more years of success. Such was not the case. Johnson died at the age of sixty-five in 1901, and soon after, the college began to flounder. The board of governors, made up of Johnson's relatives and friends, lacked the founder's energy, vision, and financial skills, and in 1905 the college was forced to close. The following year the estate was put up for auction and the Central Body for London acquired it at a reported cost of almost £36,000 ($180,000). Renamed the Hollesley Bay Farm Colony, it was used to accommodate and retrain hundreds of destitute London working men who, after being introduced to rural industries, were resettled with their families on farms in East Anglia.[24]

The loss of the Colonial College was keenly felt, particularly since public school emigration increased annually in the early 1900s. However, the loss was alleviated to some extent when the Royal Agricultural College at Cirencester, near Gloucester, inaugurated a special six-month programme for prospective colonists. Several privately endowed training centres, which catered exclusively to English public school boys, were also established in the Dominion during the Edwardian years. Of these centres, the most notable were the Berkhamsted School Farm and the Bradfield College Ranch. Both establishments offered young emigrants a practical introduction to western Canadian life and so helped to fill the void left ten years earlier when St. John's Collegiate Farm closed.

Berkhamsted School Farm was conceived following a tour the Reverend Dr. T.C. Fry, headmaster of Berkhamsted School, Hertfordshire, made with the British Association in 1901. The association, which was comprised of scholars and educators, had come to America to study educational systems and teaching techniques. After visiting schools and universities in the United States and eastern Canada, the group had swung through the Canadian West. There Dr. Fry encountered a number of public school Old Boys who had failed to "make good." Fry was disappointed and more than a little puzzled. How was it, he wondered, that healthy young men from good families and good schools had failed to succeed in a land of unlimited opportunities? Why were they apparently unable to compete with less affluent, less educated men? The doctor concluded that the youths had failed simply because they had plunged prematurely into their new careers. The youths needed to be introduced gradually to western life; they required guidance, on-the-job training, and a lifeline to the Old Country. To provide these services for Old Berkhamstedians, Fry acquired a 1,200-acre farm four miles from Red Deer in 1902.[25]

Dr. Fry purchased the property with his own funds. He also used his own money to build the two-storey frame house which was situated on a small bluff overlooking the property. The house was a large, box-like structure—functional but not fancy. On the first floor were a drawing room, a dining room, a kitchen, a pantry, and a smoking-room-cum-library, stocked with books and periodicals concerning agriculture and decorated with steel engravings of the Hertfordshire school. Upstairs were staff quarters, lockers, and cubicles for a dozen students. Outbuildings included a barn, a stable, and a windmill which was used to draw water, pulp root crops, and saw wood.

The farm school accepted Old Berkhamstedians eighteen years of age and over. The students were offered a two-year course and were charged £100, inclusive of room and board. The youths were expected to develop initiative and independence, and those who did so were entitled to a small monthly wage during their second year at the farm. It was a reasonable arrangement, and Fry had no trouble in attracting trainees. He did, however, have some problems with the staff. Since the doctor was required to spend most of his time in England, the Berkhamsted Farm School was conducted by a resident manager. The first manager, Fry's son, Basil, had little interest in the position and left within a few months to pursue a career in international politics. The second manager was the brother of a master at Berkhamsted School and the cousin of the doctor's wife. Although he had been in Canada for several years, the second manager had little experience with prairie farming; he was also, some of the trainees thought, too much of a martinet. The third manager, who was appointed in 1903, was recruited from among the trainees but being young and inexperienced, he was not long at the helm. Fortunately, the fourth manager, an American farmer, was successful. He and his wife (who served as matron, head cook, and mother-confessor) put the school farm on a profitable footing. More important, they made sure that the trainees spent their time profitably. Reveille sounded early every day except Sunday. After a hearty breakfast, the youths were divided into teams and despatched to work—some to the wheat fields, some to the dairy, others to the vegetable garden. On Dr. Fry's behalf, the new manager also purchased one hundred head of cattle and half as many pigs. They, too, formed part of the Berkhamsted School Farm curriculum.

Dr. Fry's training centre was regarded highly in England. The *Morning Post* (4 November 1904) thought it was a bold scheme and hoped that other public schools would follow the doctor's lead. Harry Whates of the London *Standard* was similarly impressed and, after a visit to the farm in 1905, described it as an admirable experiment "in colonisation as well as education." He also claimed that Dr. Fry's establishment had saved many a young English gentleman from ruin. "I met with more than one youth of the well-to-do classes who, for want of just such help as he would have got at Berkhamsted Farm, [might have] lost heart because of life in the West and gone to the bad." The school farm, he reported, allowed youths to be "initiated gently and gradually into the harsh realities of frontier life." Even though they were thousands of miles from home, the students were still "under the glamour of school traditions"; they still enjoyed the camaraderie of old school chums and still benefited from "wholesome" Old Country "influences." The boys of Berkhamsted School Farm, Whates declared, were in no danger of "slipping down to the ne'er-do-well plane of life."[26]

Neighbouring farmers, who put little store in glamorous school traditions, were less impressed, and some referred derisively to Fry's venture as "the baby farm." Nevertheless, once the managerial problems had been resolved, even the most cynical of observers had to admit that the operation was well run and well intentioned. They conceded, too, that the young emigrants did develop into reasonably competent farmers, particularly as Old Berkhamstedians annually walked away with prizes at the local agricultural fairs. Moreover, as Fry hoped and Whates noted, the boys from the "baby farm" never did go to "the bad." George R. Pearkes, who won a Victoria Cross at Passchendaele and later served as minister of defence and lieutenant governor of British Columbia, was one of many Old Berkhamstedians who enjoyed very distinguished careers in the Dominion.[27]

Bradfield College Ranch, twenty-one miles south of Calgary, also functioned as a training and reception centre for English public school boys. But it was as symbolic as it was utilitarian. The ranch was a visible expression of public school enterprise: it was designed to show that new chums from old schools could play a useful and honourable role in the Canadian West. This nobly conceived showplace was established by the Reverend Dr. Herbert Branston Gray, warden and headmaster of Bradfield College, Berkshire.[28] Gray was a man of many talents. He was an Anglican divine, widely known and respected for his liberal theological views; he was a social reformer, actively involved with the Shaftesbury Homes and other rescue missions; he was an innovative educator, who deserves to be ranked with Thomas Arnold and Edward Thring as a key figure in the development of the English public school.

Unlike many of his colleagues, Gray believed that the public schools placed too much emphasis on scholastic achievement. He especially lamented the emphasis that was placed on the classics and the lack of attention that was paid to the sciences; and, while he upheld athletic training, he believed that equal attention should be paid to metalwork, carpentry, and other manual skills. Many public school boys, he said, were, or could become, gifted tradesmen or artisans; yet because they were unsuccessful classicists they were branded as "failures." Youths so branded were then sent off to the colonies. Was it to be wondered that the youths, lacking both confidence and suitable training, subsequently failed there? Gray often put the question to his colleagues in England. He put the same question to acquaintances in Canada when he visited with members of the

British Association in 1909. Most of the public school emigrants whom Canadians dismissed as "failures," he said, were simply boys who had not received sufficient encouragement and recognition at school. He conceded that a few bad apples may have found their way into the proverbial barrel but insisted that the Tom Browns who came to the Dominion were by no means an undesirable lot.[29] To demonstrate the fact, and to put some of his ideas into practice, Gray purchased with his own funds the 2,500-acre Melrose Ranch, near Millarville, in the autumn of 1909. He rechristened it the Bradfield College Ranch and instituted on it a programme that was designed not only to train young settlers, but also to rehabilitate the unfavourable image of the gentleman emigrant.

Gray chose property in southern Alberta, rather than in Manitoba or Saskatchewan, because ranching was so popular with public school alumni. He chose the Melrose spread because of the ranch house. It was a handsome, beautifully proportioned building, two-and-one-half storeys high, with tall balconies and broad verandahs. It was large enough to accommodate a salaried manager, a full-time housekeeper, and upwards of twenty "ranch pupils." The pupils were selected from senior students who had completed the agricultural and engineering courses which Gray had instituted in his school in Berkshire. The young men, all of whom were adjudged to have been of "solid character," were charged £50 ($200) per annum and were expected to undergo two years' training before setting out on their own. As was the case at Berkhamsted Farm School to the north, Gray's pupils were able to recover a portion of their fees by assisting with household chores and other duties. During the first year they received $10 a month; during the second year their wages were doubled.

Fortunately, Dr. Gray did not experience any managerial problems, though one of his housekeepers left after being subjected to the repeated pranks of high-spirited pupils. For the most part, though, the youths were well behaved and operations proceeded smoothly. Working days at the ranch began with morning prayers and ended with "God Save the King." Between times, the pupils were kept busy at the creamery, in the vegetable

garden, in the carpentry shops, or out on the range, where Gray
ran 300 head of beef cattle, several dozen horses, and over 200
Angora goats. The ranch also included a large flock of Buff
Orpington hens, a few geese, and half a dozen pigs, so there was
never any shortage of work for the pupils to do. But neither was
there any shortage of entertainment, for Gray's colonists were
very popular in the district. They were especially popular with
the established ranchers, many of whom were still fighting a
rear-guard action against the sod-busters. The older cattlemen
regarded the boys as valuable recruits and allies and so included
the youths in their hunting parties and racing meets.[30] The
youths were also popular with Canadian and American farmers,
who were impressed by their industry. The boys were consequently included in the local baseball league and were invited to
community box-lunch picnics. The Bradfield boys reciprocated
the kindnesses extended to them by holding some of the most
memorable bachelor balls in the Millarville area.

"Dr. Gray's faith in the soundness of his school," a colleague
recalled, "was unbounded; he went into it with the ardour of a
pioneer."[31] He did indeed, for he invested a great deal of energy
and money in the ranch. The strain of travelling between Berkshire and Alberta, however, proved too much for him, and in
1910, for reasons of health, he resigned as headmaster of Bradfield College. His retirement was a blow to the college, but a
boon to the college ranch, for Gray and his wife were then able
to spend several months each year in Alberta. They also spent
time in British Columbia where the doctor, though nominally
retired, undertook a great many new responsibilities: he
preached at Christ Church cathedral in Victoria, catalogued
and reorganized the provincial legislative library, served as travelling secretary to a B.C. Government commission on taxation,
wrote the provincial budget speech of 1912, and served as con-
sultant to the newly established University of British Columbia
in Vancouver. The Bradfield College Ranch, nevertheless, remained his chief interest, and until he returned to England in
1914, he devoted as much time to it as possible.

Unquestionably, Doctors Fry and Gray did provide a valuable service to gentlemen emigrants. To a certain extent they

also helped to redeem the reputation of the Old School Tie in western Canada during the Edwardian years. But the institutions they founded catered only to students from Bradfield and Berkhamsted. Both schools were relatively small, and between them they sent less than one hundred emigrants to the Alberta training centres. By the turn of the century, there were almost one hundred public schools in Britain, and students from each were migrating to the Dominion. How, then, were Etonians, Harrovians, Wykemists, Salopians, and the alumni of the other public schools to be introduced to Canadian life? This question troubled the Headmasters' Conference, and they hoped to resolve the problem with the Public Schools' Emigration League.

The Headmasters' Conference (HMC) had been concerned about gentlemen emigrants since its founding in 1869. The headmasters began by being concerned with the emigrants' welfare, but towards the turn of the century they became more concerned with the emigrants' reputations. They feared that scapegraces were being sent willy-nilly to the colonies, and that such emigrants were bringing the whole public school system into disrepute. The problems that attended the public school man abroad were raised periodically at the annual meetings of the HMC, but it was not until 1906, after several disquieting reports on public school failures had appeared in the British press, that the headmasters decided to take some sort of positive action. They were in the midst of formulating their plans at Malvern College when, fortuitously, they were contacted by the British Public Schools Association of Canada (BPSAC).

Established in 1904, the BPSAC was composed of successful Old Boys from a number of English schools. It was based in Montreal and had chapters in Halifax, Toronto, Winnipeg, Saskatoon, Calgary, Vancouver and Victoria. The association had been formed in order to attract emigrants with capital and culture, to smooth the way for emigrant schoolboys, and to combat the unfavourable image of the remittance man in the Dominion. Accordingly, they approached the headmasters with a simple but attractive proposition: if the HMC would help to vet emigrants in the Old Country, the BPSAC would help the emigrants find suitable positions on the other side of the pond. In addition, the association offered to provide newcomers with social introductions, so that young gentlemen "might find themselves in a position to mix in good company in Canada." The HMC received the offer enthusiastically and the following year (1907) formally launched the Public Schools Emigration League (PSEL).[32]

The purpose of the league was to provide "information, guidance, and protection" to emigrants from "the Public Secondary Schools of the United Kingdom." "Every other branch of emigration has been specialised," PSEL brochures stated, "and many associations have been formed to direct and assist the poorer classes of emigrants; but hitherto no organised effort has been made on behalf of boys of the upper and middle classes who, by choice or necessity, will find their life's work in the new countries within the British Empire." To provide for these boys, the HMC engaged a full-time secretary and opened an office in London. Youths who applied to the office and who wished to emigrate under the league's auspices were first interviewed by the PSEL secretary. Next, they were required to provide transcripts of their school records, a character reference from their headmaster, and a testimonial from their clergyman. If the documents were in order, and if the interview had been successful, the youths were deemed to be "fit and worthy representatives" of their schools, their country, and the PSEL.[33]

The league did not provide its members with financial assistance; in fact, youths who registered with the PSEL were charged a nominal fee, and because of the fee the league did not qualify for the grants that the Canadian government normally gave to non-profit emigration societies. Ottawa nevertheless looked favourably upon the league and assisted it in a number of ways. The Department of the Interior, for example, along with the Grand Trunk Railway and the CPR, helped with the publication of a collection of essays entitled *The Schoolboy in Canada* (1914). The book was distributed free of charge to HMC members and to PSEL emigrants. One of the essays, by schoolmaster Cyril FitzGerald, discussed the history and resources of the Dominion. Another essay, by J. Obed Smith, a federal immigration officer, dealt with opportunities in Canada. Smith's essay, which was inspirational in tone, also dealt with gentlemen emigrants' reputations and warned readers against inappropriate attitudes and behaviour. Other essays in the book were written by the agents general of the nine provinces. All referred to the Dominion's economic growth and each drew attention to the particular advantages the provinces offered to British public school boys.

The Schoolboy in Canada was a useful reference book. More useful were the special training courses which were made available to PSEL members at the Royal Agricultural College and at the Honourable Rupert Guinness's farm in Woking, Surrey. With the assistance of the Nova Scotia government, arrangements were also made to train PSEL members on the farms owned by Guinness in Pictou County. Other arrangements were made with Alberta's Department of Agriculture, which agreed to provide places for HMC-approved youths at the High River Agricultural College, and with the government of Ontario, which supplied the league with the names of provincial farmers who were willing to hire newly arrived gentlemen.[34]

Approximately 300 boys availed themselves of the PSEL's services between 1907 and 1914. Before leaving Britain, these young emigrants were provided with certified letters of introduction from the league secretary, W.A. Evans. The letters were brief but to the point:

> Dear Sir,
>
> The bearer, Mr. [Thomas Brown] of [White Horse Vale, Berks.] was at [Greyfriar's] School from 19— to 19—, leaving it in the [Sixth] Form [Modern] Side, with a [sterling] character.
>
> He has since been employed [as a student at the Hon. R. Guinness's Emigrants' Training Farm] and is going to [Alberta] with a view of [ranching].
>
> My Committee would be greatly obliged to you if you could assist him not only in attaining this object, but with social introductions at [Calgary] and its neighbourhood.
>
> I am, dear Sir,
Yours faithfully,
London Secretary
Public Schools Emigration League[35]

Prior to their departure, the youths were also provided with a list of contacts (or "friends," as they were termed) in Canada. Unfortunately, the lists have not survived, and in HMC records the friends are simply referred to as "prominent men," "men of affairs," or "men of engrossing engagements." Most of the contacts, however, were supplied by the league's advisory committee. The chairman of that committee was Lord Strathcona, Canada's high commissioner and one of the Dominion's wealthiest men. Another member of the committee was George (later Sir George) Parkin, formerly principal of Upper Canada College in Toronto (Canada's leading "public" school) and organizing secretary of the Rhodes Trust. A third member of the committee was the Honourable T.A. Brassey. His father, the 1st Baron Brassey, was owner of the "Sunbeam" farms, which were among the largest farms in Saskatchewan. Brassey, Parkin, and Strathcona shared their duties with a dozen other prominent, influential men. These men were valuable patrons, to say the least, and the Tom Browns who came to Canada with their blessings must have been very well connected indeed.

The Public Schools Emigration League eventually expanded its operations to New Zealand, South Africa, and Australia, but until the First World War Canada remained its special focus. Even so, its work was not extensively publicized in the Dominion, and consequently it was never as well known as the Barnardo Homes or the other philanthropic immigration societies. But among the educated classes, the PSEL was known and respected, and each year the league gained strength. As league members established themselves in the country, new friends were added, new districts were covered, and new opportunities opened. By the end of the Edwardian era, the PSEL had supporters in all walks of Canadian life and had laid out an intricate Old Boy network which extended from Halifax to Victoria.

CHAPTER XI

PRO PATRIA

When the Earl of Dundonald was invited to a conference on emigration held at the Royal Colonial Institute in 1910, he spoke at length on the importance of the British public schools and the schoolboy emigrant. He said that the schools would have to adjust their curricula and train young men who would succeed in the Dominion. The earl, an Old Etonian, was not so much concerned with the reputations of the schools in Canada; rather, the former commanding officer of the Canadian militia was more concerned for the welfare of the Empire. The future of the Empire, he said, lay in the hands of the young men who were embarking upon careers in Canada and the other dominions. It was therefore important that the young men be strong, capable, conscientious colonists. The representatives of the Public Schools Emigration League who were in attendance heartily endorsed Lord Dundonald's remarks. So, too, did Canadian immigration officials who were at the meeting, and not long after the conference, an Ontario writer expressed the general sentiments of the group. "The emigrant," he wrote, "is the real custodian of the Empire's future, the living epistle of the only political religion that can preserve British unity throughout the world. By emigration the Empire is made. . . . By taking heed of emigration . . . the Empire may renew its youth." [1]

Imperial enthusiasms were at their height during the Edwardian years, and this enthusiasm gave the relationship between the Empire and the emigrant new importance. As Dr. H. B. Gray put it in 1909, in a speech dealing with public schoolboys in Canada: "The welfare of our young men and the interests of the Empire... cannot be treated apart: they are parts of one organic whole."[2] Yet although the rhetoric of empire was particularly striking during the years immediately preceding the Great War, imperialism and immigration had gone hand in hand since the 1870s. In fact, from that time onwards the spirit of empire pervaded all aspects of upper-class emigration and settlement. The same spirit excited both the British gentlemen and the English-Canadian and, next to language, was the most important factor in uniting the emigrant and his host in the Dominion. Reverence for empire also helped to redeem and enhance the image of the gentleman emigrant in Edwardian Canada. Ironically, though, it was empire—specifically, the Empire's Great War—that marked the end of the gentleman emigrant in Canada.

The half-pay officers who came to British North America after the Napoleonic Wars did not regard themselves as "imperial emigrants," although assuredly their presence in the colonies helped to maintain the imperial link. Similarly, the officers and gentlemen who came to British Columbia and to Canada West after the Crimean War were not regarded as "emissaries of empire," even though they too helped to keep the colonies within the imperial fold. The middle decades of the century were characterized by "Little Englanderism," by laissez-faire, and by indifference towards formal empire. Many British politicians regarded the colonies as expensive millstones and believed that with the advent of responsible government, the colonies would inevitably develop separately and independently of the Mother Country. Many officials in Whitehall and Westminster felt, in fact, that the British North American colonies would go the way of the United States or would, at the very least, be absorbed by the republic. But with the dawning of the "New Imperialism," indifference gave way to interest, and those who settled in the colonies or were about to settle in the colonies were regarded in a new, rather heroic light. The colonists came to be regarded as "empire builders," and prospective emigrants were hailed as "imperial crusaders."

The supernumerary gentlemen from the public schools were particularly suited for the imperial crusade. They had been raised by imperially minded headmasters like J.E.C. Welldon, of Harrow, and H.W. Moss, of Shrewsbury; they had been taught that they were "citizens of the greatest empire under heaven"; they had been inspired "with faith in the divinely ordered mission of their country and race."[3] They had been taught to appreciate tradition, to endure physical hardship and discomfort, to value teamwork and fair play. They had, in short, been imbued with the "public school spirit," a spirit that, one historian has noted, "became one of the most potent of the imperial elixirs."[4]

Major General Feilding had drunk of this elixir, and he was among the first to inspire young gentlemen emigrants with the idea of empire building. Feilding even regarded elite settlements like Cannington Manor as vital strands in the strong but silken cord that united the far-flung provinces of Greater Britain. Robert Johnson, the founder of the Hollesley Bay Colonial College, shared some of Feilding's ideas and enthusiasms. "The mission of Old Colonials," he said, was "to carry forward the flag of the great mother of Nations, to sustain her good name the world over, to open up new lands, to open new markets, to create new industries...."[5] But Johnson was also a keen advocate of imperial federation; like Cecil Rhodes, he dreamed of a federation of Anglo-Saxon peoples which would include not only Great Britain, British India, and the white settlement colonies but also the United States of America. Johnson's dream found expression in the Colonial College flag, a curious, crowded, multi-coloured banner which incorporated the stars and stripes as well as the armorial bearings of Great Britain, Canada, Australia, and the Cape Colony. His dream of an alliance of English-speaking peoples was expressed in the lectures and addresses he gave to the young men at Hollesley Bay. "Students of the Colonial College! Colonials!" he exhorted on one occasion,

> It will rest with you, the men of the rising generation, to decide whether this great and beneficent empire shall be dismembered

and destroyed, or sustained and developed. Happy indeed are
the youth of this nineteenth century! Possibilities open out before them which to their ancestors would have appeared but as
idle dreams of an enthusiast! The alliance of the English-
speaking peoples will be one step more towards the realization
of the goal foreshadowed by the most prophetic poet of our
time [Tennyson]:

"When the war drums throb no longer and the battle flags are
     furled
In the Parliament of man, the Federation of the world!"

Johnson hoped that the young men who were bound for
Canadian ranches, South African mines, and Australian sheep
stations would help implant this dream on the frontiers of the
Empire. He hoped, too, that once the young men had established themselves successfully in their new careers, they
would promote the idea of federation in the chambers of colonial legislatures around the world.[6]

Few Canadians were as keen as Johnson on a federation that
would include the United States, for Canada had been fighting
America's "manifest destiny" since the eighteenth century. However, many Canadians—George Parkin among them—were keen
on the idea of imperial federation. Others, while not committed
to a federated empire, were nonetheless excited by the imperial
idea. They felt that the Dominion's best hope for avoiding
annexation by the United States lay in the strengthening of the
ties that bound Canada with the Empire. They also felt that the
Dominion would have a more significant place on the world
stage if it remained under the imperial banner. Thus Canadian
imperialists were well-disposed towards young, imperially
minded British emigrants—on condition, of course, that the
emigrants were not supercilious and that they recognized
Canadians as equal partners in the imperial crusade. Similarly,
imperial enthusiasts in Canada looked favourably upon the
institutions and organizations which facilitated the settlement of
patriotic young Britons in the Dominion. The Berkhamsted
School Farm was one of these institutions. Enthusiasts said that
it gave "actuality to talk of Empire" and represented "a strong
bond of imperial union." The Bradfield College Ranch, which

Dr. Gray described as his "humble contribution to the cause of empire" was also highly regarded by English-Canadians. The Public Schools Emigration League—described by Parkin as "an important means of distributing the energies of young Englishmen to the different points in the Empire where they are most needed"—was regarded favourably as well.[7]

Energetic young Englishmen were particularly welcome in western Canada, where nativism, a kind of xenophobia inextricably bound up with Canadian imperialism, was most pronounced. Nativism became virulent in the West in the late 1890s, when the Liberal government launched its epic campaign for immigrants from central and eastern Europe and the United States. Clifford Sifton, the minister responsible for the campaign, believed that immigrants from the steppes of Russia, the Ukraine, and Austria-Hungary would be ideally suited for the western prairies. He also looked upon Americans who had some capital and some experience in dry-land farming as valuable settlers for the West. Many English-speaking Canadians were not convinced. Critics charged that Sifton's "stalwart peasants in sheepskin coats" were sullen, slovenly, and immoral. The impoverished, illiterate immigrants, they said, could never be assimilated properly into English-Canadian culture. As for the Americans, critics charged that they had little respect for monarchical institutions or the Canadian way of life. Overlooking the fact that approximately half of the immigrants from the United States were in fact returning Canadians, critics claimed that the "American invasion of the West" would inevitably result in the Dominion's being swallowed up by the insatiable republic.[8]

Dr. Gray of Bradfield was haunted by the same spectre. He looked, as he told his colleagues at a meeting of the Headmasters' Conference in 1909, "with unfeigned concern... upon the vast tide of foreign [i.e. European] immigration which [was] pouring into the Canadian prairies." If these immigrants did not displace English-speaking settlers, they would at the very least undermine the close relationships which had developed between Canada and the other members of the Empire. In urging his colleagues to support the work of the PSEL, the doctor also warned of the consequences of American settlement in Canada.

> They [Americans] are absorbing land and trade, and flinging giant tentacles monthly, weekly, daily, over the corpus of Western Canada. I yield to no one in my admiration of the vivid life and fiery spirit of progress of the American people; but I hold a humble brief for the British Empire, and I ask in all seriousness of the headmasters of this conference: in fifty years, in twenty years, will the flag flying over the Government Offices of Ottawa be the Union Jack or the Stars and Stripes?[9]

Thousands of miles away in British Columbia, Clive Phillipps-Wolley, an ardent supporter of imperial immigration, was asking similar questions. Would Canadians stand by and see the Dominion lost to foreigners and republicans? The reply which he, Dr. Gray, and other imperial enthusiasts received from their counterparts across Canada was encouraging. "One city-bred Englishman, if properly selected and trained," Parkin said, "[was] worth more to western Canada than all the Doukhobors put together."[10] Even the outlandish remittance man, said historian C.M. McInnis, speaking for the Alberta cattlemen, was better than "the off-scourings of Eastern European peasantry, with their slave mentality and their traditions of oppression." The humourist, Stephen Leacock, Magistrate George T. Denison of Toronto, and many other influential Canadians added to the chorus, by voicing their fears of American commercialism, continentalism, and lawlessness.[11]

And so it was that nativism and imperial sentiment diffused much of the hostility that had been directed towards English remittance men and public school boys. These were the sentiments that led nationalists like Leacock and Denison to encourage the immigration of British gentlemen in Canada. These same sentiments also found frequent expression in the English-Canadian press during the Edwardian years and in much of the popular literature of the period. A ballad by R.J.C. Stead, the Ontario-born writer who later served as an official with the Canadian government's Department of Immigration and Colonization, provides a good example of this kind of literature. "The Son of Marquis Noddle" appeared in a collection of Stead's verse entitled, appropriately, *The Empire Builders* (1908). The ballad began:

He is brand-new out from England, and he
    thinks he knows it all—
  (There's a bloomin' bit o' goggle in his eye)
The "colonial" that crosses him is going to get
    a fall—
  (There's a seven-pound revolver on his thigh).
He's a son of Marquis Noddle, he's a nephew of
    an earl,
In the social swim of England he has got 'em all
    awhirl,
He's as confident as Caesar and as pretty as a
    girl—
Oh, he's out in deadly earnest, do or die.

But by the end of the ballad, ten stanzas later, it is clear that this English emigrant, who appeared so effete and cocky is, in fact, the stuff of which great empires are made:

In a dozen years you'll find him with a section
    of his own,
  (He had to learn his lesson at the start)
With a happy wife and children he is trying to
    atone—
  (For he loves the country now with all his
    heart).
He's a son of dear old England, he's a hero, he's
    a brick;
He's the kind you may annihilate but you can
    never lick,
For he played and lost, and played and lost, and
    stayed and took the trick;
In a world of men he'll play a manly part.

Harry Whates, of the London *Standard*, said in 1906 that gentlemen emigrants were fulfilling their imperial obligations and were upholding "good traditions" in government, society, and religion by the simple act of settling in Canada and working diligently at their holdings. Mrs. Traill had said much the same thing three-quarters of a century earlier, when she sang the praises of the half-pay officers who were busy founding "peaceful villages" and "pleasant homesteads" in the backwoods.[12] But there was more to empire building than promoting agriculture and settlement. The Empire required the sword, as well as the ploughshare. Yet here, too, the gentleman emigrant could—indeed, did—play an important part. Most of the emigrants were born into a warrior class, and the martial skills they inherited were often required in the New World. Their willingness to provide these skills and services was demonstrated in 1837, when men like Samuel Strickland had dashed out of the backwoods in order to oppose the forces of "ruffianism and radicalism." Their willingness to defend the colonies was demonstrated again three decades later, when young militiamen like John Gwynn Swain had been eager to have "a go" at the Fenians who were threatening to invade Canada. Their willingness to fight for Queen and Country was also demonstrated in 1885, when newly settled ranchers like Robert Newbolt joined the Alberta Field Force during the North West Rebellion. Their eagerness to answer the call of empire and serve the new Dominion was shown yet again during the Boer War when great numbers of young Englishmen enlisted in Lord Strathcona's Horse, the Royal Canadian Regiment, and the other units that made up Canada's contingents to South Africa.[13] On each occasion the young emigrants acquitted themselves well, and even those who did not see action were accorded a hero's welcome when they returned to their offices, farms, and ranches.

To be sure, the young emigrants were not all driven by patriotism. Some enlisted for glamour, some in order to escape the drudgery of mundane jobs. Some unhappy mudpups and remittance men volunteered for overseas service in order to escape Canada without losing face. But judging from the emigrants' diaries and memoirs and from the letters written by Old Colonials who served with Canadian units in South Africa, it is apparent that many of the emigrants were indeed patriotically motivated. When they enlisted they were responding to a deeply engrained emotion. They were responding, as Phillipps-Wolley put it in his poem, "Strathcona's Cavaliers," to a "Voice" which beckoned from their very hearts.[14] A good number of the emigrants who rushed to recruiting depots at the outbreak of the First World War were responding to the same emotion and answering the same voice.

Referring to the young Englishmen who enlisted in 1914, Bob Edwards of the Calgary *Eye-Opener* is said to have remarked: "They may have been green, but they weren't yellow." Certainly the contributions and sacrifices the young men made during the Great War for Civilisation were recognized and appreciated by Canadians, and the erstwhile emigrants who resumed their careers in Canada after the war did so with a new kind of status. They were no longer regarded as greenhorn Englishmen or remittance men. They were no longer regarded as gentlemen emigrants. They were veterans.

But what price glory? As was the case during the South African war, British-born volunteers were substantially overrepresented in the Canadian Expeditionary Forces. The volunteers were not all from the gentlemen class of emigrants, but the gentlemen emigrants were well represented. Moreover, whereas many who enlisted in Canada subsequently transferred to British units, a considerable number continued to wear the Maple Leaf throughout the course of the war. The important point to consider, though, is the casualty rates among these young men. Overall, the casualty rates of World War I were substantially higher than those of the Boer War. For many of the volunteers, notably those who became commissioned officers, casualty rates were appallingly high; on some sectors of the western front the life expectancy of junior officers was a scant three months. Just how many of the young gentlemen lost their lives is unknown, since statistics are incomplete and in some cases inaccurate. But statistics in themselves cannot tell the story of the Great War and the gentleman emigrant. To appreciate something of the impact the war had on these men one has to turn the pages of the memorial books which are displayed in the chapels of the British public schools or study the honour rolls which hang in small churches like All Saints, Cannington Manor, or Christchurch, Millarville; one has to ponder the long lists of names engraved on the war memorial at Duncan, B.C. and the names inscribed on the statues, obelisks, and bronze tablets which are to be found in dozens of other small communities across Canada. Only then can one derive a sense of the war's impact.

The war most affected the young men who had emigrated

during the Edwardian years, since they were of military age. But in one way or another it also affected many of the gentlemen who had come to Canada during the Victorian years. Herbert Church, for example, was ranching at Big Creek, B.C. when the war broke out. He had resettled in British Columbia sixteen years earlier, after his brothers Dickie and Teddy drowned while attempting to cross the Athabaska River with a team of pack-horses. After their death, Herbert had not had the heart to stay on at the ranch which he had built with them; and though he had built a new life west of the Rockies, he was still haunted by his brothers' drowning. He consequently suffered from great anxiety when his eldest son enlisted in the navy. Happily, the son survived the war.

Edward ffolkes was fifty-two and living in Toronto when the war began. In the 1890s he had married one of Bishop Strachan's granddaughters and had moved to Ontario as manager of a company that manufactured farm machinery. He and his wife did not have any children, so ffolkes did not lose a son to the war. But he himself was active in war bond drives, and because so many men were overseas, he volunteered for duties that were normally undertaken by younger men. One of these duties involved patrolling the Humber River in west Toronto during the flood season. He was carrying out a patrol on 2 April 1916 when he noticed a party of linemen struggling with telephone wires which had fallen into the river. While assisting the linemen, ffolkes fell from his canoe and drowned.

William Baillie-Grohman was in his *schloss* in Austria when war was declared, and despite his Austrian heritage he was interned until 1918. However, his fellow sportsman, Warburton Pike, managed to get back to England shortly after hostilities began. Although he was fifty-three years old, "Pikey" volunteered for active service and was confident that he would be given command of one of the navy's new motor torpedo boats. His confidence rested on the fact that he had piloted his ketch, *Fleet-wing*, through hundreds of Pacific coast islands and had navigated thousands of miles of lakes and rivers in the far north. But the best the Admiralty could offer was a place with the coastal rescue service, and even that was denied to him by the medical board. Depressed, and physically worn out from many years of tramping over rough terrain, he was sent to a nursing home in Bournemouth. In a letter to a friend in British Columbia, Pike wrote that he found his confinement an intolerable strain. "I am afraid of my brain going permanently wrong if I don't get out."[15] He did get out. On 20 October 1915, he eluded his nurses and fled from the hospital under cover of darkness. He then committed suicide by stabbing himself in the heart and throwing himself into the sea.

Clive Phillipps-Wolley was also under great strain during the war, even though he received a knighthood for his services to the Navy League. As soon as war was declared, his only son was commissioned into the Royal Navy and drafted to H.M.S. *Hogue*. While patrolling off the Dutch coast on 22 September 1914, the *Hogue* was torpedoed by a German submarine. Young Phillipps-Wolley was the first Canadian officer in the British forces to be killed in action. He was acclaimed a hero, but such honours did little to console his father. To make matters worse, despite repeated applications to the army and navy, Sir Clive was denied active duty. He became increasingly embittered and depressed. "They have killed my only boy... and my oldest friends," he told an admirer in 1916. "I who was once a hot favourite for the amateur [boxing] championship (heavy weights) of England, have to stay here and rot slowly.... I am sixty-four in years but I am afraid I am an older man really. The last two years have told more than twenty should have done."[16] Two years later, Sir Clive died of a cerebral haemorrhage at his home near Duncan.

In an obituary article the Victoria *Daily Colonist* described Sir Clive as "a man of virile, rugged type." The Vancouver *World*, in an editorial written on 9 July 1918 to mark his death, said he belonged to "an older, less democratic, more rugged age." Neither the *Colonist* nor the *World* nor the Toronto *Globe* nor the many other newspapers in Canada that published Sir Edward Clive Oldnall Long Phillipps-Wolley's obituary thought they would see his type, or his age, again. And they did not.

Although many erstwhile gentlemen emigrants returned to Canada after the war, the attitudes and demeanour of most of them had altered considerably. They were more serious, more cynical than they had been in their Edwardian summer. Many were physically disabled. Few had the means or inclination to resume the rounds of hunt club suppers, shooting parties, and bachelor balls. It was just as well, for the country they returned to had also altered. It was more urbanized, more industrial. It was more democratic, more cohesive, more Canadian. The nation was also in the grip of post-war economic recession, which in itself precluded a revival of some of the institutions and activities enjoyed by previous generations of well-bred settlers.

Because of the changes brought about by the war, the Dominion was never again so attractive to the sporty, romantically inclined supernumerary gentleman. But, of course, after the war there were few such gentlemen to attract. In the first instance, the imperial spirit which had motivated and sustained so many Tom Browns during the Victorian and Edwardian years attenuated after 1919. Secondly, with the abolition of primogeniture in 1925, younger sons were able to stand as equals with respect to the family estate. More important, post-war economic exigencies in Britain forced the middle and upper classes to shed many of their prejudices regarding suitable careers for their sons. The reduced circumstances and altered attitudes of British gentlefolk prompted many of the changes that took place within the public school system during the inter-war years. Taking their cue from progressive headmasters like H.B. Gray of Bradfield and F.W. Sanderson at Oundle, the schools modernized and rationalized their curricula so as to allow public school graduates to compete for, and succeed in, a wide variety of occupations in Britain. These educational reforms removed a major "push" factor that had accounted for the exodus of public school alumni prior to 1914. Consequently, although British immigration to Canada resumed (albeit in a diminished way) in the mid-twenties, the gentleman emigrant was never again as distinctive or as prominent a part of the immigration flow.

As might be expected, the Great War affected the organizations and institutions that had catered to gentlemen emigrants. The Public Schools Emigration League shut down in 1914 and was not revived until 1920. It then became the Public Schools

Employment Bureau and thereafter devoted most of its energies to finding places for public school alumni in Britain. In the mid-1920s a "migration department" was added to the bureau, but it was a small department and was concerned mainly with assisting youths who wished to resettle in New Zealand and South Africa. The Berkhamsted School Farm closed its doors in 1914, after sending almost fifty of its Old Boys into the Canadian army. The Bradfield College Ranch also closed in 1914, and like the school farm, was never reopened. The Colonial College at Hollesley Bay changed hands a number of times before 1938, when it was acquired by His Majesty's Prison Commissioners. Since then, the estate, which had been established to train young gentlemen emigrants, has served as a borstal home and rehabilitation centre for juvenile offenders.

Lord Curzon once remarked that "the first thing an Englishman does in the outlying portions of the Empire is to make a race-course; the second, is to make a golf-course." [17] Although the former viceroy of India made the remark in jest, it nonetheless underscores a point that is often forgotten: namely, that the attitudes and activities of gentlemen emigrants in Canada were not especially unusual. There were turf clubs and race-courses in Calcutta, Cape Town, and Alexandria, just as there were in Cannington Manor, Walhachin, and Ashcroft. Just as emigrant gentlemen established university clubs, literary societies, and theatrical guilds in the backwoods and prairies so, too, did the officers and gentlemen who pitched up in the jungles and savannahs of Africa and Asia. The same rituals and formalities that ranchers in southern Alberta observed were observed by the tea planters of Ceylon. Similarly, sportsmen like Sir Clive Phillipps-Wolley, schoolboys like Edward ffolkes, half-pay officers like Dunbar Moodie, and remittance men like the fictitious Bertie Buzzard-Cholomondeley were scattered across the length and breadth of the Empire. The emigrants in Canada were but a battalion in a world-wide army, and indeed they were well aware of the fact. They were aware, too, that by importing the Anglican church and *The Times*, by clubbing together and dressing for dinner, by laying out cricket pitches and tennis courts, by holding "at homes" and hunt club suppers, by establishing cloistered, elite communities they were employing techniques used by British gentlefolk throughout the world. The techniques they employed were designed to keep up the expatriates' morale, to overawe the subject peoples, and to ensure a degree of order and comfort in strange and sometimes inhospitable environments. But a point the emigrants sometimes forgot—despite admonitions from William Stamer, Dr. Gray, and others—was that behaviour which was useful, often vital, in securing the Briton's position in the tropical dependencies was not always appropriate in the white settlement colonies. Their failure to appreciate this fact accounted for many of the difficulties that attended the progress of gentlemen emigrants in Canada.

Some of the gentlemen's difficulties also stemmed from their schooldays, for the education offered by the Victorian public schools had many shortcomings. It was idiosyncratic, archaic, and elitist; it was inordinately preoccupied with the classics and excessively devoted to athletics. Many of the schools allowed students to look "with the scorn of ignorance on manual training as being suitable only to the Helots or the Heathen"; many of the schools, as Dr. Gray lamented, failed to teach boys "any educational connection between mind and hand except how to wield the willow or kick the bladder."[18] Most schools—ancient or modern, endowed or proprietary—imbued their students with inflated notions of self-worth, a sense of nationalism which verged on arrogance, and unrealistically high expectations. These and other weaknesses of the elite education system often hampered the public school man's progress in Canada. On the other hand, the schools were above all character-building institutions, and without question their alumni did bring away moral and physical qualities which were beneficial in the Dominion. The public school men were physically fit, energetic, confident, and courageous. They were manly, muscular Christians who possessed a sense of duty to their friends, families, neighbours, and communities. It was also true, as in the cases of John Langton and the Uppingham emigrants, that traits which young gentlemen acquired in the schoolhouse could later show to good advantage in the backwoods cabin or prairie shack. By the same token, even though British gentlemen were often slow in acclimatizing themselves to conditions in Canada, most of them were nevertheless sensitive, intelligent men who ultimately learned to adjust their ideas and alter their demeanour in keeping with their new environment. Furthermore, whereas few British Old Boys succumbed completely to that individualistic, democratic, utilitarian spirit which supposedly characterized the North American frontier, most of the emigrants who remained in Canada developed attitudes and skills which enabled them to become successful settlers. This point even their critics acknowledged.[19]

The many gentlemen emigrants who did "make good" in Canada must be accounted nation builders, for individually and collectively they made significant contributions to the country. To assess their legacy in detail would require another study. But even a cursory review of some of their achievements indicates that they played a seminal role in the country's development. On the political front, for example, they provided the British North American colonies and the territories and provinces of the Dominion with a pool of articulate leaders who acknowledged public service as a duty. To be sure, their politics were usually conservative, and on occasion they appeared dogmatic, reactionary, and irrationally afraid of republicanism. Still, they represented stability, order, and respect for monarchical traditions, and their conservatism was a useful counterpoise to the liberal, radical, or demagogical ideas of their opponents. More important, most of the gentlemen who sat in Ottawa, in provincial legislatures, in municipal councils, and on local school boards were respected for their integrity and dependability. Even in the notoriously sordid world of Canadian politics, the gentlemen emigrants remained gentlemen.

Because of their temperament and training, gentlemen emigrants were not especially suited to commercial life; accordingly, few of them became plutocrats, industrial magnates, or captains of industry. Nevertheless, they contributed to the economy by providing the country with a corps of professionals, senior administrators, and white-collar employees. As in the example of James Seton Cockburn, these roles were not particularly glamorous or prestigious; they were, however, vitally important in turning the wheels of commerce and government. The emigrants also made substantial contributions in the fields of agriculture. In southern Ontario, for example, it was the half-pay officer who introduced high-quality seeds, superior breeds of livestock, and improved (mixed) farming techniques which ensured the long-term productivity of the soil.[20] Farther west, it was the gentleman emigrant who provided much of the money, the energy, and the enthusiasm necessary for developing the cattle-ranching industry in Alberta and horticulture in British Columbia. Elsewhere, gentlemen emigrants who possessed capital invested liberally in mining, in railways, and in a wide range of other primary and secondary industries. The emigrants were valuable, too, because they helped to attract British investments to the country. In fact, it was young men like John Gwynn Swain, with contacts in Scotland, and sportsmen like William Baillie-Grohman, with connections in London money markets, who were responsible for some of the three million dollars that British investors annually directed to Canada during the post-Confederation years.[21]

The mudpups also had an economic impact. Towards the end of the nineteenth century, those who were intent on justifying the premium racket claimed that farm pupils who "trained" in southern Ontario each brought, on average, £2,000 ($10,000) to the area.[22] This figure may have been inflated, though mudpups were definitely regarded as financial assets in many parts of Canada. When it was rumoured that an "agricultural academy" was to open on the giant Bell Farm at Indian Head in the mid-1880s an Assiniboia newspaper exclaimed: "The news is almost too good to be true." "How happy our farmers would be," the paper declared unabashedly on another occasion, "if they could only get hold of a pupil paying one hundred pounds premium and five dollars a week for his board."[23] Nor must we forget the thirsty, free-spending remittance men, for on occasion they, too, proved to be a financial blessing to small western communities.

On the cultural level, the emigrants' contributions were immense, for they introduced and nurtured a great many institutions and organizations that remain important elements in English-Canadian society. The Anglican church (which prior to 1955 was known as the Church of England in Canada) was often the first Old Country institution to be established in frontier communities, and in parts of Ontario and in much of western Canada, the gentleman emigrant was responsible for ensuring its development and growth. Once established, however, the English church provided succour and a spiritual focus for a cross section of the community, and as such it was never as aloof or as elitest as its parent in the Old Country. Moreover, because Church of England clergymen proved to be adaptable to local conditions and attuned to contemporary concerns, the emigrants' church developed deep roots in the Dominion. To this day the Anglican church occupies a pre-eminent place among religious groups in Canada.

Gentlemen emigrants and emigrant churchmen also left an indelible mark on Canadian education. The emigrants hailed from some of the leading schools in Britain, so it is not surprising that they were responsible for founding some of the most prestigious boys' schools in Canada. Upper Canada College, which opened in Toronto in 1829, and Bishop's College, Lennoxville (1836), a Quebec school once touted as "the Eton of Canada," are among the earliest and most respected of these institutions. Equally respected are Trinity College (1862) in Port Hope, Ontario, Bishop Ridley College (1889) in St. Catharines, and Lakefield College (1879), a school located adjacent to Samuel Strickland's property near Peterborough. In western Canada, the schools established by Anglican gentlemen include St. John's, Winnipeg (1866), University School, Victoria (1904), and the Vernon Preparatory School (1914), in the Okanagan Valley. These schools were modelled on the British public schools, though to their credit the Canadian academies have traditionally offered a broad curriculum which includes courses in modern science and commerce. Also to their credit, the Canadian private schools have never been as consciously elitist as their British models. Still, each of the private boarding schools was founded to develop the characters of Christian gentlemen, and in spite of the changes that have taken place in society since their founding, the schools have clung tenaciously to the spirit of Dr. Arnold and the philosophy of *mens sana in corpore sano.*

Dunbar Moodie's friend Tom Wilson had warned the Moodies that their "literary propensities" would bring them nothing but grief in Canada, and certainly their aesthetic sensibilities were often bruised during their first years in the country. "The sin of authorship meets with little toleration in a new country," Dunbar's wife complained. "Several persons of this class, finding few minds that could sympathize with them, and enter into literary pursuits, have yielded to despondency, or fallen victims to that insidious enemy of souls, *Canadian whisky.*"[24] More than once the Moodies yielded to despondency, but they steered clear of rye whisky, and despite their small audience they wrote prolifically. They were joint editors of the *Victoria Magazine* (1847–48) and, in company with Samuel Strickland and Mrs. Traill were among the mainstays of Canada's first successful literary journal, the *Literary Garland* (1838–51). Tiger Dunlop also contributed to this journal, and his contemporary, John Langton, wrote learned papers on silviculture and ethnology. These backwoods littérateurs and scholars provided the main fillip for the arts in eastern Canada, just as their liberally educated compatriots provided the impetus behind organizations such as the Ft. Macleod Literary and Historical Society (1884) and the Regina Literary and Musical Society (1885) in the prairie West. Across the Rockies, men like Clive Phillipps-Wolley helped promote popular literature on the Pacific slope. In fact, until the turn of the present century—and possibly later—educated Britons who had resettled in Canada were the country's most popular and successful writers.[25] And when the Canadian public was not reading works by the gentlemen emigrants, they were reading about them, for the novels of Ralph Connor, Harold Bindloss and others constituted a distinct, and decidedly popular, genre during the Edwardian years.

Many of the emigrants who nurtured the country's earliest intellectual societies helped launch the country's earliest athletic clubs, and a fair number of these clubs survive. Gentlemen still play cricket in Victoria's Beacon Hill Park, and on the grounds of Rideau Hall in Ottawa. Lawn tennis, introduced by Anglo-Indian officers in the late 1870s, still has devotees, while several Canadian rowing clubs, established by Oxbridge emigrants, command respect at Henley. Polo, alas, has all but disappeared, and most of the hunts are now drag-hunts, hardly the thing to have excited the likes of Clement Cornwall. But some of the Victorians' turf clubs survive, and there is no shortage of golf.

Gentlemen's havens such as the Union Club in Victoria and the Ranchmen's Club in Calgary, the Navy League, rod and gun clubs, the Masonic Lodge—these and sundry other organizations and institutions are legacies of the gentlemen emigrants in Canada. But the emigrants' influence is not confined to tangible, readily identifiable institutions and organizations. Their influence manifests itself in subtler ways. It is apparent in some of the regional accents in Canada, in the reserved nature of many English-speaking Canadians, in the conservative outlook which prevails in parts of the country. These characteristics are not, of course, solely attributable to the British gentlemen who settled in Canada; however, as Lindsey Russell, Canada's Deputy Minister of the Interior, realized almost a century ago, the emigrants were a contributing factor. In a letter written to the prime minister in 1883, concerning Military Colonization Company settlers like Robert Newbolt, Russell predicted that the gentlemen ranchers would do more than develop the rangelands of the North West Territory. They would also, he said, "have a good influence for refinement" and would "tend by their contribution to the 'breed' towards rounding off the coarser corners of the future western national type of Canadian."[26] And so they did, by implanting some of their attitudes, interests, and traditions on the unformed frontier. In fact, it was the presence of Newbolt and his Uppingham colleagues, and the presence of the Church brothers and Edward ffolkes, that, more than anything else, made the Canadian West appreciably different from the American West. By the same token, it was the presence of men like Samuel Strickland who helped make Ontario different from upstate New York, and men like John Clapperton and the Cornwall brothers who made British Columbia distinct from the state of Washington.

Indeed, although the Great War effectively marked the end of the gentleman emigrant in Canada, the style of life which the emigrants imported has proved to be remarkably enduring. *Maclean's*, "Canada's National Magazine," discovered this in the mid-1950s when it sent a reporter to Duncan in search of the longstockings. The longstockings were still there, clad in Norfolk jackets and sensible brogues; they were still reading the *Field* and *Horse and Hound;* they were still playing cricket and maintaining a way of life which the magazine's reporter imagined had been buried in 1914 and reinterred in 1939.[27] That generation of longstockings has now died, but their interests and cultural values have been passed on in a diluted but still recognizable form to their children and neighbours. There is, consequently, an atmosphere of gentility in some parts of the Cowichan Valley, just as there is a delicate but perceptible air of Old World refinement and culture on some of the Gulf Islands, in parts of the Okanagan valley, in the foothills of Alberta, and in parts of southern Ontario. In many of the small communities that were peopled by gentlemen emigrants there is (to paraphrase Rupert Brooke) Beauty yet to find, and Certainty, and Quiet kind. And while the village clocks do not stand at ten to three, there is honey still for tea.

Even though they clung to many of the attitudes that characterized their class in the Old Country, most of the emigrant gentlemen who settled in these communities managed to adapt to the demands of the New Land. But some of their compatriots were intractable fellows who, figuratively speaking, remained expatriates and exiles. In Canada, the reputation of the gentleman emigrant still derives largely from the Tom Browns—or, one should say, the Bertie Woosters—who, despite the efforts that were made on their behalf, remained unwilling or unable to take their place in the mainstream of Canadian society.

During his tour of Canada in the early 1900s, Rudyard Kipling discovered that these gentlemen—the inveterate remittance men—were a source of exasperation to many Canadians. His hosts regaled him with tales of the emigrants' idiosyncracies, their shortcomings, and their follies. He even heard the hoary tale of the fastidious gentleman who was found dying of thirst beside a river because he didn't have a cup. Kipling listened attentively and nodded understandingly but when asked to comment, replied that a country as large, as diverse, and as dynamic as Canada could easily accommodate such characters. Indeed, he maintained that the Dominion actually benefited from such emigrants. "Every new country," he said, "needs—vitally needs—one-half of one per cent of its population trained to die of thirst rather than drink out of their hands."[28]

Kipling may well have been right, for even the eccentric, inexpedient gentlemen emigrants enriched Canadian society. They added levity and variety to the Canadian frontier. They added a gentler tone and a softer hue to many backwoods and prairie communities. Certainly the Dominion would have been a harsher, less colourful, less interesting place without them.

NOTES

The following abbreviations have been used in these notes:

ACFPA (Anglo-Canadian Farm Pupil Association)

AHR *(Alberta Historical Review)*

BCHQ *(British Columbia Historial*

CHA (Canadian Historical Association)

CHR *(Canadian Historical Review)*

GAI (Glenbow-Alberta Institute)

HMC (Headmasters' Conference)

OAC (Ontario Agricultural College)

PABC (Provincial Archives of British Columbia)

RGS (Royal Geographical Society)

M/H USA (A.S. Morton manuscripts/A.E.M. Hewlett collection, University of Saskatchewan Archives)

INTRODUCTION

1. G. Kitson Clark, *The Making of Victorian England* (1973), p. 255.

2. Brian Gardner, *The Public Schools: An Historical Survey* (1973), and Jonathan Gathorne-Hardy, *The Public School Phenomenon* (1977), both provide good introductions to the British public school system.

3. Leslie Stephen, "Thoughts of an Outsider: Public Schools," *Cornhill Magazine* 27 (March 1873):283.

4. Michael S. Cross, "The Age of Gentility: The Formation of Aristocracy in the Ottawa Valley," CHA *Historical Papers* 1967, pp. 105–17.

5. Frank Musgrove, *The Migratory Elite* (1963), p. 19.

6. Brinley Thomas, *Migration and Economic Growth* (1954), pp. 59–63.

7. A detailed account of female emigration during the period is to be found in A. James Hammerton, *Emigrant Gentlewomen: Genteel Poverty and Female Emigration, 1830–1914* (1978).

I: PIONEER GENTLEMEN

1. The term "half-pay officer" may be considered a figurative expression, since in most instances an officer's pension was less than 50 per cent of his regular salary. On active service, Dunbar Moodie's pay and allowances would have been approximately £50 or £60 per annum. See Gwyn Harries-Jenkins, *The Army in Victorian Society* (1977), pp. 71–73, 89–91, on wages and half-pay officers.

2. Susanna Moodie, *Roughing It in the Bush* (1852; introduction to 3rd ed., 1854), p. xv.

3. Ibid., p. 244.

4. Ibid., pp. 87–88.

5. Catharine Parr Traill, *The Backwoods of Canada* (1836), p. 24.

6. Moodie, *Roughing It*, pp. xviii, 563.

7. Samuel Strickland, *Twenty-Seven Years in Canada West* (1853), vol. 1, p. 31.

8. W. H. Graham, *Tiger Dunlop* (1962), p. 116.

9. Patrick Shirreff, *A Tour Through North American* (1835), p. 123.

10. W. A. Langton, ed., *Early Days in Upper Canada* (1926), p. 22.

11. Ibid., pp.93–94.

12. Mrs. Moodie's sense of relief is most evident in her second book, *Life in the Clearings versus the Bush* (1853).

13. Audrey Y. Morris, *The Gentle Pioneers* (1973), pp. 167–209.

14. Langton, *Early Days*, p. 90.

15. Moodie, *Roughing It*, pp. xix, 34, 44–45, 247.

16. Langton, *Early Days*, p. 90.

17. Traill, *The Backwoods of Canada*, pp. 74, 105, 272.

18. Ibid., p. 271.

19. Anna Jameson, *Winter Studies and Summer Rambles in Canada* (1838), vol. 2, p. 133.

20. H.H. Langton, ed., *A Gentlewoman in Upper Canada* (1950), p. 154.

21. One gentleman who left Canada because of an unhappy spouse was the Reverend Isaac Fiddler. On returning to England in 1833 he ruefully advised his married readers that only those who had "dutiful and obedient wives, disposed like themselves to temporary difficulties and self-denials for ultimate and certain benefit" should contemplate resettling in the colony. Quoted in *Early Travellers in the Canadas, 1791–1867* (1955), ed. Gerald Craig, p. 95.

22. *Letters From Muskoka, by an Emigrant Lady* (1878), pp. 50, 186.

23. Gerald M. Craig, *Upper Canada: The Formative Years, 1784–1841* (1963), pp. 236–37.

24. S.R. Mealing, "The Enthusiams of John Graves Simcoe," CHA *Annual Report* 1958, p. 58; W.S. Shepperson, *British Emigration to North America: Projects and Opinions in the Early Victorian Period* (1957), p. 37.

25. *Canada in 1849; or the Emigrant Churchman* (1850), quoted in *The Great Migration* (1963), by Edwin C. Guillet, p. 40.

26. Paul W. Gates, "Official Encouragement to Immigration by the Province of Canada," *CHR* 15 (March 1934):30; Norman Macdonald, *Canada: Immigration and Colonization, 1841–1903* (1966), p. 53.

27. W.H.G. Kingston, *Western Wanderings,* (1856), vol. 2, p. 38.

28. Charles Good, "British Columbia and How I Got There," *Kingston's Magazine for Boys* 4 (1862), quoted in *Victoria: A History in Architecture* (1979), by Martin Seggar and Douglas Franklin, pp. 13–14.

II: GENTLEMEN ADVENTURERS

1. Margaret A. Ormsby, *British Columbia: a History* (1971), pp. 80, 85.

2. Ibid., pp. 100–101.

3. Willard E. Ireland, "Captain Walter Colquhoun Grant: Vancouver Island's First Independent Settler," *BCHQ* 17 (1953): 87–95.

4. Dorothy Blakey Smith, ed., *The Reminiscences of Doctor John Sebastian Helmcken* (1975), p. 290.

5. James E. Hendrickson, "Two Letters from Walter Colquhoun Grant," *BC Studies* 26 (Summer 1975):13.

6. Grant's first paper, "Description of Vancouver Island," appeared in the Royal Geographical Society *Journal,* 27 (1857); his second paper, "Remarks on Vancouver Island," was published in the RGS *Journal,* 31 (1861).

7. Ormsby, *British Columbia,* p. 187.

8. Details of Clapperton's adventures are taken from his journal and diary. John Thomas Wilson Clapperton (pseud. Artemus Ward), "Jottings from our first seven years in British Columbia, 1862–69," PABC, Victoria.

9. Ibid., p. 4.

10. Ibid, pp. 24–25.

11. R. Byron Johnson, *Very Far West Indeed* (1872), p. 46.

12. C.R. Maier, ed., "A Letter from New Westminster," *The Beaver,* Autum 1976, p. 44.

13. Johnson, *Very Far West Indeed,* pp. 195–96. Johnson's book contains a number of questionable tales and several characters who are clearly fictitious. The book was, however, one of the most popular accounts of the Cariboo. It went through no less than four editions in 1872 and into a fifth in 1873. A Dutch edition (1873) and at least two French editions were also published.

14. Matthew Macfie, a Congregationalist minister who arrived in Victoria in 1859, was one of those who criticized the governor's policies in making appointments. Macfie warned "gentlemen of education and breeding... without funds and trained to no particular employment" that they would have a hard time in British Columbia. Macfie, *Vancouver Island and British Columbia: Their History, Resources, and Prospects* (1865), pp. 406–7, 412–13, 495.

15. Margaret A. Ormsby, "Some Irish Figures in Colonial Days," *BCHQ* 14 (1950): 63–64, 70–71.

16. New Westminster *Mainland Guardian*, 14 July 1888.

17. Hester E. White, "John Carmichael Haynes," *BCHQ* 4 (1940): 196.

18. R.E. Gosnell, *A History of British Columbia* (1906), pp. 650–51, 694–95; Ormsby, "Some Irish Figures," pp. 76–78.

19. Edward Philip Johnson, "The Early Years of Ashcroft Manor," *BC Studies* 5 (Summer 1970):5.

20. Viscount Milton and W.B. Cheadle, *The North-West Passage by Land* (1865), p. 355. Jargon and colloquialisms presented problems for many British gentlemen. Recognizing this, the Reverend Mr. Macfie dealt with such terms as "on the make," "fizzled out," and "skedaddled" in *Vancouver Island and British Columbia*, p. 416.

21. M.B. Begbie to James Douglas, 25 April 1859, Colonial Correspondence, PABC, Victoria, quoted in "Interlude or Industry? Ranching in British Columbia, 1858–1885," by John S. Lutz, *B.C. Historical News* 13 (Summer 1980):4.

22. Johnson, "Early Years of Ashcroft Manor," pp. 6, 8–9.

23. Journal of Clement Francis Cornwall: The Story of the Coyote Hounds, 1868–1888, pp. 35–36, PABC, Victoria.

24. Dorothy Blakey Smith, ed., *Lady Franklin Visits the Pacific Northwest* (1974), p. 81.

III: SUPERNUMERARY GENTLEMEN

1. Donald Read, *England 1868–1914: The age of urban democracy* (1979), p. 235; F.M.L. Thompson, *English Landed Society in the Nineteenth Century* (1963), pp. 290, 303, 308–18.

2. T.W. Bamford, *Rise of the Public Schools* (1967), pp. 210–22.

3. W.J. Reader, *Professional Men* (1966), pp. 66–67, 192, 208.

4. For a witty but cogent view of the phenomenon see Michael Young, *The Rise of the Meritocracy* (1965), especially pp. 11–39.

5. Bamford, *Rise of the Public Schools*, pp. 18–36.

6. F. Musgrove, "Middle Class Education and Employment in the Nineteenth Century," *Economic History Review*, 2d. ser., 12 (1959):99–111.

7. Bamford, *Rise of the Public School*, p. 62; Walter E. Houghton, *The Victorian Frame of Mind, 1830–1870* (1975), pp. 141, 190. For a perceptive view of the problem see A.J. Meadows and W.H. Brock, "Topics Fit for Gentlemen: The Problem of Science in the Public School Curriculum," in *The Victorian Public School* (1975), eds. Brian Simon and Ian Bradley, pp. 95–114. J.A. Mangan's essay, "Athleticism: A Case Study of the Evolution of an Educational Ideology," published in the same volume, is also useful when considering the philosophy of the public schools and the advent of the supernumerary gentleman.

8. Bracebridge Hemyng, *Jack Harkaway at Oxford* (1872), p. 144.

9. S.H. Jeyes, "Our Gentlemanly Failures," *Fortnightly Review* 61 (1 March 1897):388.

10. Jacob Van Der Zee, *The British in Iowa* (1922), pp. 158–59.

11. T.H.S. Escott, *England: Its People, Polity, and Pursuits* (1881), p. 511.

12. W. Feilding, "What Shall I Do With My Son?" *Nineteenth Century* 13 (April 1883): 578–96; idem, "Whither Shall I Send My Son?" *Nineteenth Century* 14 (July 1883): 65–77.

13. Bamford, *Rise of the Public Schools*, p. 210; F. Musgrove, *The Migratory Elite* (1963), pp. 21, 173; Reader, *Professional Men*, pp. 212–14; private correspondence.

14. Harvey J. Philpot, *A Guide Book to the Canadian Dominion* (1871), pp. 63–120.

15. William Stamer, *The Gentleman Emigrant* (1874), vol. 1, p. 122.

16. John J. Rowan, *The Emigrant and Sportsman in Canada* (1876), p. 32.

17. Geraldine Coombe, *Muskoka past and present* (1976), pp. 231–32.

18. Doug Owram, *Promise of Eden* (1980), pp. 125–48; Norman Macdonald, *Canada: Immigration and Colonization, 1841–1903* (1966), pp. 30–48.

19. Daniel M. Gordon, *Mountain and Prairie: From Victoria to Winnipeg* (1880), p. 309.

20. Quoted in *The English Public School* (1929), by Bernard Darwin, p. 21.

21. E.M., "Sport in the Canadian North-West," (Letter) The *Field* 49 (21 October 1882): 575.

IV: EMIGRANT SCHOOLBOYS

1. John G. Swain, *Letters From John Gwynn Swain to His Mother* (1869), p. 104.

2. Ibid., p. 9.

3. Ibid., pp. 9, 13.

4. Ibid, pp. 52, 58.

5. Ibid, pp. 82, 96.

6. Ibid., pp. 78, 82.

7. Ibid., p. 109.

8. James Seton Cockburn, *Canada For Gentlemen* (1885), p. 8.

9. Ibid., pp. 38, 48.

10. Ibid., p. 23.

11. Ibid., p. 36.

12. I am indebted to Dr. David H. Newsome, Master of Wellington College, and to Mr. C.M. Baker, Wellington College archivist, for providing me with details concerning DelaFosse's school record.

13. Frederick M. DelaFosse (pseud. Roger Vardon), *English Bloods* (1930), pp. 10–11.

14. Ibid., pp. 11–12. Although Frederick made light of the gift, the Cockle's Antibilious Pills he received before leaving for Canada were most appropriate. The tablets were made famous in the 1870s by Col. Frederick Burnaby, the balloonist, pugilist, traveller, and soldier. Burnaby, the Victorian's beau ideal of the gentleman adventurer, extolled the invigo-

rating qualities of the pills following his celebrated ride to Khiva (in Asia Minor) in 1875–76. He also advertised the fact that he depended on the tablets while reporting on the Russian-Turkish war of 1877 and on his many aerial ascents. Thanks to Burnaby, Cockle's Antibilious Pills and high adventure were closely linked in the public mind.

15. DelaFosse, "Reminiscences of a Vagabond," Thunder Bay Historical Society, 18th & 19th *Annual Reports* (1926–28), 62–75.

16. I am grateful to Mr. J.A. Bently of Haileybury College for providing me with ffolkes's school record. I am also grateful to Professor Alexander M. Ross, late of McMaster University, for identifying ffolkes as the author of *Letters From A Young Emigrant in Manitoba* (1883).

17. Edward ffolkes, *Letters from a Young Emigrant*, p. 176.

18. Qu'Appelle lays claim to having the first cricket club and hunt club west of Winnipeg. John Hawkes, *The Story of Saskatchewan and Its People* (1924), vol. 2, p. 824. For details of cultural and athletic organizations elsewhere in the wheat lands, see L.O. Armstrong, *Southern Manitoba and Turtle Mountain Country* (1880), p. 10; A.G. Bradley, *Canada in the Twentieth Century* (1903), pp. 265, 283; Robert B. Hill, *Manitoba: History of Its Early Settlement* (1890), pp. 639–86; and "Sporting Clubs of the North West Territory," *The Emigrant* 1 (September 1886):101.

19. H.A. McGusty, *Two Years in Manitoba and the North-West Territory* (1891), p. 11.

20. R.E.W. Goodridge, *A Year in Manitoba* (1882), p. 70.

21. R.E.W. Goodridge, *The Colonist At Home Again* (1889), p. 15. In a letter to Premier Thomas Greenway, Goodridge declared that his first book, *A Year in Manitoba*, had been "exceedingly well-received [in England] and was the means of bringing out ... a large number of superior class settlers." "In fact," the captain said, without any hint of modesty, "it is doubtful if any other *one single agency* has every done so much for the country before." Goodridge to Greenway, 11 June 1889, Thomas Greenway Papers, Provincial Archives of Manitoba, Winnipeg.

22. Goodridge, *The Colonist at Home Again*, p. 61.

V: HIGH-CLASS COWBOYS

1. Herbert Grange, *An English Farmer in Canada* (1904), p. 61; Charles Hanbury-Williams, "The American Invasion of Canada," *Monthly Review* 21 (May 1903): 51; Moira O'Neill [Mrs. Walter Skrine], "A Lady's Life on a Ranche," *Blackwood's Edinburgh Magazine* 163 (January 1898):3.

2. Calgary *Herald*, 12 November 1884, quoted in "The Rancher and the City: Calgary and the Cattlemen, 1883–1914," by L.G. Thomas, *Transactions of the Royal Society of Canada* 6 (June 1968): 206.

3. I am indebted to Dr. David H. Breen, of the University of British Columbia, for information on the character and development of Alberta's ranching industry. In this chapter I have drawn on Dr. Breen's Master's thesis and Ph.D. dissertation and on several of his published articles, all of which are listed in the bibliography. I am also greatly indebted to Professor Lewis G. Thomas, professor emeritus of the University of Alberta,

for information and advice regarding the complexion of the ranching community.

4. In the 1880s Lister-Kaye's Canadian Agriculture, Coal, and Colonisation Company also had extensive holdings in Assiniboia. The ranching districts of present-day Saskatchewan, however, tended to be dominated by American-based companies. British companies—who, it may be noted, often used the archaic *ranche* spelling—were concentrated farther west. For details of the industry in Saskatchewan see Don G. McGowan, *Grassland Settlers* (1975), and Simon M. Evans, "American Cattlemen in the Canadian Range, 1874–1914," *Prairie Forum* 4 (Spring 1979): 121–35.

5. George B. Elliot, "Small Ranching in Alberta," *The Emigrant 1* (1 September 1886): 95; Thomas, "The Rancher and the City," pp. 209–13; High River Pioneers' and Old Timers' Association, *Leaves From the Medicine Tree* (1960), p. 155.

6. Moira O'Neill, "A Lady's Life on a Ranche," pp. 15–16.

7. James Francis Hogan, *The Sister Dominions* (1896), p. 90.

8. For details on the Church brothers see Alfred J. Church, ed., *Making a Start in Canada* (1889); A.J. Church, "Settling in Canada," *Macmillan's Magazine* 61 (November 1889): 41–44; and H.E. Church, *An Emigrant in the Canadian Northwest* (1929).

9. G.G. Ramsay, "Over the Rocky Mountains by the Canadian Pacific Line in 1884," *Macmillan's Magazine* 51 (December 1884): 122.

10. Church, *Making a Start*, p. 200.

11. H.A. McGusty, *Two Years in Manitoba and the North-West Territory* (1891), pp. 18–19.

12. Alexander Stavely Hill, *From Home to Home* (1884), p. 418.

13. Angus McKinnon, "Bob Newbolt, Pioneer 1884," pp. 15–16, GAI, Calgary; T. Bland Strange, *Gunner Jingo's Jubilee* (1893), pp. 389, 407–9.

14. Moira O'Neill, *Songs of the Glen of Antrim* (1910), pp. 58–59, quoted in *Our Foothills* (1975), ed. Lewis G. Thomas, p. 7.

15. J.L. Douglass, "Journal of a Four Months' Holiday to Canada and the United States," p. 25, GAI, Calgary.

16. Ralph Connor, *The Sky Pilot* (1899), pp. 27–29.

17. C.W. Holliday, *The Valley of Youth* (1948), pp. 183–84; David Mitchell and Dennis Duffy, eds., *Bright Sunshine and a Brand New Country*, Sound Heritage Series, no. 8 (1979), p. 12.

VI: NATURE'S GENTLEMEN

1. Clive Phillipps-Wolley, *The Trottings of a Tenderfoot* (1884), p. 49.

2. W. Henry Barneby, *Life and Labour in the Far Far West* (1884), p. 151.

3. M. Maturin Ballou, *The New Eldorado* (1889), pp. 87–88. See also Henry Tanner, *British Columbia: The Advantages It Offers for Emigration Purposes* (1887): "In no part of Canada is the English language equally pure, the rural homes of the West of England so strikingly reproduced, or the rule of the road in driving so correctly observed [as in Victoria]" (p. 2).

4. Barneby, *Life and Labour*, p. 133.

5. Gordon Elliott, ed., and Lillian Gustafson, comp., *Memories of the Chemainus Valley* (1978), pp. 20–27.

6. Derek Reimer, ed., *The Gulf Islanders*, Sound Heritage Series, no. 5 (1976), p. 17.

7. Margaret A. Ormsby, "Fruit Marketing in the Okanagan Valley of British Columbia," *Agricultural History* 9 (1935):82; idem, "The History of Agriculture in British Columbia," *Scientific Agriculture* 20 (1939):65.

8. J.T. Bealby, *Fruit Ranching in British Columbia* (1909), p. 12; Margaret A. Ormsby, *British Columbia: a History* (1971), p. 354; J.F.S. Redmayne, *Fruit Farming in the "Dry Belt" of British Columbia* (1909), p. 10.

9. C.W. Holliday, *The Valley of Youth* (1948), p. 183.

10. David Mitchell and Dennis Duffy, eds., *Bright Sunshine and a Brand New Country*, Sound Heritage Series, no. 8 (1979), p. 32.

11. J.K. Nesbitt, "Old Homes and Families," Victoria *Daily Colonist,* 9 May 1948.

12. R.E. Gosnell, "Warburton Pike (An Appreciation)," Victoria *Daily Colonist*, 30 October 1915.

13. Mabel E. Jordan, "The Kootenay Reclamation and Colonization Scheme and William Adolphe Baillie-Grohman," *BCHQ* 20 (1956): 187–220.

14. W.A. Baillie-Grohman, *Fifteen Years' Sport and Life in the Hunting Grounds of Western America and British Columbia* (1900), p. 319.

VII: REMITTANCE MEN

1. W.S. Caine, *A Trip Round the World in 1887–8* (1888), p. 41; Alexander A. Boddy, *By Ocean, Prairie, and Peak* (1896), p. 87.

2. John Sandilands, *Western Canadian Dictionary and Phrase-Book* (1912), p. 8.

3. H. Frank Lawrence, "Early Days in the Chinook Belt," *AHR* 13 (Winter 1965): 16–17

4. Philip J. Thomas, "B.C. Songs," *British Columbia Library Quarterly* 26 (July 1962):26.

5. Mary E. Inderwick, "A Lady and her ranch," *AHR* 15 (Autumn 1967): 6–7.

6. Howard Angus Kennedy, *New Canada and the New Canadians* (1907), p. 107.

7. W.H.P. Jarvis, *The Letters of a Remittance Man to His Mother* (1907), pp. 3, 8, 51.

8. L.V. Kelly, *The Range Men* (1913), p. 242; Ken Liddell, "The Remittance Man," Saskatoon *Western Producer,* 4 June 1959.

9. William Ward Spinks, *Tales of the British Columbia Frontier* (1933), p. 5; Jack Mould, *Stump Farms and Broadaxes* (1976), pp. 18–19.

10. Frank G. Carpenter, "Sporty Town is Calgary," Boston *Sunday Globe,* 11 March, 1906.

11. Kelly, *The Range Men,* p. 243; A.G. Hopkins, *Go West, Young Man, I Did,* (1955), p. 14.

12. Catharine Parr Traill, *The Backwoods of Canada* (1836), p. 272; Susanna Moodie, *Life in the Clearings,* (1853), p. xxxi; Fred M. DelaFosse, "Reminiscences of a Vagabond," Thunder Bay Historical Society, 18th & 19th *Annual Reports* (1926–28):63; Edward ffolkes, *Letters From a Young Emigrant* (1883), p. 45.

13. Hamilton B. Chipman, "The Garry Club," *The Beaver,* Autumn 1957, p. 50; J.S. Woodsworth, *Strangers Without Our Gates* (1909), p. 49.

14. Alfred O. Legge, *Sunny Manitoba* (1893), p. 198; Beecham Trotter, *A Horseman and the West* (1925), pp. 200–201; *The Times* (London), 31 January 1894; H.R. Whates, *Canada: The New Nation* (1906), p. 159.

15. John G. Donkin, *Trooper and Redskin in the Far North-West* (1889), p. 90.

16. Dr. G.D. Stanley, *A Round-Up of Fun in the Foothills* (n.d.), pp. 13–16.

17. Kelly, *The Range Men,* p. 241. See also Dr. Frank Gilbert Roe, "Remittance Men," *AHR* 2 (January 1954): 3–12.

18. C.W. Holliday, *The Valley of Youth* (1948), p. 182.

19. H.A. McGusty, *Two Years in Manitoba and the North West Territory* (1891), pp. 25–26; A.S. Morton MSS, A.E.M. Hewlett Collection, University of Saskatchewan Archives, Saskatoon (hereinafter noted as M/H, USA, Saskatoon].

20. John Foster Fraser, *Canada As It Is* (1905), p. 228.

21. J.G. Swain, *Letters from John Gwynn Swain to His Mother* (1869), p. 35.

22. Holliday, *Valley of Youth,* pp. 327–28.

23. Although formal marriages—*à la façon du pays*—between white fur traders and native Indians had been common in North America since the sixteenth century, the practice was deplored from about 1850 onwards. British gentlemen who "went native" were denounced in the harshest terms. Contemporary attitudes were perhaps most evident in E.M. Royle's play *The Squaw Man* (1905), which dealt with an aristocratic English rancher who marries an Indian maiden in Wyoming. Cecil B. DeMille made his directorial debut with Royle's play when he made a film entitled *The Squaw Man* in 1914. So successful was the film that DeMille made two other versions, in 1918 and 1931. The last version, a "talkie," was released in Britain as *The White Man.* A novel by Julie Opp Faversham, entitled *The Squaw Man* (1906), also resulted from Royle's play, and in 1917 Wallace Reid starred in a motion picture called *The Squaw Man's Son.* The theme obviously fascinated the British and American public.

24. Edna Kells, Pioneer Interviews: Stories of Bill Lees, p. 171; Stories of Mrs. Wallace J. Eddy, p. 169; GAI, Calgary.

25. H.H. Bashford, *The Manitoban* (1904), p. 44.

26. Ibid., p. 106

27. Harvey J. Philpot, *A Guide Book to the Canadian Dominion* (1871), pp. 96–98.

28. William Stamer, *The Gentleman Emigrant* (1874), vol. 1, pp. 47–48.

29. John J. Rowan, *The Emigrant and Sportsman in Canada* (1876), pp. 4, 12, 16.

30. *The Emigrant* 1 (1 July 1886):38; Kennedy, *New Canada*, p. 100.

31. Emily P. Weaver, *Canada and the British Immigrant* (1914), p. 277; Herbert Branston Gray, *The Public Schools and the Empire* (1913), pp. 20–21.

VIII: CLOISTERED COLONISTS

1. C.L. Johnstone, *Winter and Summer Excursions in Canada* (1896), p. 131.

2. W. Feilding, "What Shall I Do With My Son?" *Nineteenth Century* 13 (April 1883): 585.

3. Ibid.: John J. Rowan, *The Emigrant and Sportsman in Canada* (1876), p. 15.

4. William Stamer, *The Gentleman Emigrant* (1874), vol. 1, p. 47.

5. Literature dealing with gentlemen's colonies in the United States is extensive. Basic works include W.H.G. Armytage, "A Public School Paradise," *Queen's Quarterly* 57 (Winter 1950): 530–36; R.T. Berthoff, *British Immigrants in Industrial America* (1953), pp. 107–21; Nyle H. Miller, ed., "An English Runnymede in Kansas," *Kansas Historical Quarterly* 41 (Spring-Summer 1975): 22–62, 183–224; W.S. Shepperson, *Emigration and Disenchantment* (1965), pp. 113–25; and Jacob Van Der Zee, *The British in Iowa* (1922).

6. E.M. Pierce to J.A. Donaldson, 2 June 1883, John A. Macdonald Papers, PAC, Ottawa.

7. J.A. Donaldson to Sir John A. Macdonald, 7 October 1882, John A. Macdonald Papers, PAC, Ottawa; Mrs. George Shaw Page, "Life in Old Country Settlements: The Settlement of Cannington Manor," in *The Story of Saskatchewan and Its People* (1924), ed. John Hawkes, vol. 2, pp. 787–88.

8. E.M. Pierce to J.A. Donaldson, 2 June 1883, John A. Macdonald Papers, PAC, Ottawa.

9. E.M. Pierce, "A Canadian Settler's Story," letter to the press reprinted in *Allan Line's Handbook of Information and Advice for Emigrants* (1887), pp. 14–16; E.M. Pierce to John Stanier, 21 June 1887, Stanier Papers, PAC, Ottawa.

10. Frank Kidd, "Old Cannington Manor," 22 May 1927, p. 4, M/H, USA, Saskatoon.

11. I am indebted to Miss Margaret De Motte of the Central Library, Manchester, England; to Mrs. H.S. Beckton of Victoria, B.C.; and to Mr. Garth Pugh of the Saskatchewan Department of Culture and Youth, Regina, for information on the Beckton brothers. Details concerning the Becktons' Didsbury Stock Farm are taken from pioneers' reminiscences in M/H, USA, Saskatoon.

12. Kidd, "Old Cannington Manor," p. 6.

13. John G. Donkin, *Trooper and Redskin in the Far North-West* (1889), pp. 254–55.

14. Verbatim Notes From Old Timers: no. 25, William Humphreys; no. 43, Charles J. Couper, M/H, USA, Saskatoon.

15. Verbatim Notes: no. 43, Charles J. Couper.

16. Verbatim Notes: no. 9, William Laing.

17. Harold Bindloss, *Harding of Allenwood* (1915), pp. 20–21; idem, *Winston of the Prairie* (1907), pp. 52, 87. Several of Bindloss's novels were published under different titles, with slight differences in the text, in Britain and the United States. *Winston of the Prairie* was published in Britain as *The Imposter* (1907). *A Sower of Wheat* (1901) was revised and re-issued in 1909 in the United States as *Lorimer of the Northwest*.

18. Verbatim Notes: no. 31, Mrs. P. Taylor, M/H, USA, Saskatoon.

19. Verbatim Notes: no. 22, C. Royal Dawson; no. 28, T.L. Neish; Charles J. Couper, "Forty-Five Years in Canada; Being Reminiscences Recalled at Random of My Life in Saskatchewan and B.C.."; A.S. Morton, "Confidential Note," 23 February 1932; A.E.M. Hewlett, *A Too Short Yesterday* (1970), p. 41.

20. Diary of Basil G. Hamilton, 1896, pp. 100–104, GAI, Calgary.

21. See A.W. Rasporich, "Utopian Ideals and Community Settlements in Western Canada, 1880–1914," in *The Canadian West: Social Change and Economic Development* (1977), ed. Henry C. Klassen, pp. 39–44.

22. Kathleen Munro, "The Tragedy of Walhachin," *Canadian Cattleman* 18 (May 1955): 7–31; Elsie G. Turnbull, "The Ghost of Walhachin," *B.C. Outdoors* 28 (1972):24–29; Florence McNeil, "Walhachin," (poem) in *Walhachin*, p. 3.

23. Nelson A. Riis, "Settlement Abandonment: A Case Study of Walhachin, B.C." (Master's thesis, University of British Columbia, 1970), and Riis, "The Walhachin Myth: A Study in Settlement Abandonment," *BC Studies* 17 (Spring 1973):3–25. I have relied on Riis's studies for details concerning the economic and geographic aspects of Walhachin.

24. "Walhachin," B.C. Horticulturist Estates Co. Papers, pp. 5–6, vertical file, PABC, Victoria.

25. Arthur S. Jennings, *Walhachin, British Columbia* (n.d.), p. 11.

26. Ibid., p. 23.

27. Riis, "The Walhachin Myth," p. 18.

28. John S. Weir, "Walhachin: A Romantic Adventure or a Glorious Con?" *Kamloops Daily Sentinel,* 25 June 1977.

IX: MUDPUPS & PREMIUM HUNTERS

1. A.G. Bradley, "Farm Pupils in the Colonies," *Macmillan's Magazine* 62 (July 1890): 194–96.

2. Samuel Strickland, *Twenty-Seven Years in Canada West* (1853), vol. 2, p. 319.

3. Charles Weld, *A Vacation Tour of the United States and Canada* (1855), p. 110.

4. Horton Rhys (pseud. Morton Price), *A Theatrical Trip for a Wager* (1861), pp. 66–69, quoted in *The Valley of the Trent* (1957), by Edwin C. Guillet, p. 422.

5. C.H. Clementi, "Mutius V. Clementi," *Report of the Ontario Land Surveyors' Association*, no. 41 (1926):103.

6. Edward ffolkes, *Letters From a Young Emigrant in Manitoba* (1883), pp. 3–4. Patteson was captain of the first Canadian cricket XI and founder of the Ontario Jockey Club. He had been assistant provincial secretary and managing editor of the *Toronto Mail* before taking up his appointment as Toronto's postmaster in 1879. Patteson appears in ffolke's *Letters* as "Mr. Smith."

7. Frederick DelaFosse, *English Bloods* (1930), pp. 13–25.

8. Ibid., p. 213.

9. Ibid., p. 219.

10. A.J. Church, "Settling in Canada," *Macmillan's Magazine* 61 (November 1889):40.

11. For details on the Church brothers' daily routine at Collingwood see A.J. Church, ed., *Making A Start in Canada* (1889).

12. H.E. Church, *An Emigrant in the Canadian Northwest* (1929), p. 6.

13. *The Emigrant* 1 (1 October 1886): 110; 1 (17 December 1886): 169.

14. John G. Donkin, *Trooper and Redskin in the Far North-West* (1889), pp. 4–5.

15. Frank Hall, ed., "The Letters of Arthur Sherwood," *Manitoba Pageant* 16 (Winter 1971):10.

16. H.E. Church, *An Emigrant,* pp. 29–31.

17. Joe Lewis, "The Remittance Men." *Calgary Albertan*, 31 October 1955; Lewis G. Thomas, ed., *Our Foothills* (1975), pp. 213–14.

18. Verbatim Notes from Old Timers: no. 26, Arthur LeMesurier; no. 36, Mrs. P. Taylor (née Bryce); Mrs. A.E.M. Hewlett, *Cannington Manor Historic Park* (1966), p. 16, M/H, USA, Saskatoon.

19. J.F.S. Redmayne, *Fruit Farming in the "Dry Belt" of British Columbia* (1909), p. 70.

20. Raven Barratt's autobiographical novel, *Coronets and Buckskins* (1957), deals with gentlemen emigrants at Squamish on Howe Sound. "Most mud-pups," Barratt recalled, "married lady helps and had a family which they supported by bits from the old country and working on the road or in a logging camp. Sometimes a mudpup would inherit money and even a title. It was just as well to treat them all kindly" (p. 164).

21. *The Times* (London), 19 February 1885.

22. On the Birchall case see Victor Speer, *Memoirs of a Great Detective* (1905), and W.S. Wallace, *Murders and Mysteries* (1931); on the ACFPA see "The Farm-Pupil Swindle," *Truth* (London) 34 (21 December 1893): 1340.

23. H.B. Small to J.G. Colmer, 5 June 1889, and Sir Charles Tupper to J. Reade, 15 December 1893, Department of the Interior (Immigration Branch) Records, PAC, Ottawa.

X: OLD BOYS & OLD COLONIALS

1. James Aspdin, *Our Boys: What Shall We Do With Them?* (1889), pp. 21–22; A.G. Bradley, "Farm-Pupils in the Colonies," *Macmillan's Magazine* 62 (July 1890): 193–94.

2. "A Word to Genteel Emigrants," *Chamber's Edinburgh Journal* 17 (28 February 1852): 143–44.

3. Patrick A. Dunae, "'Making Good': The Canadian West in British Boys' Literature, 1890–1914," *Prairie Forum* 4 (Fall 1979): 170 – 71.

4. W. Feilding, "Whither Shall I Send My Son?" *Nineteenth Century* 14 (July 1883): 66–67.

5. Willaim Stamer, *The Gentleman Emigrant* (1874), vol. 1, p. 27.

6. John J. Rowan, *The Emigrant and Sportsman in Canada* (1876), p. 8.

7. Edward ffolkes, *Letters From a Young Emigrant in Manitoba* (1883), pp. 25, 15.

8. A.M. Ross, "An Emigrant at OAC," *Guelph Alumnus,* Autumn 1974, p. 11.

9. ffolkes, *Letters, p.* 27.

10. Ibid., p. 8.

11. Lucy H. Murray, "St. John's College, Qu'Appelle, 1885–1894," *Saskatchewan History* 9 (Winter 1958): 18–29.

12. Henry Greig, "St. John's Mission, Qu'Appelle," *Western World,* August 1892, quoted in "St. John's College," by L.M. Murray, p. 21.

13. I am indebted to Mrs. Marion B. Ingram, Richmond Hill, Surrey, England; to Mr. H.F. Ferguson, Administrative Officer, H.M. Borstal and Detention Centre, Woodbridge, Suffolk, England; and to Surgeon Captain H.E.B. Curjel, Royal Navy (retired), Hollesley, Suffolk, England, for providing me with information concerning Robert Johnson and the Colonial College.

14. Robert Johnson, "The Origin of the Colonial College," *Colonia: The Colonial College Magazine* 1 (April 1889): 4–5.

15. *Boy's Own Paper* 23 (17 November 1900): 111

16. A.E. Manning-Foster, "When You Leave School: Farming," *Captain* 1 (September 1899): 620–23.

17. Johnson, "Origin of the Colonial College," p. 6.

18. K.J. Neale, *The 'Colony' Suffolks: The Origin and History of the 'Colony Stud' of Suffolk Horses* (1975), pp. 16–17.

19. *Colonia* 1 (December 1891):456.

20. H.A. McGusty, *Two Years in Manitoba and the North-West Territory* (1891) pp. 1–2.

21. *Colonia* 1 (August 1891): 424–25.

22. *Colonia* 1 (December 1890): 134; (December 1891): 446–47; 5 (April 1898): 5–7; Ida Clingan, *The Virden Story* (1957), p. 23.

23. *Extracts from Press Notices of Colonia* (1896), pp. 2–3. See also the *Daily Graphic* (London), 6 January 1890; *Education* (London), January 1891, and *The Times* (London), 2 September 1901.

24 *The Times* (London), 17 December 1906.

25. On Fry and the Berkhamsted School Farm see Herbert Grange, *An English Farmer in Canada* (1904), pp. 60–64; Mrs. J.L. Richards, "Story of School-farm named Berkhampstead [sic]," Red Deer *Advocate*, 24 July 1971; and Colonel A.L. Wilson, "Berkhamsted Farm," [unpublished MS, in possession of the author].

26. H.R. Whates, *Canada: The New Nation* (1906), p. 162.

27. See R.H. Roy, "A Berkhamsted Boy in the Foothills," *AHR* 20 (Summer 1972): 17–29.

28. For details of Gray's career and the College Ranch see *Dictionary of National Biography*; E.J. Park, "Bradfield Ranch," in *Our Foothills* (1975), ed. Lewis G. Thomas, pp. 265–68; and Selina Gray, ed., *Gray of Bradfield: A Memoir* (1931), pp. 63–93.

29. Herbert Branston Gray, *The Public Schools and the Empire* (1913), pp. 145–47.

30. Previously, some of the ranchers in the foothills had considered the possibility of opening a training and/or reception centre for British public school boys, in order to reinforce the position of the aristocratic cattlemen in the West. The most ambitious of the proposals came from A.E. Cross who in 1904 circulated a prospectus for a "Ranche School" among members of the Ranchmen's Club. See "General Idea of Proposed Ranche School," A.E. Cross Papers, GAI, Calgary; and David H. Breen, "The Turner Thesis and the Canadian West: A Closer Look at the Ranching Frontier," in *Essays on Western History* (1976), ed. Lewis H. Thomas, pp. 147–58.

31. Gray, ed., *Gray of Bradfield*, p. 66.

32. *The Times* (London), 12 December 1906; *Report of the 34th Meeting of the Headmasters' Conference, 1906* (1907), pp. 6–10. [Hereinafter noted as *HMC Report*.]

33. *HMC Report 1909*, pp. 152–55, Appendix F; *HMC Report 1910*, pp. 131–33, Appendix F.

34. *HMC Report 1907*, p. 125; *HMC Report 1910*, pp. 112–13; *HMC Report 1911*, p. 100; George H. Williams, *Careers for Our Sons* (1911), pp. 424–25; Cyril FitzGerald, *The Schoolboy in Canada* (1914), p. 147.

35. *HMC Report 1907*, p. 128, Appendix E.

XI: PRO PATRIA

1. "The Emigration Conference," *United Empire Journal* 1 (July 1910): 510–18; Arthur Hawkes, "The Imperial Emigrant and His Political Religion," *Nineteenth Century and After* 71 (January 1912): 112.

2. *HMC Report 1909*, p. 14.

3. J.E.C. Welldon, "Schoolmasters," in *Unwritten Laws and Ideals of Active Careers* (1899), ed. E.H. Pitcairn, p. 284; Mary Moss, *Moss of Shrewbury* (1932), pp. 130–41.

4. A.P. Thornton, *The Imperial Idea and Its Enemies* (1966), p. 90.

5. "The Colonial College: A Retrospect and a Forecast," *Colonia* 3 (February 1895): 228.

6. "The Alliance of the English-Speaking Peoples," *Colonia* 1 (December 1895): 468–721.

7. H.R. Whates, *Canada: The New Nation* (1906), p. 163; Herbert B. Gray, *The Public Schools and the Empire* (1913), pp. 24–25; *HMC Report 1907*, p. 9.

8. Robert Craig Brown and Ramsay Cook, *Canada, 1896–1921: A Nation Transformed* (1974), p. 164; Norman Macdonald, *Canada: Immigration and Colonization, 1841–1903* (1966), pp. 228–34, 266–69; Charles Hanbury-Williams, "The American Invasion of North-Western Canada," *Monthly Review* 11 (May 1903): 48–61; "Canada: Under What Flag?" *Monthly Review* 26 (January 1907): 30–45.

9. *HMC Report 1909*, p. 14.

10. Carl Berger, *The Sense of Power* (1971), p. 151.

11. C.M. MacInnes, *In the Shadow of the Rockies* (1930), p. 329; Berger, *Sense of Power,* pp. 151, 161 and *passim.*

12. Whates, *Canada: The New Nation*, p. 163; Catharine Parr Traill, *The Backwoods of Canada* (1836), p. 24.

13. Carman Miller, "A Preliminary Analysis of the Socio-economic Composition of Canada's South African War Contingents." *Histoire sociale/Social History* 8 (November 1975): 219–37.

14. Clive Phillipps-Wolley, *Songs of an English Essau* (1902), p. 76.

15. Warburton M. Pike to Marshall Bond, 28 September 1915, Marshall Bond Correspondence, PABC, Victoria.

16. Clive Phillipps-Wolley to W.D. Walker, 5 April 1916, Vertical File, PABC, Victoria.

17. Quoted in *Britain's Imperial Century 1815–1914* (1976), by Ronald Hyam, p. 151.

18. Gray, *Public Schools and the Empire*, p. 21.

19. Even the fictitious remittance men reformed and "made good." Reggie Brown, of W.H.P. Jarvis's *Letters of a Remittance Man to His Mother*, married a Winnipeg girl, joined the Salvation Army, and became a successful Canadian. Clarence de Brown-Jones married a beautiful Montreal lady and was blessed with a dozen children. The son of R.J.C. Stead's Marquis of Noddle became a manly western rancher, while Bertie Buzzard-Cholomondeley, of *Eye-Opener* fame, emerged in later years as one of Calgary's leading citizens.

20. Kenneth Kelly, "The Transfer of British Ideas on Improved Farming to Ontario During the First Half of the Nineteenth Century," *Ontario History* 63 (June 1971):111–12; idem, "Notes on a Type of Mixed Farming

Practised in Ontario During the Early Nineteenth Century," *Canadian Geographer/Le Géographe canadien* 17 (Fall 1973): 215–17.

21. D.G. Paterson, *British Direct Investment in Canada, 1890–1914* (1976), p. 8.

22. D. Armstrong to the Hon. J.H. Pope, 19 April 1885, Department of the Interior (Immigration Branch) Records, PAC, Ottawa.

23. *Qu'Appelle Vidette,* 5 March 1885 and 1 April 1886, quoted in "The Bell Farm," by E.C. Morgan, *Saskatchewan History* 19 (Spring 1966): 51.

24. Susanna Moodie, *Life in the Clearings* (1853), p. 44.

25. J. Paul Grayson and Linda Grayson, "The Canadian Literary Elite: A Socio-Historical Perspective," *Canadian Journal of Sociology/Cahiers canadiens de sociologie* 3 (Summer 1978): 291–308; Carl F. Klinck, ed., *Literary History of Canada*, vol. 1, *Canadian Literature in English* (1976), pp. 138–76; E.A. McCourt, *The Canadian West in Fiction* (1970), pp. 12, 31–33.

26. Lindsey Russell to John A. Macdonald, 13 June 1883, John A. Macdonald Papers, PAC, Ottawa, quoted in *Promise of Eden,* (1980), by Doug Owram, p. 143.

27. Mackenzie Porter, "The Last Stronghold of the Longstockings," *Maclean's Magazine,* 2 April 1955, pp. 30–31, 80–81.

28. Rudyard Kipling, *Letters to the Family* (1908), pp. 36–37.

BIBLIOGRAPHY

PRIMARY SOURCES

Armstrong, L.O. *Southern Manitoba and Turtle Mountain Country.* Winnipeg: n.p., 1880.

Aspdin, James. *Our Boys: What Shall We Do With Them?; or, Emigration—The Real Solution of the Problem.* Manchester: John Heywood, 1889.

Baillie-Grohman, W.A. *Camps in the Rockies.* London: Sampson Low, Marston, Searle & Rivington, 1882.

———. *Fifteen Years' Sport and Life in the Hunting Grounds of Western America and British Columbia.* London: Horace Cox, 1900.

Ballou, M. Maturin. *The New Eldorado.* Boston: Houghton Mifflin, 1889.

Barneby, W. Henry. *Life and Labour in the Far, Far West: Being Notes of a Tour in the Western States, British Columbia, Manitoba, and the Northwest Territory.* London: Cassell, 1884.

Bashford, H.H. *The Manitoban: A Romance.* London: John Lane, 1904.

Bealby, J.T. *Fruit Ranching in British Columbia.* London: Adam & Charles Black, 1909.

Berkhamsted, Hertfordshire, England. Colonel A.L. Wilson. "Berkhamsted Farm." Typescript, n.d.

Bindloss, Harold. *Harding of Allenwood.* Toronto: Mcleod & Allen, 1915.

———. *Lorimer of the Northwest.* New York: Frederick A. Stokes, 1909.

———. *A Sower of Wheat.* London: Chatto & Windus, 1901.

———. *Winston of the Prairie.* New York: Grosset & Dunlap, 1907.

Binnie-Clark, Georgina. *A Summer on the Canadian Prairie.* London: Edward Arnold, 1910.

Boddy, Alexander A. *By Ocean, Prairie and Peak.* London: Society for Promoting Christian Knowledge, 1896.

Bradley, A.G. *Canada in the Twentieth Century.* London: A. Constable, 1903.

———. "Farm-Pupils in the Colonies." *Macmillan's Magazine* 62 (July 1890):193–98.

———. "Gentlemen Emigrants." *Macmillan's Magazine* 58 (May 1888): 30–40.

Brittain, Harry. *Canada: There and Back.* London: Privately printed by John Lane at The Bodley Head, 1908.

Butler, William Francis. *The Great Lone Land: A Narrative of Travel and Adventure in the North-West of America.* 1872. 14th ed. London: Sampson Low, Marston, 1891.

Caine, W.S. *A Trip Round the World in 1887–8.* London: George Routledge, 1888.

Calgary. GAI. J.L. Douglass. "Journal of a Four Months' Holiday to Canada and the United States [1886]."

Calgary. GAI. Basil G. Hamilton. "Diary, Saskatchewan area, 1896."

Calgary. GAI. Edna Kells. Pioneer Interviews.

Calgary. GAI. Angus McKinnon. "Bob Newbolt, Pioneer 1884."

Canada. Department of Agriculture. *An Official Handbook of Information Relating to the Dominion of Canada.* 1890.

"Canada: Under What Flag?" *Monthly Review* 26 (January 1907):30–45.

Carpenter, Frank G. "Sporty Town is Calgary." Boston *Sunday Globe,* 11 March 1906.

Church, Alfred J., ed. *Making a Start in Canada: Letters From Two Young Emigrants.* London: Seeley, 1889.

———. "Settling in Canada." *Macmillan's Magazine* 61 November 1889):40–44.

Church, H.E. *An Emigrant in the Canadian Northwest.* London: Methuen, 1929.

Cockburn, James Seton. *Canada for Gentlemen: Being Letters From James Seton Cockburn.* London: Army and Navy Co-operative Society, Printed for Private Circulation, 1885.

Colonia: The Colonial College Magazine [Woodbridge, Suffolk, England]. 1889–1902.

Connor, Ralph. *The Sky Pilot: A Tale of the Foothills.* Toronto: Westminster, 1889.

DelaFosse, Frederick M. [pseud. Roger Vardon]. *English Bloods.* Ottawa: Graphic Publishers, 1930.

———. "Reminiscences of a Vagabond." Thunder Bay Historical 18th and 19th *Annual Reports* (1926–28):62–75.

Donkin, John G. *Trooper and Redskin in the Far North-West: Recollections of Life in the North-West Mounted Police, Canada, 1884–1888.* London: Sampson Low, Marston, Searle & Rivington, 1889.

Dunlop, William. *Statistical Sketches of Upper Canada for the Use of Emigrants, by a Backwoodsman.* London: John Murray, 1832.

Edwards, Bob. "Letters from a badly made son to his father in England." Calgary *Eye-Opener,* 24 October 1903 to 30 April 1904.

Elkington, E. Way. *Canada: The Land of Hope.* London: Adam & Charles Black, 1910.

The Emigrant: A Journal Devoted to the Interests of Emigration to the Canadian Northwest [Winnipeg]. 1886–88.

"The Emigration Conference." *United Empire Journal* 1 (July 1910): 510–18.

Escott, T.H.S. *England: Its People, Polity, and Pursuits.* London: Cassell, Petter, Galpin, 1881.

Faversham, Julie Opp. *The Squaw Man.* New York: Grosset & Dunlap, 1906.

Feilding, William-Henry-Adelbert. "What Shall I Do With My Son?" *Nineteenth Century* 13 (April 1883):578–86.

———. "Whither Shall I Send My Son?" *Nineteenth Century* 14 (July 1883):65–77.

ffolkes, Edward G.E. *Letters From a Young Emigrant in Manitoba.* London: Kegan Paul, Trench, 1883.

FitzGerald, Cyril. *The Schoolboy in Canada.* London: Northern Printers, 1914.

Fraser, John Foster. *Canada As It Is.* London: Cassell,1905.

Geikie, Cunningham. *The Backwoods of Canada.* 4th ed. London: Strahan, 1879.

Gill, E.A. Wharton. *A Manitoba Chore Boy: The Experiences of a Young Emigrant Told From His Letters.* London: Religious Tract Society, 1912.

Goodridge, R.E.W. *The Colonist At Home Again; or, Emigration Not Expatriation.* London: William Dawson & Sons, 1889.

———. *A Year in Manitoba: being the experiences of a retired officer in settling his sons.* 2d ed. London: W. & R. Chambers, 1882.

Gordon, Daniel M. *Mountain and Prairie: From Victoria to Winnipeg.* London: Sampson Low, 1880.

Gosnell, R.E. *A History of British Columbia.* [Chicago]: Lewis, 1906.

———. "Warburton Pike (An Appreciation)." Victoria *Daily Colonist,* 30 October 1915.

Grange, Herbert. *An English Farmer in Canada.* London: Blackie & Son, 1904.

Gray, Herbert Branston. *The Public Schools and the Empire.* London: Williams & Norgate, 1913.

Hanbury-Williams, Charles. "The American Invasion of North-Western Canada." *Monthly Review* 11 (May 1903):49–61.

Hawkes, Arthur. "The Imperial Emigrant and His Political Religion." *Nineteenth Century and After* 71 (January 1912):112–32.

Headmasters' Conference, Annual Reports. 1900–14.

Hemyng, Bracebridge. *Jack Harkaway at Oxford.* London: E.J. Brett, 1872.

Hill, Alexander Stavely. *From Home to Home: Autumn Wanderings in the North-West, in the Years* 1881, 1882, 1883, 1884. London: Sampson Low, 1885.

Hill, Robert B. *Manitoba: History of Its Early Settlement, Development, and Resources.* Toronto: William Briggs, 1890.

Hogan, James Francis. *The Sister Dominions: Through Canada to Australia by the New Imperial Highway.* London: Ward & Downey, 1896.

Hopkins, A.G. *Go West, Young Man, I Did.* Ilfracombe, Devon: Arthur H. Stockwell, 1955.

Hughes, Thomas. "Rugby, Tennessee." *Macmillan's Magazine* 43 (February 1881):310–15.

———. *Tom Brown at Oxford.* London: Macmillan, 1861.

———. *Tom Brown's Schooldays.* London: Macmillan, 1857.

Jameson, Anna. *Winter Studies and Summer Rambles in Canada.* 3 vols. London: Saunders & Otley, 1838.

Jarvis, W.H.P. *The Letters of a Remittance Man to His Mother.* London: John Murray, 1907.

Jennings, Arthur S. *Walhachin, British Columbia: In the Heart of the "Dry Belt" for Commercial Fruit Growing.* London: B.C. Horticultural Estates Ltd., n.d.

Jeyes, S.H. "Our Gentlemanly Failures." *Fortnightly Review* 61 (1 March 1897):387–98.

Johnson, R. Byron. *Very Far West Indeed: A Few Rough Experiences on the North-West Pacific Coast.* London: Sampson Low, Marston, Low & Searle, 1872.

Johnstone, C.L. *Winter and Summer Excursions in Canada.* London: Digby, Long, 1894.

Kelly, L.V. *The Range Men: The Story of the Ranchers and Indians of Alberta.* Toronto: William Briggs, 1913.

Kennedy, Howard Angus. *New Canada and the New Canadians.* London: Horace Marshall, 1907.

Kingston, W.H.G. *Western Wanderings; or, A Pleasure Tour in the Canadas.* 2 vols. London: Chapman & Hall, 1856.

Kipling, Rudyard. *Letters to the Family.* Toronto: Macmillan, 1908.

Legge, Alfred O. *Sunny Manitoba — Its People and Its Industries.* London: T. Fisher Unwin, 1893.

Leighton, Robert. *Sergeant Silk, The Prairie Scout.* London: Jarrold & Sons, 1913.

Letters From Muskoka by An Emigrant Lady. London: Richard Bentley & Son, 1878.

Lizars, Robin, and MacFarlane, Kathleen. *In the Days of the Canada Company.* Toronto: William Briggs, 1896.

"Lofty." *Adventures and Misadventures; or, An Undergraduate's Experiences in Canada.* London: J. Bale, Sons & Danielson, 1922.

"Mac." *The Englishman in Canada (A Satire).* Toronto: Belford, 1880.

Macfie, Matthew. *Vancouver Island and British Columbia: Their History, Resources and Prospects.* London: Longman, Green, Longman, Roberts & Green, 1865.

McGusty, H.A. *Two Years in Manitoba and the North-West Territory.* Frome, Somerset: Harvey & Woodland, 1891.

Manning-Foster, A.E. "When You Leave School: Farming." *Captain* 1 (September 1899):620–23.

Milton, William Fitzwilliam, Viscount, and Cheadle, W.B. *The North-West Passage by Land.* London: Cassell, Petter & Galpin, 1865.

Moodie, J.W.D. *Scenes and Adventures as a Soldier and Settler During Half a Century.* Montreal: John Lovell, 1866.

Moodie, Susanna. *Life in the Clearings versus the Bush.* London: Richard Bentley, 1853.

——. *Roughing It in the Bush; or, Forest Life in Canada.* 1852. Reprint. Toronto: Bell & Cockburn, 1913.

O'Neill, Moira [Mrs. Walter Skrine]. "A Lady's Life on a Ranche." *Blackwood's Edinburgh Magazine* 163 (January 1898):1–16.

Osborn, E.B. *Greater Canada: The Past, Present, and Future of the Canadian North West.* London: Chato & Windus, 1900.

Ottawa. PAC. RG76, vol. 12. Department of the Interior (Immigration Branch) Records.

Ottawa. PAC. MG25 A. vol. 394. John A. Macdonald Papers.

Ottawa. PAC. MG29 C78. John Stanier Papers.

Phillipps-Wolley, Clive. *One of the Broken Brigade.* London: Smith, Elder, 1897.

——. *Snap: A Legend of Lone Mountain.* London: Longman, Green, 1890.

——. *Songs of an English Essau.* London: Smith, Elder, 1902.

——. *A Sportsman's Eden.* London: Richard Bentley & Son, 1888.

——. *The Trottings of a Tenderfoot.* London: Richard Bentley & Son, 1884.

Philpot, Harvey J. *Guide Book to the Canadian Dominion, Containing Full Information for the Emigrant, the Tourist, the Sportsman, and the Small Capitalist.* London: Edward Stanford, 1871.

Pike, Warburton Mayer. *The Barren Ground of Northern Canada.* London: Macmillan, 1892.

——. *Through the Sub-Arctic Forest.* London: Edward Arnold, 1896.

Pitcairn, E.H. ed. *Unwritten Laws and Ideals of Active Careers.* London: Smith, Elder, 1899.

Ramsay, G.G. "Over the Rocky Mountains by the Canadian Pacific Line in 1884." *Macmillan's Magazine* 51 (December 1884):120–29.

Redmayne, J.F.S. *Fruit Farming on the "Dry Belt" of British Columbia: The Why and the Wherefore.* London: Times Book Club, 1909.

Rowan, John J. *The Emigrant and Sportsman in Canada, Some Experiences of an Old Country Settler.* London: Edward Stanford, 1876.

Sandilands, John. *Western Canadian Dictionary and Phrase-Book.* Winnipeg: Telegram Job Printers, 1912.

Saskatoon. University of Saskatchewan Archives. A.S. Morton manuscripts, A.E.M. Hewlett collection.

Shirreff, Patrick. *A Tour Through North America; Together with a Comprehensive View of the Canadas and United States, as Adopted for Agricultural Emigration.* Edinburgh: Oliver & Boyd, 1835.

Southesk, James Carnegie, Earl of. *Saskatchewan and the Rocky Mountains: A Diary and Narrative of Travel, Sport, and Adventure During a Journey Through the Hudson's Bay Company's Territories, in 1859 and 1860.* 1875. Reprint. Edmonton: Hurtig, 1969.

Speer, Victor. *Memoirs of a Great Detective: Incidents in the Life of John Wilson Murray.* Toronto: Fleming H. Revell, 1905.

Stamer, William. *The Gentleman Emigrant: His Daily Life, Sports, and Pastimes in Canada, Australia, and the United States.* 2 vols. London: Tinsley Brothers, 1874.

Stead, Robert J.C. *The Empire Builders and Other Poems.* Toronto: William Briggs, 1908.

Stephen, Leslie. "Thoughts of an Outsider: Public Schools." *Cornhill Magazine* 27 (March 1873):281–92.

Stewart, Basil. *The Land of the Maple Leaf; or, Canada As I Saw It.* London: George Routledge & Sons, 1908.

Stock, A.B. *Ranching in the Canadian West.* London: Adam & Charles Black, 1912.

Stock, Ralph. *Confessions of a Tenderfoot.* London: Grant Richards, 1913.

Strange, T. Bland. *Gunner Jingo's Jubilee.* London: Remington, 1893.

Strickland, Samuel. *Twenty-Seven Years in Canada West; or, The Experiences of an Early Settler.* 2 vols. London: Richard Bentley, 1853.

Swain, John Gwynn. *Letters From John Gwynn Swain to His Mother. Written On His Entrance Into Life: Aged Seventeen. Giving a Description of His Voyage to Canada and Adventures at Lake Superior.* [Edinburgh]: Printed for Private Circulation, 1869.

Sykes, Ella C. *A Home Help in Canada.* London: Smith, Elder, 1912.

Talbot, Frederick A. *Making Good in Canada.* London: Adam & Charles Black, 1912.

Tanner, Henry. *British Columbia: The Advantages it Offers for Emigration Purposes.* London: G. Kenning, 1887.

Traill, Catharine Parr. *The Backwoods of Canada: Being Letters From the Wife of an Emigrant Officer, Illustrative of the Domestic Economy of British America.* 1836. Reprint. Toronto: McClelland & Stewart, 1929.

———. *The Canadian Settler's Guide.* 5th ed. Toronto: Old Countrymen Office, 1855.

Victoria. PABC. Marshall Bond Correspondence.

Victoria. PABC. John Thomas Wilson Clapperton [pseud. Artemus Ward]. "Jottings From Our First Seven Years in British Columbia, 1862–69."

Victoria. PABC. Clement Francis Cornwall Diaries, 1862–73.

Victoria. PABC. Clive Phillipps-Wolley Correspondence.

Ward, Mrs. Humphrey. *Canadian Born.* London: Smith, Elder, 1910.

Watney, Charles. "Why the Englishman is Despised in Canada." *National Review* 50 (November 1907:431–43.

Weaver, Emily P. *Canada and the British Immigrant.* London: Religious Tract Society, 1914.

Weld, Charles Richard. *A Vacation Tour in the United States and Canada.* London: Longman, Brown, Green, & Longman, 1855.

Whates, H.R. *Canada: The New Nation. A Book for the Settler, the Emigrant and the Politician.* London: J.M. Dent, 1906.

Williams, George H. *Careers for Our Sons.* London: Simpkin, Marshall, 1911.

Winnipeg. Provincial Archives of Manitoba. MG13.E1. Thomas Greenway Papers.

Woodsworth, James S. *Strangers Within Our Gates; or, Coming Canadians.* 1909. Reprint. Toronto: University of Toronto Press, 1972.

"A Word to Genteel Emigrants." *Chamber's Edinburgh Journal* 17 (28 February 1852):143–44.

SECONDARY SOURCES

Armytage, W.H.G. "A public school paradise." *Queen's Quarterly* 57 (Winter 1950):530–36.

Athearn, Robert G. *Westward the Briton: The Far West, 1865–1900, As Seen By British Sportsmen and Capitalists, Ranchers and Homesteaders, Lords and Ladies.* Lincoln: University of Nebraska Press, 1953

Bamford, T.W. *Rise of the Public Schools. A Study of Boys' Public Boarding Schools in England and Wales from 1837 to the Present Day.* London: Nelson, 1967.

Barman, Jean. "Growing Up British in British Columbia: The Vernon Preparatory School, 1914–1946." In *Schooling and Society in Twentieth Century British Columbia,* edited by J. Donald Wilson and David C. Jones, pp. 119–138. Calgary: Detselig Enterprises, 1980.

Barratt, Raven. *Coronets and Buckskin.* Boston: Houghton Mifflin, 1957.

Berger, Carl. *The Sense of Power: Studies in the Ideas of Canadian Imperialism, 1867–1914.* Toronto: University of Toronto Press, 1971.

Berthoff, Rowland Tappan. *British Immigrants in Industrial America: 1790–1950.* Cambridge, Mass.: Harvard University Press, 1953.

Blue, John. *Alberta: Past, Present, Historical and Biographical.* 3 vols. Chicago: Pioneer Historical Publishing, 1924.

Breen, David H. "The Canadian West and the Ranching Frontier, 1875–1927." Ph.D. dissertation, University of Alberta, 1972.

———. "The Cattle Compact: The Ranch Community in Southern Alberta, 1881–1896." Master's thesis, University of Calgary, 1969.

————. "The Ranching Frontier in Canada, 1875–1905." In *The Prairie West to 1905: A Canadian Sourcebook,* edited by Lewis G. Thomas, pp. 217–28. Toronto: Oxford University Press, 1975.

————. "The Turner Thesis and the Canadian West: A Closer Look at the Ranching Frontier." In *Essays on Western History,* edited by Lewis H. Thomas, pp. 147–58. Edmonton: University of Alberta Press, 1976.

Brown, Robert Craig, and Cook, Ramsay. *Canada, 1896–1921: A Nation Transformed.* Toronto: McClelland & Stewart, 1974.

Carrington, Philip. *The Anglican Church in Canada: A History.* Toronto: Collins, 1963.

Carrothers, W.A. *Emigration from the British Isles.* London: P.S. King, 1929.

Carr-Saunders, A.M., and Wilson, P.A. *The Professions.* London: Oxford University Press, 1932.

Chadwick, Owen. *The Victorian Church.* 2 vols. London: Adam & Charles Black, 1970.

Chipman, Hamilton B. "The Garry Club." The *Beaver* (Autumn 1957):49–52.

Clark, G. Kitson. *The Making of Victorian England.* London: Methuen, 1973.

Clementi, C.H. "Mutius V. Clementi." *Report of the Ontario Land Surveyors' Association* 41 (1926):103–4.

Clingan, Ida. *The Virden Story.* Virden, Man.: Empire Publishing, 1957.

Coleman, Terry. *Passage to America. A History of Emigrants From Great Britain and Ireland to America in the Mid-Nineteenth Century.* London: Hutchinson, 1972.

Coombe, Geraldine. *Muskoka past and present.* Toronto: McGraw-Hill Ryerson, 1976.

Craig, Gerald M., ed. *Early Travellers in the Canadas, 1791–1867.* Toronto: Macmillan 1955.

————. *Upper Canada: The Formative Years, 1784–1841.* Toronto: McClelland & Stewart, 1963.

Cross, Michael S. "The Age of Gentility: The Formation of an Aristocracy in the Ottawa Valley." Canadian Historical Association *Historical Papers,* 1967, pp. 105–17.

Darwin, Bernard. *The English Public School.* London: Longman, Green, 1929.

Dunae, Patrick A. "'Making Good': The Canadian West in British Boys' Literature, 1890–1914." *Prairie Forum* 4 (Fall 1979):165–81.

England, Robert. "Disbanded and Discharged Soldiers in Canada Prior to 1914." *Canadian Historical Review* 27 (March 1946):1–18.

Evans, Simon M. "American Cattlemen on the Canadian Range, 1874–1914." *Prairie Forum* 4 (Spring 1979):121–35.

Gardner, Brian. *The Public Schools: An Historical Survey.* London: Hamish Hamilton, 1973.

Gates, Paul W. "Official Encouragement to Immigration by the Province of Canada." *Canadian Historical Review* 15 (March 1934):24–38.

Gathorne-Hardy, Jonathan. *The Public School Phenomenon, 597–1977.* London: Hodder & Stoughton, 1977.

Gossage, Caroline. *A Question of Privilege: Canada's Independent Schools.* Toronto: P. Martin, 1977.

Graham, W.H. *Tiger Dunlop.* London: Hutchinson, 1962.

Gray, Selina, ed. *Gray of Bradfield: A Memoir.* London: Oxford University Press, 1931.

Grayson, J. Paul, and Grayson, Linda. "The Canadian Literary Elite: A Socio-Historical Perspective." *Canadian Journal of Sociology/Cahiers canadiens de sociologie* 3 (Summer 1978):291–308.

Guillet, Edwin C. *The Great Migration: The Atlantic Crossing by Sailing-ship Since 1770.* 2d ed. Toronto: University of Toronto Press, 1963.

——. *The Pioneer Farmer and Backwoodsman.* 2 vols. Toronto: Ontario Publishing, 1963.

——. *The Valley of the Trent.* Toronto: Champlain Society, 1957.

Gustafson, Lillian, comp., and Elliott, Gordon, ed. *Memories of the Chemainus Valley: A History of People.* Chemainus Valley Historical Society, 1978.

Hall, Frank, ed. "The Letters of Arthur Sherwood." Preface by S.W. Jackman. *Manitoba Pageant* 16 (Winter 1971):2–24.

Hammerton, A. James. *Emigrant Gentlewomen: Genteel Poverty and Female Emigration, 1830–1914.* London: Croom Helm, 1978.

Harries-Jenkins, Gwyn. *The Army in Victorian Society.* London: Routledge & Kegan Paul, 1977.

Hawkes, John. *The Story of Saskatchewan and Its People.* 2 vols. Chicago/Regina: S.J. Clarke, 1924.

Hendrickson, James E. "Two Letters From Walter Colquhoun Grant." *B.C. Studies* 26 (Summer 1975):3–15.

Hewlett, A.E.M. *Cannington Manor Historic Park.* Regina: Saskatchewan Diamond Jubilee and Canada Centennial Corporation, 1965.

——. "England on the Prairies." The *Beaver* (December 1952):20–25.

——. *A Too Short Yesterday.* Saskatoon: Western Producer, 1970.

Higginbotham, John D. *When the West Was Young.* Toronto: Ryerson Press, 1933.

High River Pioneers' and Old Timers' Association. *Leaves From the Medicine Tree.* Lethbridge: Lethbridge Herald, 1960.

Holliday, C.W. *The Valley of Youth.* Caldwell, Idaho: Caxton Printers, 1948.

Houghton, Walter E. *The Victorian Frame of Mind, 1830–1870.* London: Yale University Press, 1975.

Hyam, Ronald. *Britain's Imperial Century, 1815–1914: A Study of Empire and Expansion.* London: B.T. Batsford, 1976.

Inderwick, Mary E. "A Lady and Her Ranch." *Alberta Historical Review* 15 (Autumn 1967):1–9.

Ireland, Willard E. "Captain Walter Colquhoun Grant: Vancouver Island's First Independent Settler." *British Columbia Historical Quarterly* 17 (1953):87–125.

James, N.B. *The Autobiography of a Nobody.* Toronto: J.M. Dent, 1947.

Jameson, Sheilagh S. "Women in the Southern Alberta Ranch Community, 1881–1914." In *The Canadian West: Social Change and Economic Development,* edited by H.C. Klassen, pp. 63–78. Calgary: University of Calgary Press/Comprint, 1977.

Johnson, Edward Philip. "The Early Years of Ashcroft Manor." *BC Studies* 5 (Summer 1970):3–23.

Johnson, Stanley C. *A History of Emigration from the United Kingdom to North America.* 1913. Reprint. London: Frank Cass, 1966.

Johnston, Lukin. *Beyond the Rockies: Three Thousand Miles by Trail and Canoe Through Little-Known British Columbia.* London: J.M. Dent, 1929.

Jordan, Mabel E. "The Kootenay Reclamation and Colonization Scheme and William Adolphe Baillie-Grohman." *British Columbia Historical Quarterly* 20 (1956):187–220.

Kelly, Kenneth. "Notes on a Type of Mixed Farming Practised in Ontario During the Early Nineteenth Century." *Canadian Geographer/Le Geographe canadien* 17 *(Fall* 1973):205–19.

———. "The Transfer of British Ideas of Improved Farming to Ontario During the First Half of the Nineteenth Century." *Ontario History* 63 (June 1971):103–112.

Klink, Carl F., ed. *Literary History of Canada.* 2d ed., vol. 1, *Canadian Literature in English.* Toronto: University of Toronto Press, 1976.

Langton, H.H. ed. *A Gentlewoman in Upper Canada: The Journals of Anne Langton.* Toronto: Clarke, Irwin, 1964.

Langton, W.A. ed. *Early Days in Upper Canada: Letters of John Langton.* Toronto: Macmillan, 1926.

Lawrence, H. Frank. "Early Days in the Chinook Belt." *Alberta Historical Review* 13 (Winter 1965):9–19.

Lewis, Joe. "The Remittance Man." Saskatoon *Western Producer,* 4 June 1959.

Lutz, John S. "Interlude or Industry? Ranching in British Columbia, 1859–1885." *B.C. Historical News* 13 (1980):2–10.

McCourt, Edward A. *The Canadian West in Fiction.* Rev. ed. Toronto: Ryerson Press, 1970.

McCormack, Ross. "Cloth Caps and Jobs: The Ethnicity of English Immigrants in Canada, 1900–1914," In *Ethnicity, Power and Politics in Canada,* edited by Jorgen Dahlie and Tissa Fernando, pp. 38–55. Toronto: Methuen, 1981.

Macdonald, Norman. *Canada, 1763–1841: Immigration and Settlement.* London: Longman, Green, 1939.

———. *Canada: Immigration and Colonization, 1841–1903.* Aberdeen: Aberdeen University Press, 1966.

McGowan, Don C. *Grassland Settlers: The Swift Current Region During the Era of the Ranching Frontier.* Regina: Canadian Plains Research Center, 1975.

MacInnes, C.M. *In the Shadow of the Rockies.* London: Rivingtons, 1930.

Macleod, R.C. *The North-West Mounted Police and Law Enforcement, 1873–1905*. Toronto: University of Toronto Press, 1975.

McNeil, Florence. *Walhachin*. Fredericton, N.B.: Fiddlehead Books, 1972.

Mack, Edward C. *Public Schools and British Opinion Since 1860*. New York: Columbia University Press, 1941.

Mack, Edward C., and Armitage, W.H.G. *Thomas Hughes: The Life of the Author of Tom Brown's Schooldays*. London: Ernest Benn, 1952.

Maier, C.R., ed. "A Letter From New Westminster." The *Beaver* (Autumn 1976):42–44.

Mangan, J.A. "Athleticism: A Case Study of the Evolution of an Educational Ideology." In *The Victorian Public School. Studies in the Development of an Educational Institution*, edited by Brian Simon and Ian Bradley, pp. 147–67. Dublin: Gill & Macmillan, 1975.

Meadows, A.J., and Brock, W.H. "Topics Fit for Gentlemen: The Problem of Science in the Public School Curriculum." In *The Victorian Public School: Studies in the Development of an Educational Institution*, edited by Brian Simon and Ian Bradley, pp. 95–114. Dublin: Gill & Macmillan, 1975.

Mealing, S.R. "The Enthusiasms of John Graves Simcoe." Canadian Historical Association *Annual Report*, 1958, pp. 50–62.

Miller, Carman. "A Preliminary Analysis of the Socio-economic Composition of Canada's South African War Contingents." *Histoire sociale/Social History* 8 (November 1975):219–37.

Miller, Nyle H., ed. "An English Runnymede in Kansas." *Kansas Historical Quarterly* 41 (Spring-Summer 1975):22–62, 183–224.

Mitchell, David, and Duffy, Dennis, eds. *Bright Sunshine and a Brand New Country: Recollections of the Okanagan Valley, 1890–1914*. Sound Heritage Series, no. 8. Victoria: PABC, 1979.

Morgan, E.C. "The Bell Farm." *Saskatchewan History* 19 (Spring 1966):41–60.

Morris, Audrey Y. *Gentle Pioneers: Five Nineteenth-Century Canadians*. Don Mills, Ontario: PaperJacks, 1973.

Moss, Mary. *Moss of Shrewsbury: A Memoir, 1841–1917, by His Wife*. London: Sheldon Press, 1932.

Mould, Jack. *Stump Farms and Broadaxes*. Saanichton, B.C.: Hancock House, 1976.

Munro, Kathleen. "The Tragedy of Walhachin." *Canadian Cattleman* 18 (May 1955):7, 30–31.

Murray, Lucy H. "St. John's College, Qu'Appelle, 1885–1894." *Saskatchewan History* 11 (Winter 1958):18–29.

Musgrove, Frank. "Middle-Class Education and Employment in the Nineteenth Century." *Economic History Review* 2d ser., 12 (1959–60): 99–111.

———. *The Migratory Elite*. London: Heinemann, 1963.

Neale, K.J. *The 'Colony' Suffolks: The Origin and History of the 'Colony Stud' of Suffolk Horses*. Surbiton, Surrey: The Home Office, 1975.

Nesbitt, J.K. "Old Homes and Families." Victoria *Daily Colonist*, 9 May 1948.

Ormsby, Margaret A. *British Columbia: a History.* Toronto: Macmillan, 1971.

———. "Fruit Marketing in the Okanagan Valley of British Columbia." *Agricultural History* 9 (1935):80–97.

———. "The History of Agriculture in British Columbia." *Scientific Agriculture* 20 (1939):61–72.

———. "Some Irish Figures in Colonial Days." *British Columbia Historical Quarterly* 14 (1950):61–82.

Owram, Doug. *Promise of Eden: The Canadian Expansionist Movement and the Idea of the West, 1856–1900.* Toronto: University of Toronto Press, 1980.

Paterson, D.G. *British Direct Investment in Canada, 1890–1914.* Toronto: University of Toronto Press, 1976.

Porter, Mackenzie. "The Last Stronghold of the Longstockings." *Maclean's Magazine,* 2 April 1955, pp. 30–31, 80–81.

Purdy, J.D. "The English Public School Tradition in Nineteenth-Century Ontario: In *Aspects of Nineteenth-Century Ontario: Essays presented to James J. Talman,* edited by F.H. Armstrong, et al, pp. 237–52. Toronto: University of Toronto Press, 1974.

Rasporich, A.W. "Utopian Ideals and Community Settlements in Western Canada, 1880–1914." In *The Canadian West: Social Change and Economic Development,* edited by Henry C. Klassen, pp. 37–62. Calgary: University of Calgary/Comprint, 1977.

Read, Donald. *England 1868–1914: The age of urban democracy.* London: Longmans, 1979.

Reader, W.J. *Professional Men: The Rise of the Professional Classes in Nineteenth-Century England.* London: Weidenfeld & Nicolson, 1966.

Reimer, Derek, ed. *The Gulf Islanders.* Sound Heritage Series, no. 5. Victoria: PABC, 1976.

Riis, Nelson A. "Settlement Abandonment: A Case Study of Walhachin, B.C." Master's thesis, University of British Columbia, 1970.

———. "The Walhachin Myth: A Study in Settlement Abandonment." *BC Studies* 17 (Spring 1973):3–25.

Roe, Frank G. "Remittance Men." *Alberta Historical Review* 2 (January 1954):3–12.

Ross, A.M. "An Emigrant at OAC." *Guelph Alumnus* (Autumn 1974):8–11.

Roy, R.H. "A Berkhamsted Boy in the Foothills." *Alberta Historical Review* 20 (Summer 1972):17–29.

Segger, Martin, and Franklin, Douglas. *Victoria: A History in Architecture, 1843–1929.* Watkins Glen, N.Y.: American Life Foundation and Study Institute, 1979.

Shepperson, W.S. *British Emigration to North America: Projects and Opinions in the Early Victorian Period.* Minneapolis: University of Minnesota Press, 1957.

———. *Emigration and Disenchantment: Portraits of Englishmen Repatriated From the United States.* Norman: University of Oklahoma Press, 1965.

Smith, Dorothy Blakey, ed. *Lady Franklin Visits the Pacific Northwest.* Victoria: PABC, 1974.

———. *The Reminiscences of Doctor John Sebastian Helmcken.* Vancouver: University of British Columbia Press, 1975.

Spinks, William Ward. *Tales of the British Columbia Frontier.* Toronto: Ryerson Press, 1933.

Stanley, Dr. George Douglass. *A Round-Up of Fun in the Foothills. Sketches of Turn-of-the-Century High River.* [Calgary]: Privately printed, n.d.

Tait, Terence D. "Haileybury: The Early Years." *Ontario History* 55 (1963): 193–204.

Thomas, Brinley. *Migration and Economic Growth. A Study of Great Britain and the Atlantic Economy.* Cambridge, England: At the University Press, 1954.

Thomas, Gregory E.G. "The British Columbia Ranching Frontier, 1858–1896." Master's thesis, University of British Columbia, 1976.

Thomas, Lewis G., ed. *Our Foothills.* Calgary: Millarville, Kew, Priddis, and Bragg Creek Historical Society, 1975.

———. "The Rancher and the City: Calgary and the Cattlemen, 1883–1914." *Transactions of the Royal Society of Canada.* 6. Series IV. Section II. (June 1968):203–15.

Thomas, Lewis H. "British Visitors' Perceptions of the West, 1885–1914." In *Prairie Perspectives* 2, edited by Anthony W. Rasporich and Henry C. Klassen, pp. 181–96. Toronto: Holt, Rinehart & Winston, 1973.

Thomas, Philip J. "B.C. Songs." *British Columbia Library Quarterly* 26 (July 1962):17–29.

Thompson, F.M.L. *English Landed Society in the Nineteenth Century.* London: Routledge & Kegan Paul, 1963.

Thornton, A.P. *The Imperial Idea and Its Enemies: A Study in British Power.* London: Macmillan, 1966.

Trotter, Beecham. *A Horseman and the West.* Toronto: Macmillan, 1925.

Turnbull, Elsie G. "The Ghost of Walhachin." *B.C. Outdoors* 28 (1972): 24–29.

Van Der Zee, Jacob. *The British in Iowa.* Iowa City: State Historical Society, 1922.

Wallace, W.S. *Murders and Mysteries.* Toronto: Macmillan, 1931.

Weir, Joan S. "Walhachin: A Romantic Adventure or a Glorious Con?" *Kamloops Daily Sentinel,* 25 June 1977.

White, Hester E. "John Carmichael Haynes." *British Columbia Historical Quarterly* 4 (1940):183–201.

Wilkinson, Rupert. *The Prefects: British Leadership and the Public School Tradition.* London: Oxford University Press, 1964.

Young, Michael. *The Rise of the Meritocracy, 1870–2033. An Essay on Education and Equality.* Harmondsworth, Middlesex: Penguin, 1965.

INDEX

Aberdeen, 7th Earl of (John Campbell Gordon), 103–4, 113–14, 165

Alaska, 119

Alberta, 81, 86, 87–105, 113, 123, 129, 132, 140, 142, 161, 169, 185–86, 203, 209–10, 220, 228, 230, 234

Alberta Field Force, 100, 222

Alberta Ranche Company, 89

Anglesey, 6th Marquis of (Charles Henry Alexander), 168–69

Anglican Church, 91, 100, 107, 108, 152, 208, 227, 231. *See also* Church of England

Anglo-Canadian Farm Pupil Association (ACFPA), 189–90, 191, 192, 200

Angus, Richard Bladworth, 70

Anson, the Rt. Rev. the Hon. Adelbert J.R., 198–200

Army, reforms, 49, 51, 52

Army and Navy Co-operative Society, 78

Arnold, Dr. Thomas, 53, 208, 232

Arthur, Chester, 76

Ashcroft Manor, B.C., 45, 46, 163, 227

Aspdin, James, 192–93, 194, 196

Assiniboia, 84, 86, 88, 89, 123, 128, 151, 157, 198, 203, 230. *See also* North West Territory; Saskatchewan

Australia, 8, 48, 149, 201, 214, 217, 218. *See also* New South Wales

Baillie-Grohman, William Adolphe, 120–22, 224, 230

Bar S Ranch, Alta., 100

Barkerville, B.C., 39, 43, 45

Barnardo immigrants, 189, 214

Barneby, William Henry, 106, 109

Barr Colony. *See* Lloydminster, Sask.

Bashford, Sir Henry H., 142

Bass, Sir William Arthur Hamer, 2nd Bt., 163, 164, 168

Bassano, Alta., 101

Bath, C. Avon, 61

Beaconsfield, Man., 83

Beauclerc, Osborne de Vere (12th Duke of St. Albans), 119
Beaufort, 8th Duke of (Henry Charles Fitzroy Somerset), 46
Beckton, Ernest, 154–56
Beckton, Frances (née Pierce), 156
Beckton, Herbert ("Bertie"), 154–56
Beckton, Joseph, 154
Beckton, William ("Billy"), 154–56
Begbie, Sir Matthew Baillie, 38, 42, 45
Belleville, Ont., 24, 26
Benwell, Frederick, 190
Berkhamsted School, Herts., 205–8, 211
Berkhamsted School Farm, Alta., 205–9, 218, 227
Big Creek, B.C., 224
Bindloss, Harold, 102, 156–58, 184, 232, 247n.
Birch, Arthur, 40
Birchall, Reginald, 190–91
Birtle, Man., 84
Bishop Ridley College, St. Catharines, Ont., 231
Bishop's College, Lennoxville, P.Q., 231
Black, Col. H.B., 19
Blackfoot Indians, 88
Blair, John, 108
Boddy, the Rev. Alexander A., 124–25
Boer War. *See* South African War
Bournemouth, Dorset, 225
Bowchase Ranch, Alta., 100
Bracebridge, Ont., 62, 179
Bradfield College, Berks., 208–10, 211, 226
Bradfield College Ranch, Alta., 205, 208–10, 218–19, 227
Bradley, Andrew Granville, 175–76 181, 182, 193, 194, 196
Brandon, Man., 84, 133, 184
Brassey, the Hon. Thomas A., 214

Brew, Chartres, 42–43
Brighton, Sussex, 107
British-American Horse Ranche, 197
British American Land Company, 29
British Association, 205, 209
British Columbia, 1, 10, 31, 37–47, 60, 103–23, 125, 130, 158, 162, 163, 165, 188, 203, 204, 210, 216, 220, 230, 223
British Columbia Development Association (BCDA), 163–66, 168
British Columbia Fruit Lands Ltd., 204
British Columbia, University of, 210
British Public Schools Association of Canada (BPSAC), 211–12
Brooke, Rupert, 234
Bryce, William ("Scotty"), 187–88
Buck Lake, Ont., 180
Buckler, Eric, 186
Bullock, Henry Wright, 112–13, 118
Burchell, Henry, 111
Burdett-Coutts, Baroness Angela, 107
Butler, Sir William Francis, 65

Caine, William Sprostan, 124
Calgary, Alta., 88, 92, 94, 95, 98, 100, 127, 132, 138, 167, 185, 197, 208, 211, 213
Cambridge University, 53, 104, 150, 180
Canada Company, 20, 21
Canada East, 29. *See also* Lower Canada; Quebec
Canada North West Land Company, 204
Canada West, 29, 31, 216. *See also* Ontario; Upper Canada
Canadian Agricultural, Coal, and Colonization Co., 89, 243n.
Canadian Northern Pacific Railway, 163

Canadian Pacific Railway (CPR), 63,
70, 77, 81, 88, 103, 107, 114, 122,
141, 152, 153, 160, 163, 198, 212
Canadian Wildlife and Conservation
Commission, 197
Cannington, Ont., 152
Cannington, Som., 152
Cannington Manor, Sask., 151–62,
163, 169–70, 187–88, 204, 217,
223, 227
Cape Colony, 14, 15, 217. *See also*
South Africa
Cape Town, 227
Cariboo gold rush (1861–66),
37–38, 44–45, 103, 107
Carlyle, Thomas, 21
Cassiar Central Railway Company,
119
Castletown, 2nd Baron (Bernard
Edward Barnaby FitzPatrick), 89
Central Body for London, 205
Ceylon, 227
Charlottetown, P.E.I., 8
Charterhouse School, Surrey, 4
Cheadle, Dr. Walter Butler, 45
Cheltenham, Glos., 61
Cheltenham College, Glos., 4,
53, 154
Chemainus Valley, B.C., 110–11,
188
Chetwynd, Sir Talbot, 164
Chilcotin district, B.C., 42, 105
Church, the Rev. Alfred John, 93,
94, 97, 181–82, 193
Church, George Edward ("Teddy"),
97, 203, 224, 233
Church, Herbert Edmund, 92–98,
101, 108, 124, 181–83, 185–86,
188, 193, 224, 233
Church, Richard A. ("Dickie"),
92–98, 108, 181–83, 185–86,
188, 193, 224, 233
Church of England, 49, 50, 157, 231.
See also Anglican Church

Civil Service, reforms, 49, 51, 52
Clapperton, John Thomas Wilson,
38, 39, 41, 47, 233
Clifford, the Hon. Walter, 183–84
Clifton College, Bristol, C. Avon,
53, 60, 153, 154
Close, William, 150, 163, 165
Cobble Hill, B.C., 110
Cobourg, Ont., 22, 23
Cochrane, Alta., 102
Cochrane Ranch Co., 89–90
Cockburn, Henry, 74–76, 79
Cockburn, James Seton, 74–79, 230
Coldstream Ranch, B.C., 44, 104
Collingwood, Ont., 94, 181, 182,
183, 185
Colonial College, Hollesley Bay,
Suffolk, 200–205, 217–18,
222, 227
Comox, B.C., 94
Connor, Ralph (the Rev. Charles
Gordon), 102–3, 138, 232
Corfield, B.C., 110
Cork, Ireland, 42
Cornwall, the Rev. A.G., 44
Cornwall, Clement Francis, 44–47,
103, 124, 233
Cornwall, Henry Pennant, 44–47,
103, 233
Cowichan Valley, B.C., 109–10,
188, 234
Crimean War, 10, 31, 42, 43, 51, 59,
216
Cross, A.E., 197, 250n.
Curtis, Matthew, 154
Curzon, George Nathaniel (1st
Marquis Curzon of Kedleston),
227

Dakota Territory, 104
Dease Lake, B.C., 119
De Cosmos, Amor, 41
De Winton, Maj. Gen. Sir Francis
Walter, 89

DelaFosse, Frederick Montague
(pseud. Roger Vardon), 79–82,
124, 137, 179–81, 188
DelaFosse, Lt. Col. Henry George,
79, 80, 179
Denison, George T., 220
Didsbury, Manchester, 154–55
Dominion Lands Act (1872), 63
Dominion Police, 190
Donkin, John George, 156, 184, 188
Donnally, J.P., 72, 73
Douglas, Sir James, 32, 40, 41, 109
Douglass, Charles Linzee, 101
Douglass, Gordon Cecil, 101
Douglass, J.L., 101
Douglass, Leslie Victor, 101
Duncan, B.C., 109, 110, 111, 117,
130, 223, 225, 234
Dundonald, 12th Earl of (Douglas
MacKinnon Baillie Hamilton
Cochrane), 215
Dunlop, Dr. William ("Tiger"), 20,
21, 24, 131, 232
Durham School, Co. Durham, 60

East Retford, Notts., 93
Eastbourne, Sussex, 107
Eastern Townships, P.Q., 8, 29, 75
Edinburgh, Scotland, 13, 68, 71, 73,
189
Edmonton, Alta., 119, 137
Edwards, Bob, 139, 223
Elizabeth College, Guernsey, 121
Elphinstone, the Hon. Mountstuart
("Monty"), 204
Escott, Thomas Hay Sweet, 58–59
Esquimalt, B.C., 37, 47, 107, 110
Esquimalt and Nanaimo Railway,
109
Eton College, Berks., 4, 53, 55, 102,
145, 154, 166, 178, 198, 211, 215,
231
Evans, W.A., 213

Feilding, John Basil, 197
Feilding, Maj. Gen. the Hon.
William-Henry-Adelbert, 58–59,
148–49, 169, 170, 193–94, 201, 217
Fenian Brotherhood, 70, 222
Fenwick, Rear Adm. W.H., 116
Fettes College, Edinburgh, 53, 154
ffolkes, Edward George Everard,
82–84, 124, 137, 178–79, 185,
196–98, 224, 227, 233
ffolkes, the Rev. Henry Edward
Browne, 82
ffolkes, Robert Walling Everard, 198
ffolkes, Sir William Everard
Browne, 4th Bt., 82
ffolkes, Sir William Hovell, 3rd Bt.,
82
FitzGerald, Cyril, 212
Fort Macleod, Alta., 87, 89, 97, 100
Fort Macleod Literary and
Historical Society, 232
Fort Resolution, N.W.T., 119
Fort William, Ont., 72, 73
Franklin, Lady Jane, 47
Fraser River gold rush (1858),
37–38, 42, 107
Fry, Basil, 206
Fry, the Rev. Dr. Thomas Charles,
205–8, 210

Galiano Island, B.C., 111
Galt, John, 20
Gang Ranch, B.C., 105
Garry Club, Winnipeg, 137
Gibson, Hugh, 68, 70–71, 137
Gladstone, Man., 84
Glasgow, Scotland, 20, 73
Goderich, Ont., 20, 21, 22
Goodridge, Capt. Richard E.,
84–86, 88, 90, 242n.
Gordon, the Rev. Dr. Daniel Miner,
63
Grand Trunk Railway, 76, 212

Grant, Lt. Col. Colquhoun, 34
Grant, Gen. Sir Lewis, 34
Grant, Capt. Walter Colquhoun, 34–37, 47, 51, 108
Gravenhurst, Ont., 179
Gray, the Rev. Dr. Herbert Branston, 208–10, 216, 219–20, 226, 228
Great War. *See* World War I
Greenock, Scotland, 20, 68
Greig, Henry, 199
Grey, 4th Earl (Albert Henry George Grey), 114, 165
Grosse Isle, P.Q., 25
Guelph, Ont., 20, 83, 137, 179, 195–98
Guinness, the Hon. Rupert, 213
Guisachan Ranch, B.C., 103, 104

Hadley Ranch, Alta. 92, 97
Haileybury College, Herts., 53, 60, 82, 84, 179, 197
Halifax, N.S., 8, 123, 211, 214
Hamilton, Basil, 160
Harrow School, Mx., 4, 49, 53, 54, 59, 154, 211, 217
Harvey, Adam, 78
Hawaii, 36
Haynes, John Carmichael, 43, 46, 47
Head, Sir Francis Bond, 29
Headingly, Man., 85
Headmasters' Conference (HMC), 4, 57, 211–14, 219
High River, Alta., 91, 92, 98, 100, 138, 139
High River Agricultural College, Alta., 213
High River Horse Ranche, 98
Hill, Alexander Stavely, 98
Hogan, James Francis, 92
Hollesley Bay Farm Colony, 205
Hoodstown, Ont., 62
Hope, B.C., 39

Houghton, Capt. Charles Frederick, 43, 44, 47
Hudson's Bay Company (HBC), 32, 33, 34, 36, 37, 62, 118
Hudson's Hope, B.C., 119
Hughes, Thomas, 5, 55–56, 150–51, 163
Huntsville, Ont., 62
Huron Tract, 20

Idaho, 99
Ilfracombe, Ont., 62
Inderwick, F.C., 132
Inderwick, Mary Ella (née Lees), 132, 141
India, 3, 19, 20, 217
Indian Head, Sask., 230
Iowa, 198

Jameson, Anna, 28, 29, 31
Jameson, H.B., 203
Jarvis, William Henry Pope, 133
Jeyes, Samuel Henry, 56, 57, 59
Johnson, Richard Byron, 39–41, 239
Johnson, Robert, 200–202, 204–5, 217–18
Johnstone, C. Laura, 147, 170

Kamloops, B.C., 45, 162
Kelly, Leroy Victor, 134, 139
Kelowna, B.C., 188
King William's College, Isle of Man, 154
King's Lynn, Norfolk, 82
Kingston, William Henry Giles, 31
Kipling, Rudyard, 115, 234–35
Klondike gold rush, 117, 161, 204
Kootenay Valley, B.C., 114, 120, 122, 130, 135, 188

Lakefield, Ont., 177–78
Lakefield College, Ont., 231

Langton, John, 22, 24, 25, 26, 28, 228, 232

Lansdowne, 5th Marquis of (Henry Charles Keith Petty-Fitzmaurice), 132

Lascelles, the Hon. F.C., 203

Lathom, Earl of (Edward Bootle-Wilbraham), 89

Laurier, Sir Wilfrid, 167

Law Society, 50

Leacock, Stephen, 220

Leighton, Robert, 101

Leith, Scotland, 13

Le Mars, Iowa, 150, 155, 163, 165

Lethbridge, Alta., 92

Lillooet, B.C., 39, 44, 45

Lister-Kaye, Sir John Pepys, 3rd Bt., 89, 243n.

Liverpool, Lancs., 60, 74, 75, 191

Lloydminster, Sask., 161–62

Lockhart, John Gibson, 21

London, Ont., 189

Loretto School, Musselburgh, Scotland, 154

Lower Canada, 9, 13, 29. *See also* Canada East; Quebec.

Loyalists, United Empire, 8, 18, 30

Lytton, Sir Edward Bulwer, 42, 43

McBride, Sir Richard, 165, 169

Macdonald, Sir John A., 152

McGusty, Henry Alexander, 84, 98, 140, 203–4

McInnis, C.M., 220

MacPherson, Sir David Lewis, 77–78, 152

Magdalene College, Cambridge, 44

Malvern College, Worcs., 53, 211

Manchester, 22, 154

Manitoba, 60, 62, 82–86, 90, 113, 123, 125, 128, 133, 134, 142, 145, 147, 159, 172, 179, 181, 198, 203, 209

Manor, Sask., 161

Maple Bay, B.C., 110

Marjoribanks, the Hon. Coutts, 103–4

Marlborough College, Wilts., 53, 60, 64, 154, 166

Marpole, Richard, 141

Martin, Captain, 179–81

Martley, Capt. John, 43, 44, 47, 103

Martley, Mary, 47

Medical profession, reforms, 50, 52

Merriott, Somerset, 151, 152

Merritt, B.C., 41

Merton College, Oxford, 178

Military and Naval Settlers' Act, 1863, 44

Military Colonization Company (MCC), 98, 99, 100, 233

Military Settlers' Proclamation Act, 1861, 43–44,

Millarville, Alta., 92, 186, 209, 210, 223

Milton, Viscount (William Fitzwilliam), 45, 47

Minnedosa, Man., 84

Minnesota, 189

Mont Head Ranche Co., 89

Montana, 99

Montreal, P.Q., 8, 21, 23, 60, 69, 70, 75, 76, 77, 79, 124, 125, 126, 197, 211

Montreal Veterinary College, 197

Moodie, John Wedderburn Dunbar, 13, 14, 15, 16, 23, 24, 25, 36, 51, 227, 232, 238n.

Moodie, Susanna (née Strickland), 13, 14, 15, 16, 17, 18, 19, 24, 25, 26, 27, 29, 85, 137, 232

Moose Mountain Trading Company, 153, 160

Moosomin, Sask., 151, 155, 160

Morden, Man., 83

Morris, Man., 84
Mosquito Creek, Alta., 91
Moss, the Rev. Henry Whitehead, 217
Murray, John Wilson, 190
Muskoka district, Ont., 28, 31, 62, 81, 82, 123, 137, 179–81

Napoleonic Wars, 1, 10, 14, 216
Naramata, B.C., 114
Navy League of Canada, 117, 225, 233
Nelson, B.C., 117
Nevada, 41
New Brunswick, 8, 9, 29
New South Wales, 15, 16. *See also* Australia
New Westminster, B.C., 37, 38, 39, 40, 42
New York, 233
New Zealand, 8, 214, 227
Newbolt, Robert, 99–101, 222, 233
Nicola Valley, B.C., 41, 104
North Fork Ranch, Alta., 132
North West Cattle Company, 89
North West Mounted Police, 64–65, 87, 97, 138, 152, 156, 184
North West Stockman's Association, 100
North West Territory, 10, 62, 92, 105, 138, 147, 183, 184, 233. *See also* Alberta; Assiniboia; Saskatchewan
Norwich, Norfolk, 14, 15, 19
Nova Scotia, 8, 29, 33, 190, 197, 213

Oak Lake, Man., 84, 98
Okanagan Valley, B.C., 43, 103, 104, 113–15, 163, 164, 168, 188, 234
Oliver, John, 169

Ontario, 1, 8, 10, 62, 80, 94, 95, 123, 128, 175, 178, 183, 188, 197, 213, 215, 230, 231, 233, 234
Ontario Agricultural College, Guelph, 83, 179, 195–98
Ontario Provincial Police, 189
Oregon, 32, 35, 118
Orkney Isles, 14, 17, 22, 24
Ormskirk, Lancs., 22
Osoyoos, B.C., 43
Ottawa, Ont., 77–79, 126, 152, 189, 229, 233
Ottawa Valley, 31, 123
Oundle School, Northants., 226
Oxford University, 17, 53, 97, 98, 118, 132, 190, 198
Oxley Ranche Company, 89, 90, 98, 186

Panama, 34, 35, 38
Papillon, the Rev. T.C., 64, 65
Parkin, Sir George Robert, 214, 218, 219, 220
Patteson, Thomas Charles, 178–79, 248n.
Payne, Charles, 118
Peachland, B.C., 114
Pearkes, Maj. Gen. George R., 208
Pemberton, Charlotte, 46
Pemberton, Joseph Despard, 46
Penticton, B.C., 113
Perth, Ont., 132
Peterborough, Ont., 18, 20, 21, 22, 47, 60, 81, 231
Phillipps-Wolley, Sir Edward Clive Oldnall Long, 106, 115–17, 118, 119, 121, 122, 142, 185, 220, 222, 225, 227, 232
Philpot, Harvey J., 61, 144
Pierce, Capt. Edward Mitchell, 151–53, 156–61, 163, 167, 187
Pierce, Lydia Bishop (née Bowdage), 151, 152

Pike, Warburton Mayer ("Pikey"),
  117–20, 122, 224–25
Pincher Creek, Alta., 91, 132, 142
Port Arthur, Ont., 81
Portage la Prairie, Man., 83, 84,
  137, 185
Primogeniture, 49, 60, 226
Prince Albert, Sask., 184
Prince Edward Island, 8, 29, 33,
  60
Public Schools Emigration League
  (PSEL), 211–14, 215, 219, 226
Public Schools Employment Bureau,
  226–27
Purser, Reginald ("Tony"), 155

Qu'Appelle, Sask., 65, 84, 85, 147,
  198
Quebec (province), 8, 9, 74
Quebec City, P.Q., 13, 25, 69
Quesnel, B.C., 40
Quorn Hunt, Leics., 98
Quorn Ranch, Alta., 98, 101, 185,
  186, 203

Racey, Arthur G., 126
Ranchmen's Club, Calgary, 100,
  197, 233
Rapid City, Man., 84
Rebellions: of 1837, 29, 33, 222;
  Riel (1869/70), 60; North
  West (1885), 100, 222
Red Deer, Alta., 98, 206
Redmayne, John Fitzgerald
  Studdert, 164–65, 188
Regina, Sask., 127, 160
Regina Literary and Historical
  Society, 232
Rhodes, Cecil, 203, 217
Rhys, Capt. Horton, 178
Ricardo, W. Crawley, 104
Roosevelt, Theodore, 119, 120
Rose, the Rev. A.W.H., 30

Rossall School, Lancs., 4, 53, 116
Rowan, John J., 62, 65, 145, 149,
  170, 195
Royal Agricultural College, Glos.,
  205, 213
Royal Colonial Institute, 215
Royal Military Academy,
  Woolwich, 22, 52
Royal Military College, Sandhurst,
  80
Royal Naval College, Greenwich, 52
Rugby School, War., 4, 49, 53, 59,
  84, 98, 118, 119, 204
Rugby, Tenn., 150–51, 163
Runnymede, Kansas, 150, 151, 159,
  164
Russell, Lindsey, 233

St. Andrew's Society, 78
St. John's, Nfld., 69, 125
St. John's Collegiate Farm,
  Qu'Appelle, 198–200, 205
St. John's Divinity College,
  Qu'Appelle, 198, 200
St. John's School, Winnipeg, 231
Saltspring Island, B.C., 111, 112, 118
San Francisco, 35, 37, 39
Sanderson, Frederick William, 226
Sarnia, Ont., 72
Saskatchewan, 84, 103, 135, 140,
  155, 161, 209, 214. *See also*
  Assiniboia; North West
  Territory
Saskatchewan Livestock and Stock-
  breeders' Association, 187
Saskatoon, Sask., 211
Saturna Island, B.C., 111, 118
Sault Ste. Marie, Ont., 73
Savigny, Hugh P., 71, 73
Scott, W.E., 165
Sedbergh School, Cumbria, 53
Selous, Frederick, 119
Shearman, Henry, 189

Sheep Creek, Alta., 96, 98, 186
Sherbrooke, P.Q., 75
Sherwood, Arthur, 185
Shoal Lake, Man., 84
Shrewsbury School, Salop, 4, 49, 154, 211, 217
Sicamous, B.C., 114
Sifton, Sir Clifford, 129, 219
Simcoe, John Graves, 30
Similkameen district, B.C., 43, 46, 104
Skrine, Agnes (née Higginson) (pseud. Moira O'Neill), 91, 100–101, 141
Skrine, Walter Claremont, 100–101
Smith, J. Obed, 212–13
Sooke, B.C., 35
Souris, Man., 84
South Africa, 8, 14, 201, 214, 218, 227. *See also* Cape Colony
South African War (1889–1902), 97, 161, 222–23
South Pender Island, B.C., 111
Southampton, Hants, 35, 191
Southesk, 9th Earl of (James Carnegie), 65
Stamer, William, 58, 61, 145, 149, 150, 169, 194–95, 201, 228
Stanley of Preston, 1st Baron (Frederick Arthur Stanley), 189
Stead, Robert James Campbell, 220
Stephen, Sir Leslie, 5, 44
Stonewall, Man., 84
Strachan, Capt. James, 71–73
Strachan, the Rt. Rev. John (Bishop of Toronto), 71, 72
Strange, Maj. Gen. Thomas Bland, 98, 99, 100
Strathcona and Mount Royal, 1st Baron (Donald Alexander Smith), 214, 222
Strickland, Mary, 20
Strickland, Samuel, 19, 20, 21, 22,
24, 47, 131, 176–78, 192, 222, 231, 232, 233
Strickland, Thomas, 14, 19
Sturgeon Lake, Ont., 22
Sturrock, Charles, 186
Summerland, B.C., 114
Swain, John Gwynn, 68–74, 77, 137, 141, 222, 230

Telegraph Creek, B.C., 119
Texada Island, B.C., 94
Texas, 88, 118
Thetis Island, B.C., 111
Thompson River Valley, B.C., 45, 104, 162, 163, 164, 168, 188
Thring, the Rev. Edward, 99, 100, 208
Toronto, Ont., 20, 31, 47, 60, 69, 70, 71, 72, 73, 79, 124, 125, 126, 151, 152, 178, 211, 214, 220, 224, 231
Toronto Literary Society, 21
Toronto, University of, 23
Traill, Catharine Parr (née Strickland), 16, 17, 18, 19, 22, 26, 27, 29, 31, 136, 220, 232
Traill, Lt. Thomas, 16, 17, 22, 26, 27, 29, 51
Trinity College, Cambridge, 22, 44
Trinity College, Dublin, 46
Trinity College, Port Hope, Ont., 231
Tupper, Sir Charles, 190–91
Turner, John Herbert, 120
Turtle Mountain, Man., 84

Union Club, Victoria, B.C., 108, 115, 118, 233
United States of America, 8, 34, 64, 149–50, 158, 169, 189, 190, 205, 216, 217–20
University College, London, 93

University School, Victoria, B.C., 231

Upper Canada, 9, 15, 16, 18, 19, 21, 22, 25, 29, 136. *See also* Canada West; Ontario

Upper Canada College, Toronto, 214, 231

Uppingham School, Rutland, 53, 60, 99, 100, 101, 228, 233

Van Horne, Sir William Cornelius, 77

Vancouver, B.C., 107, 111, 114, 122, 124, 130, 141, 166, 169, 188, 210, 211

Vancouver Island, 10, 31, 32, 33, 34, 36, 37, 46, 47, 94, 95, 130, 188

Vernon, B.C., 44, 113, 114, 130, 141, 188

Vernon, Charles Albert, 43, 44, 103

Vernon, Forbes George, 43, 44, 103, 104

Vernon Preparatory School, B.C., 231

Victoria, B.C., 32, 35–47, 61, 106–13, 115–18, 120–22, 123, 130, 169, 203, 210, 211, 214, 232, 243n.

Victoria, Kansas, 150, 151, 163

Virden, Man., 183, 204

Wakefield, Edward Gibbon, 33, 36

Walhachin, B.C., 162–70, 188, 228

Walrond Cattle Ranche Ltd., 89, 186

Walrond-Walrond, Sir John, 1st Bt., 89

Ward, Mrs. Humphrey (Mary Augustus Arnold), 102

Ware, John, 97

Washington (state), 233

Weld, Charles Richard, 177

Welldon, the Rt. Rev. James Edward Cowell, 217

Wellington College, Berks., 53, 79, 179

Western Canada Ranching Company, 105

Westholme, B.C., 111

Westminster School, London, 4

Whates, Harry R., 207, 208, 221

Whitby, Ont., 19

Williams Creek, B.C., 37

Wilson, John (pseud. Christopher North), 21

Wilson, Tom, 15, 16, 232

Winchester College, Hants, 4, 49, 53, 211

Windsor, N.S., 8

Winnipeg, Man., 81, 85, 113, 124, 125, 127, 128, 132, 133, 137, 155, 183

Woking, Surrey, 213

Woodbridge, Suffolk, 200

Woodstock, Ont., 190

Woodsworth, James Shaver, 137

World War I, 1, 8, 162, 168–69, 214, 216, 222–27, 234

Wyoming, 121

Yale, B.C., 39, 42, 43

Yarborough, 4th Earl of (Charles Alfred Worsley Pelham), 155

York. *See* Toronto

Yukon Territory, 119